PRAISE FOR

The Elephants and I

During the fifty years since I first went to Africa, I have collected or been given a considerable number of books written by those who have been to Africa but very few stand out in my memory as being exceptional. I was privileged therefore to be asked to contribute a few words to this very special book written by a great lady who writes with such dedication, feeling and passion for the gentle giants of Africa. ... [Sharon] writes as only someone who has Africa in her blood can, of the despair and the delights of the so-called dark continent. Wildlife deserves a better deal than it is getting from Man, the most lethal animal on the planet and when I leave Africa now after every visit I cry tears of joy and anger. Sharon's book will, I know, bring similar feelings to the reader.

DAVID SHEPHERD OBE, FRSA, FOUNDER OF THE
DAVID SHEPHERD WILDLIFE FOUNDATION, UK

Sharon Pincott is the Joy Adamson of Zimbabwe. It takes a very special person to battle the loneliness and isolation of the African bush. Sharon's passionate commitment to the Presidential Elephants – in the face of soaring political tensions ... – is contagious. We salute her courage and dedication. Her book gives rare and important insights ... This vivid, first-hand account ... is heart-breaking.

WILF MBANGA, EDITOR, *THE ZIMBABWEAN*

What a remarkable piece of writing! In *The Elephants and I*, Sharon Pincott takes us on an incredible journey into the very heart and soul of Africa, its natural splendour and, of course, the gentle giants that traverse the continent. Such a tale is long overdue. While many have been lured by Africa's wildlife and beauty, few have managed to capture this splendour with such finesse and grandeur. It is in the joy, the sorrow and the lonely reality of a country and a species in serious trouble that Sharon is able to remind us of what it was like.

JASON BELL-LEASK, DIRECTOR, INTERNATIONAL FUND FOR
ANIMAL WELFARE, SOUTHERN AFRICA

Sharon Pincott has written a memoir worthy of her elephant friends.
A very moving story.

GARETH PATTERSON, INTERNATIONAL BEST-SELLING AUTHOR OF *LAST OF THE FREE*

Sharon Pincott had the courage to leave a cushy life ... the grit to stand up against [those] who looked the other way as the earth's largest land mammals were slaughtered ... But perhaps what took the most pluck was for her to write this story openly ... if everyone had the spunk of Sharon Pincott we would have few conservation problems on our earth.

DELIA OWENS, PH.D AND CO-AUTHOR OF THE INTERNATIONAL
BEST-SELLER *CRY OF THE KALAHARI*

A heart-rending story, set in difficult times: Sharon Pincott exudes passion, courage and dedication as she tells it like it really is. And there's still room for humour amongst the tragedy – you'll be inspired!

NICHOLAS DUNCAN, PRESIDENT, SAVE FOUNDATION OF AUSTRALIA

Sharon's story speaks of a genuine passion and enthusiasm for her new African home – joy at discovering a new world ... While the tale of a modern girl giving up city life for the faraway African bush is a few decades past qualifying for remarkable, it is lifted by the fact that she chose to swap a secure life in suburban, comfortable Australia for one of increasing political uncertainty in Zimbabwe ... finding herself pitted against land-invading 'settlers' and snares while seeking to protect her increasingly persecuted elephants. This [book] is for those who look out of the window at work, wondering 'what if' they pursued their dreams.

ANGUS BEGG, CNN AWARD-WINNING JOURNALIST/TV PRODUCER, SOUTH AFRICA

After reading [this] book you will feel as though you have been to Africa and experienced the wonderful world that it truly is.

ROB FABER, MANAGING EDITOR, *THE ELEPHANT*, THE NETHERLANDS

The Secret meets *Born Free* in this story of an Australian woman's bond with 'The Presidential Elephants of Zimbabwe' and her efforts to stay positive and protect them in a time of political upheaval, poaching and land invasions ... Final impression: a courageous and determined conservationist outlasts fear and intimidation to stay on and fight for her beloved animals.

BRITISH AIRWAYS *COMAIR* MAGAZINE

Sharon Pincott's *The Elephants and I* masterfully combines a tale of the struggle to conserve Zimbabwe's 'Presidential Elephants' with a portrait of what life in Zimbabwe is like; it is a passionate and touching read.

BIG ISSUE, SOUTH AFRICA

... Sharon Pincott is a remarkable woman; courageous, stoic, determined and resourceful. Her story of her trials and tribulations, and the fun times, in Zimbabwe makes good reading.

DAVID HOLT-BIDDLE, *SOUTH COAST HERALD*, SOUTH AFRICA

THE
ELEPHANTS
AND I

THE
ELEPHANTS
AND I

PURSUING A DREAM IN
TROUBLED ZIMBABWE

Sharon Pincott

First published by Jacana Media (Pty) Ltd in 2009
Reprinted in 2009

10 Orange Street
Sunnyside
Auckland Park 2092
South Africa
+2711 628 3200
www.jacana.co.za

ISBN 978-1-77009-649-3

Set in Sabon 10.5/15pt
Printed by CTP Book Printers, Cape Town
Job No. 001034

A portion of this text appeared in a different, and much more
reserved, form in two self-published Zimbabwe-only-edition
books of journal entries: *In An Elephant's Rumble* and
A Year Less Ordinary.

See a complete list of Jacana titles at www.jacana.co.za

For my elephant friends
May you always walk this earth

And for Andy
Without whom I might never have
found the courage to jump

Contents

Author's Note xi

Maps xii

Preface xiii

Part I: Before the Elephants 1

Extravagance Down Under 2

Life-Changing Events 11

Part II: A New Beginning 19

Arrival in the Hwange Bush 20

Wildlife Outings 31

Meeting the Elephants 43

2001 at a Close 53

Homeland of Choice 61

Part III: Mandlovu 67

Kanondo: A Place of Timeless Peace 68

My Friends the Elephants 73

Lady of the Estate 80

My Home in the Hwange Bush 86

Part IV: An Adopted Child of Africa 97

Company in Paradise 98

Favourite Ladies, Endangered Offspring 108

Animal Antics 123

Learning about Elephants 129

Part V: Land Reform Hits Home 137

    The Ongoing Poaching Nightmare 138

    Cry of Kanondo 143

    The Dark Side of Africa 160

Part VI: The Aftermath 169

    Awaiting the Return of the Land 170

    Tranquillity or More Trouble? 185

    Deadly Snares Galore 194

    Grim Future 203

    Revival 211

    Friends, Fun and Fantasies 222

    L Family Cheer 235

    Drought and Despair 243

Part VII: Lost Hope 255

    Spy Allegation and Degradation 256

    The 12th of Never 267

Afterword 271

Glossary 276

Acknowledgements 278

Author's Note

The Presidential Elephants of Zimbabwe, although habituated to the presence of people, are wild, free-roaming animals. While I'm privileged to enjoy a close, perhaps intimate, relationship with these grey giants, it must be recognised that this is the result of many thousands of hours of contact. When among people unknown to them, their behaviour may be unpredictable. Close contact should never be initiated with these, or any other, elephants without a highly experienced person present.

AFRICA

TUNISIA
MOROCCO
ALGERIA
LIBYA
EGYPT
WESTERN
SAHARA
MAURITANIA
MALI
NIGER
CHAD
SUDAN
ERITREA
DJIBOUTI
SENEGAL
GAMBIA
GUINEA
BISSAU
GUINEA
BURKINA
FASO
NIGERIA
CENTRAL
AFRICAN
REPUBLIC
ETHIOPIA
SOMALIA
SIERRA
LEONE
IVORY
COAST
GHANA
TOGO
BENIN
CAMEROON
EQUATORIAL
GUINEA
GABON
CONGO
RWANDA
UGANDA
KENYA
LIBERIA
DEMOCRATIC
REPUBLIC
OF CONGO
BURUNDI
TANZANIA
ANGOLA
ZAMBIA
MALAWI
MOZAMBIQUE
ZIMBABWE
NAMIBIA
BOTSWANA
SOUTH AFRICA

ZIMBABWE

MANA POOLS
NATIONAL PARK
LAKE KARIBA
HARARE
(capital)
VICTORIA FALLS
DETE
VUMBA
HWANGE ESTATE
HWANGE
NATIONAL
PARK
GREAT ZIMBABWE
BULAWAYO
MATOPO HILLS

Preface

If we fail nature, we shall have failed ourselves
and the generations that come after us.
And judgement will be very harsh on us.
MAASAI ELDER

Another fine African day draws to a close as I sit on the rooftop of my faithful old Range Rover. A gentle breeze cools my body as I breathe in the quiet beauty of the summer sunset. Ahead, the blood red sun will soon touch the horizon. An elephant family is feeding close by, expertly snaking their trunks around dried clumps of grass, kicking with giant front feet to help loosen their supper from the ground. Dust, tinged pink and gold in the fading light, floats high into the air. Baboons sit silhouetted on termite mounds, while flocks of guineafowl scamper about, busy with evening chatter. A grove of acacias, old and wise like the elephants, stands guard over the approaching night.

I lower myself into my 4x4 and call out, 'Come on Lady, come girl, come here my girl.'

Lady is a fully grown jumbo who roams freely in the wilds of Africa. She's one of a clan of wild elephants said to be protected by a 'presidential decree'. Born wild. Living wild, with no fences to restrain her. The matriarch of a family of 17, Lady comes to me when I call her, like a familiar friend.

Her massive, placid form is soon beside my door. I look into her amber-coloured eyes, so filled with wisdom and warmth. Her incredibly long eyelashes, dark and mesmerising, are momentarily tinted ochre by the warm glow of the setting sun. I slowly reach my arm towards her, and gently place my hand on her trunk.

I am the first human to earn her complete trust. Some say she has bestowed on me the status of 'honorary elephant' – and I am moved and deeply honoured.

The smell of life around me is so intense that I can almost reach out and touch it, and I feel the freedom of being, right now, the only human around. I sit quietly, reflecting. I'm here in the exalted company of the largest land mammals on earth. I had once dreamed of being in such extraordinary company and now I am living my dream. Life has meaning and I have large grey friends.

Eight years ago (or maybe it was 80; it often seems difficult to be sure) I was living an extravagant life Down Under, in a world filled with countless material pleasures. There was family, friendship and fun, but somehow the rest of it lacked real meaning. Wild Africa, half a world away, beckoned. Like a powerful magnet, it drew me in – naive, a dreamer, unaware of the commitment or involvement that it would bring.

'Zimbabwe?' my family and friends had asked, bewildered. 'You're going to live in *Zimbabwe?*'

Zimbabwe, in the dawn of the new millennium, was not where many people chose to be. Yet I resolved to invest my hopes and my dreams in this troubled country, a land in dire need of both hope *and* dreams. And I was initially rewarded with a sense of fulfilment and contentment like I had never experienced before. Elephants were the reason I'd left my large suburban home in Brisbane, Australia, to live in a small hut in the Zimbabwean bush. They were the reason I'd given up a high-flying corporate life as an Information Technology (IT) specialist.

I could not know, though, from my idyllic early days of intimate wildlife encounters, sundowners, campfires and savannah breezes, that I would eventually find myself embroiled in challenges way beyond my imagination.

Nevertheless, here I remained – a million miles from my childhood home, yet completely at home.

Through the deepening twilight I glance to my right at the grove of towering acacia trees. Perhaps, I muse, like these acacias, having a thorny hide had helped me to survive here. But why, I wonder, do

I choose hardships that, as a volunteer, I'm not obliged to endure? In these unlikely surroundings, comforted at this moment by the rich sounds and smells of the African veld at dusk, I ponder how on earth I got to where I am now.

I think back to my childhood, my career, and the events and people that were pivotal in me choosing this unusual life. So much has happened since then. Had I known what lay ahead, would I ever have come to this place? Probably not, I admit to myself. But given the chance, would I do it again? Yes, absolutely yes – of that I'm certain.

I remember a friend once commenting, 'There's a tragic appeal in lost causes.'

Is that what this was, a lost cause?

Whatever it was, this place – filled with poignant beauty and wonder, and with elephants – was now my home. In time, I felt a profound sense of responsibility towards my four-legged friends and so, even when disillusionment and fear became my constant companions, and the First World beckoned, I trudged on.

Having been so warmly accepted by the giants of the wild, there were many times that my spirit soared with joy. But there were many other trying times when I felt my resolve crumble under the weight of unbearable sadness.

Yet, despite everything, while driving through the Zimbabwean veld – on my daily mission to protect my elephant friends – I always tried to remember to make space on the seat beside me. For hope.

PART I

Before the Elephants

Extravagance
Down Under

From the open door of my thatched hut I gaze out at the sunrise. Playful vervet monkeys are swinging in the trees. Close by, I hear an elephant rumble. The night just past had belonged to the lions, their powerful calls shattering the deep silence of midnight. Now, as always at first light, the red-billed francolins claim centre-stage, welcoming the morning with their boisterous cackling. It is a setting far removed from my days of high-flying corporate deals, unthinking extravagance and peak-hour traffic – and yet, it's not entirely unlike that of my first home.

Australia, New Zealand and Zimbabwe have all, at different times in my life, been 'home' to me. They are so diverse, but all are loved, filled with memories of great joy, sadness, and inspiration too. Australia is where I was born, and where I spent the first 30 years of my life.

I come originally from Grantham, a tiny country town in the Lockyer Valley in sunny south-east Queensland – the largest of Australia's eastern states. I lived there as a child on my parents' vegetable farm in a wooden house perched on wooden stilts, prudently designed to catch the breeze. The sprawling fields outside sometimes lay freshly ploughed, although they more frequently boasted a cover of bright green leaves as far as my young eyes could see.

I grew up with three sisters. First-born was Genevieve. Just one year later came Deborah, followed by me and then Catherine. When we were old enough, we woke at dawn and crawled out of bed to earn pocket money washing cucumbers, or rubbing the husks off dried pumpkin seeds. More often though, we crawled out of bed to catch

2

cabbages, which were cut and then thrown to us by our father. These were packed into big square wooden crates and transported to markets in Brisbane, the thriving capital of Queensland.

From a tender age I was at ease with the outdoors and with animals, finding even the most peculiar creatures endearing. I grew up finding pleasure in the little things, intensely curious of the natural world. I'd lie on my back and decipher the faces in the billowing clouds, or follow the passage of a wind-blown leaf. When standing in the inky darkness I always gazed up at the Southern Cross and at the silver dust of the Milky Way, marvelling at the splendour of the night sky.

There were always plenty of animals to keep me amused and I treasured their quiet company. We had cats, guinea pigs that lived under the sharp-edged pampas grass, and a pink and grey galah that said 'hello cocky'. Wild birds nested on the beams under our house and in my innocence I climbed up and placed my fingers on the eggs, feeling their smoothness and warmth.

I frequently wandered down to the nearby creek – a much-loved place of sand, stones and mottled shade – and there I stroked the thin grubs that lived on the lantana bushes, gracefully arching their backs as they moved. They felt soft and gentle, like the wings of butterflies. I never liked to see any animals die and always felt distressed whenever I awoke to find large lifeless flying foxes hanging upside down, electrocuted, on tall power lines outside my bedroom window.

Occasionally, on weekend outings, we visited a captive wildlife sanctuary where I fed the kangaroos and wondered at the idleness of the koalas. Some of the other animals, I soon discovered, were anything but idle. I have vivid memories of one visit when an exotic monkey, with an odd partiality for red, pulled down my pants. I was mortified. I stood naked from the waist down, red pants around my ankles, howling loudly, and acutely aware of the laughter. A secretly sensitive child, back then it didn't seem to me to be a particularly funny affair. But still I adored the cute monkey.

When the winds blew cold my sisters and I huddled on the floor of our lounge-room under home-made feather covers, eager to watch *Hogan's Heroes*, *Gilligan's Island* and *Skippy the Bush Kangaroo* on television.

The African wildlife documentaries, which were regularly screened, made a strong impression on me. I could not bear the predatory scenes though, and eventually couldn't bring myself to watch these parts at all.

I looked forward to regular visits from Aunty Pam, my mother's youngest sister. I would sit cross-legged on the lawn, quietly listening, fascinated by her tales from when she was a nurse on a missionary station in New Guinea.

One day, I dreamed, I too would go to a strange, foreign land.

In the meantime, my days were filled with schooling. Although I always achieved high grades, school was not where I wanted to be. I never graduated, but instead accepted a job in the office of the secondary school I'd attended, which ended my days on the farm.

Suddenly, my childhood belonged to yesterday.

I was quietly ambitious, with an independent spirit, and soon found myself accepting a job in Brisbane. There I rented a room from an elderly lady, and once again set to work. Soon after, I accepted a promotion to Canberra, Australia's political capital where I celebrated my 21st birthday in the company of friends. These included my new toy poodle puppy Chloe, who shared my life, my joys and griefs, for the next 17 years. She was delightfully affectionate, fluffy, fat and unclipped – the only 'child' in my life plan.

With Chloe for company, I continued my climb up the business-world ladder, eventually working in the Office of the Prime Minister and Cabinet (which became the first fully electronic office in Australia) and shortly after that for Wang (the computer giant of the day). Life was a whirl of activity. I modelled part-time, which made me so obsessed with maintaining my figure that I often survived on only an apple a day. Then one day, while dressed in a bright yellow miniskirt for a product promotion (enduring wolf-whistles from red-blooded Aussie blokes and feeling decidedly famished) I realised this modelling scene wasn't for me after all.

Restless, I was soon on the move again – this time to Sydney with its world-renowned opera house, sparkling harbour and more promising career prospects. The quiet country ambience of my childhood was now a million miles away. I lived life at a fast pace, constantly seeking to better myself, and never considering that I should slow down.

Although I didn't feel the need to be married, I took this step while living in Sydney. He was a budding barrister and for a while we shared fun times. Within two short years though, we'd drifted apart. Some may consider it strange that I've kept his surname, but changing it has simply never seemed important.

I loved my work and channelled all my energy into it. Eventually I found myself in the lofty position of National Director of IT for the international accountancy firm Ernst & Young. Career-wise, I had it all. I travelled round Australia and around the world. I owned a townhouse in the fashionable suburb of Bondi Junction and delighted in baskets of seafood on Bondi Beach, always with Chloe at my side.

Yet by 1993, at the age of 31, I felt my life had become repetitious. So, after much thought, I resigned from my prestigious job, said goodbye to dear friends, and flew (taking Chloe with me) to Auckland, on New Zealand's North Island, to live with a tall handsome man who'd shared my bond with Ernst & Young and my passion for working in the field of IT. His style was reflected in the countless bunches of long-stemmed red roses he showered upon me and in the chauffeur-driven limousine and French champagne that awaited Chloe and me on our arrival at Auckland airport. (All *three* of us savoured that delectable champagne!) We lived in a trendy penthouse apartment overlooking Auckland harbour – a BMW and a red sports-car parked in one garage, a white Lamborghini in another – and we flew together around the world, relishing all of the very best, so I thought, that life had to offer.

It was a chance visit to Ernst & Young in Johannesburg, South Africa, later in 1993 that changed my life as I knew it. We hadn't planned to visit a game park – despite my early love of nature it didn't even occur to me to do so – yet when we arrived at Johannesburg International Airport, malaria tablets were thrust into our hands and we were whisked away for a weekend in the Kruger National Park. And there I was spellbound. There, I felt instantly at home.

What I remember most vividly about this weekend safari is the huge bull elephant; the only one we encountered. He looked magnificent, ancient and infinitely wise as he browsed among the trees in the distance. I was haunted by that elephant, drawn like a moth to a flame, and longed to return to the wilds of Africa.

Return we did, to the likes of the famed private game reserves of Londolozi and MalaMala – because, in keeping with our lifestyle, only the best would do. We sat for hours, watching distant elephants, while I became increasingly enthralled.

Little did I know then what destiny had in store for me.

Between my personal travels, I worked in Auckland as an independent IT consultant and while contracted long-term to Air New Zealand my first-class trips around the globe continued. They were filled with friendship, fun and laughter, but all I ever *really* wanted to do was to go back to Africa. My doting partner accompanied me, but he hadn't been bitten by the same bug as I had. I often found myself lounging with him on a quiet beach in Mauritius, or elsewhere, secretly pining for the wild African animals that I desperately longed to be near.

I took some comfort in New Zealand's spectacular remote places, and in its animal life – the whales, penguins, albatrosses, gannets, and even the ungainly little lambs in green pastures, frolicking among daffodils tinted the colour of sunshine, that signalled the start of spring.

I was the one who changed. Our priorities were no longer the same. I had fallen suddenly out of love with my high-flying life and we drifted irrevocably apart. I'd spent four memorable years in New Zealand, but once again I was packing up. I returned with Chloe to Australia, where I bought a lovely suburban home in Brisbane, worked a contract or two, and returned to Africa whenever I could.

Chloe endured a somewhat unstable 'doghood', moving from city to city and country to country, spending countless days in the homes of others. A lesser dog may not have coped well, but all her minders loved and cared for her and she was perfectly content. She was my best buddy and I always promised her that, one day, she would come with me to Africa.

Our Brisbane home was filled with beautiful things. It was a modern design, open plan with cathedral ceilings, light, airy and chic, decorated throughout with photographs and mementos of Africa. There was a sparkling pebble-surfaced swimming pool in our backyard, lined with palm trees and surrounded by an assortment of African animals moulded from concrete.

My friends thought I had it all. Yet a fire burned in my belly for Africa, and no matter how often I visited, I lived with a fierce longing to return. I was *always* planning my next trip, and living on memories of my last – elephant giants, majestic and free, wandering with great dignity across the open plains, rumbling their contact calls; the exquisite reflections of elegant giraffes enjoying their evening drink; the deep throaty call of a black-maned lion, part of the splendid dusk symphony.

The African bush was where I felt whole.

As Africa beckoned – my enthusiasm for my career already gone – my liking for the lifestyle I still led quickly began to fade too. Frequent shopping sprees provided only fleeting pleasure, temporarily masking the unsettled feeling I had. Too much that cannot be bought was still missing from my life. I began to feel like a stranger in my own home. I heard the call of Africa as I watered my pot plants and mowed the lawn. I heard it as I relaxed with friends, drinking wine. I heard it as I sorted my wildlife photographs. Indeed I heard it in everything I did. Every day I would close my eyes longingly, trying to recall the colours of the African veld.

Somehow, I decided, I needed to spend more time in the wild Africa that I loved. Over the next four years I managed this by volunteering part-time on wildlife conservation projects, juggling this new-found passion with bouts of contract work in Australia that supported these adventures.

Before I'd left New Zealand, my girlfriends had, with wine in hand, helped me fill out an application form for my first three-month stint – on a remote, uninhabited island in the middle of Lake Victoria, Uganda, in Africa's east (that is, east of the continent's belly). They'd seen Africa infect my blood and knew it was slowly laying claim to my heart and soul, although they couldn't imagine how I'd ever cope without a hairdryer! Having wished me Godspeed, they wondered aloud whether I would survive unscathed in this far-off primitive place.

To the astonishment of many, I revelled in voluntary work with chimpanzees and a lion in Uganda; elephants, painted hunting dogs and hippos in Zimbabwe; migratory birds in Kenya; and cheetahs in Namibia. I cherished the company of animal-loving folk and enjoyed forming new friendships with people from around Africa, and the world.

Time and again I found myself in Zimbabwe, a land-locked country in southern Africa. It was the African country in which I felt safest travelling alone. There I met a petite Englishwoman, Karen Paolillo. Karen lived for the hippos of the Turgwe River in south-eastern Zimbabwe, all of which she knew by name. She cherished her independent lifestyle and, I quickly recognised, had both spirit and spunk. Surrounded by licensed sport-hunters she needed every drop of it, and more, to survive.

Voluntary work in Hwange National Park in western Zimbabwe, on the eastern edge of the Kalahari Desert, landed me in the company of elephant, painted hunting dog and hyena researchers. I established an instant rapport with one of the hyena researchers named Julia Salnicki – a bright, fun-loving woman with a passion for the African bush, and an energy that I admired and found infectious.

Something of a legend in this area was John Foster, the happy hermit of the Hwange bush, not yet ready to join his wife Del in a retirement home in town. I first met John when I volunteered for a few weeks on an elephant project. He struck me as a fascinating character, full of colourful stories and more than a little eccentric. Visitors always risked catching him stark naked, sometimes on the roof of his dilapidated bush home. I came to know John well, and to rely on his long experience in the African bush.

I made other good friends around Hwange National Park. Among them was Zimbabwean-born Deline Adlam (known as Dinks), who managed the Main Camp restaurant. Gracious and charming, she moved from table to table, ensuring that everything was perfect. Her warm laughter was contagious and I admired her politeness and sincerity. We quickly became friends and I looked forward to visiting her whenever I found myself in Hwange.

Living in a small National Parks settlement named Umtshibi, inside the park, were the wildlife capture and relocation warden Andy Searle and his wife Laurette, whom I came to know as Lol. Perhaps more than anyone else, they helped to open my eyes to an exciting new world, intensifying my love of Africa's wildlife. Spending time with Andy, Lol and their young son Drew, sharing extraordinary wildlife adventures, was a great privilege and a joy.

I felt as if I'd known Andy all my life; indeed we were strangers for only a moment. I admired his dedication to the wildlife of Africa and respected his quiet ways, while enjoying it when he clowned around. During my visits to the national park we had many lively discussions about elephants, our views often conflicting. It didn't matter though. There were snare removals to attend to, collarings and translocations to be done, all of which I was privileged to be part of. There were also unforgettable flights over the park in the National Parks helicopter. A frightening incident years earlier, while flying in a four-seater single-engine plane from Tanzania to Kenya in East Africa, had left me somewhat fearful of light aircraft, but Andy was a cautious pilot. His thorough pre-flight checks always comforted me and his years of experience and skill as a pilot never failed to alleviate my anxiety.

While I have fond memories of all our shared wildlife escapades, I particularly treasure the lion cub relocation that we stumbled into together. Two cubs had become separated from their radio-collared mother (a collar Andy had fitted) and would not survive much longer on their own. So Andy decided on the spur of the moment to capture both of them by hand, which proved relatively easy given their weakened state.

'Hold this,' said Andy as he walked towards me, casually carrying one of the cubs by the scruff of the neck.

'Hold *that*?' I muttered in disbelief. 'Well, okay...' I grabbed the cub in the same way.

So it was that on a day when I had simply been enjoying the splendour of Hwange National Park, I found myself on the back of an open 4x4 with Andy, each of us holding a truly wild lion cub. These cubs were not sedated. They were not sleeping. They were alert and feisty, although thin and vulnerable. We struggled to hold them, as one might battle with an overgrown domestic cat.

While Lol was at the wheel, Andy and I spoke of nothing ordinary on that open-air drive across the African plains towards the mother of the cubs. As we held them, we tried to memorise every detail – their whiskers, their almond shaped eyes and the colouring of their tails.

I knew then that, somehow, I would spend more time among the animals of Africa.

Some time later, in 1999, I was delighted to be able to reciprocate the warmth and generosity shown to me by Andy and Lol. During their visit to Australia, I took them to Fraser Island, the world's largest sand island. As a child, I'd enjoyed many family holidays on this World Heritage wilderness just off Australia's eastern coastline. Now I felt privileged to share it with special friends. We drove in a 4x4 along the white, sandy beach and then turned inland to view more of the stunning landscape.

I organised a joy-flight over the island, aware of Andy's yearning to connect with things from the air, giving him a birds-eye view of the sweeping beaches, the gigantic mobile sand dunes, the spectacular rocky outcrops that jut into the sea, the crystal clear freshwater lakes, the dense rainforests and the wind-sculpted cliffs of coloured sands. I remained on the ground, watching the plane take off from the beach in front of me, the pilot flying low and eventually landing back on the firm, damp sand just metres from the rolling waves.

For several days Andy and Lol thoroughly enjoyed the Australian wilderness, and I was thrilled to share a piece of my homeland with them.

A few days later I drove them to Brisbane airport for their flight back to Africa, desperately wishing I was going with them. Australia had so much beauty of its own, but my heart was elsewhere.

Life-Changing Events

When not among the African wildlife, I relied on e-mails for news of the wild Africa I loved so much. But the e-mail I received the following year, on a balmy autumn morning in March 2000, brought news that I never dreamed I'd have to face. There'd been a helicopter accident, while tracking rhino in Hwange National Park.

Andy, alone in the chopper, was dead.

Seated in an office block in Brisbane, I stared at my computer screen, reading and re-reading just this first line of the message.

'It can't be true,' I whispered over and over.

Yet it was.

My decision to fly to Zimbabwe wasn't a fully conscious one. I woke up two mornings after receiving the news, tired and miserable after another restless night, and knew that I had to get on a plane – even if it meant breaking my work contract. Already I felt that Andy's death would somehow greatly impact my future life.

I never imagined that a trip to Africa could be so sad. Memories churned over in my mind, none bringing comfort. John and Del were waiting at Victoria Falls airport to meet me, where tears replaced the usual joy. We reminisced a little during the two-hour drive to Hwange National Park, but mostly we tried to make sense of this tragic loss. Through the window I watched the countryside pass me by. The summer rains had been kind, but it no longer felt like the Zimbabwe that I loved.

We drove straight to the park's Main Camp entrance, where the friendly boom-gate attendant who always remembered me was on duty. He beamed at me, a bright broad smile, before realising that I must have come to say goodbye to Warden Searle. His smile dissolved as he shook my hand in the triple movement African way, not letting it go for some time. The pain in my face transferred to his and he opened the boom-gate without asking any questions.

The road to Umtshibi seemed long. We stopped on the way to let Julia, who lived in a research cottage inside the park, know that I'd arrived. Our sombre greeting reflected our shock and disbelief. When we finally arrived at Umtshibi I sat quietly with Lol, knowing there was little I could say to comfort her.

I'd been offered accommodation at the rustic Miombo Lodge, by people I hadn't met. United by grief, we were instantly friends. Exhausted after my long journey, I turned in early. I hadn't slept properly for days, and now I was jetlagged as well. The elephants didn't care though. They slurped and rumbled noisily beside the small waterhole just metres from my tree-lodge.

'I have to get some sleep,' I murmured to myself as I tossed and turned. Then I thought of Andy, and how he'd fully understood my love of the elephants. I couldn't wish them away. He would never have believed it.

I forced myself out of bed at dawn and tried to prepare myself for the funeral of the person who'd enriched my feeling for Africa like no other. I went to Julia's cottage and, from the surrounding bush, picked bright yellow daisy-like wildflowers for Andy's grave.

It was a long, slow, silent drive along the railway line to where Andy was to be buried. I had travelled this same route with him the previous year while trying to find a snared zebra. I wondered what would happen to these injured animals now. Who would care enough to save them?

Andy was to be buried on the private land of 'The Hide' safari camp, bordering Hwange National Park. There are no fences here; it is home to Hwange's wildlife. How appropriate for Andy to be laid to rest in the area he loved so much; in the land to which he belonged. From beneath the magnificent ebony tree where he was to be buried, he could still enjoy the animals in the sunset – those he had dedicated his life to saving.

Safari vehicles were everywhere. Perhaps two hundred people were already waiting. Julia, another friend and I walked, with heavy hearts, across a clearing of green grass towards the ebony tree. Sad, familiar faces acknowledged us as we passed beyond the tree and the freshly dug grave to where two tents had been put up as protection from the sun and possible rain. To our left were black faces, and white ones to our right, a separation that I noticed even in this time of grief. Without words, we joined our African friends on the left, and the separation melted away. Their singing and dancing brought more tears to my eyes. I sat on a wooden bench, holding on tightly to a small ceramic lion cub – bought in memory of the 'family reunited' adventure that Andy and I had shared.

Andy's coffin arrived, carried by friends. We were outdoors under African skies without stained-glass windows, a thundering organ or even a priest. A member of Lol's family led the service. After acknowledging the beautiful surroundings, an anecdote was shared. While helping to dig his grave the day before, one of Andy's men was overheard saying, 'What a fitting site for our chief.' Many Umtshibi men and women were there, and Andy had indeed been their chief.

The service was an unforgettable tribute to an extraordinary man. Lol bravely shared many tales about the man she loved. When she talked about Andy's men, she asked for an interpreter – to make sure that everyone understood. As she spoke, tears fell from the faces of those sitting all around me.

An invitation was then extended for others to say a few words. The tributes flowed from close friends and family. Although I hadn't planned to say anything, I suddenly found myself side-stepping past my seated friends and walking up to the microphone. There I shared the fact that Andy was my hero. My own words tore at my heart as I struggled to convey how much I'd miss him.

Soon, people around me began singing 'Rock of Ages' while Andy's scouts paid a final tribute, their rifles pointed skyward. Andy's National Parks beret and belt were officially handed over to his grief-stricken parents. There was a final salute in honour of their son, and then the coffin was lowered.

Lol and Drew approached Andy's open grave. Lol threw the first handful of soil onto the coffin while Drew, holding his mother's hand, looked down in bewilderment. Eventually he took his own handful of soil and watched as it landed on his daddy's coffin below.

I watched my own trembling hands reach out for some soil. 'See you just now' – Andy's final words to me – I repeated to him, as I released my handful of earth.

Back at Miombo Lodge it seemed easier to stay awake than go to bed and face the night. I sat with a friend around a log fire, under the star-filled sky, talking and reminiscing. Unexpectedly, it began to rain. We could hear raindrops pelting the ground around us and could see them falling into the swimming pool, yet we weren't getting wet. I guess there was a logical explanation, but it felt as though Andy was up there holding a huge umbrella over us, protecting us. We gazed at the sky and smiled.

I spent the next day driving alone in Hwange National Park. There was more rain – drops that would stimulate new life. Even so, the park felt empty and lonely. I knew it would never feel quite the same again. A piece of my Africa was gone forever.

I drove around until late in the afternoon, stopping to watch dung beetles roll their balls of elephant dung and families of guineafowl feeding. I was unhappy and confused. Out loud I asked Andy for a sign – something to let me know that everything was okay with him.

As I rounded the next bend in the road I caught my breath. It was one of the most beautiful sights I'd ever seen in Africa. The sun had peeped through the heavy clouds and more than 20 giraffes were mingling peacefully in this glorious twilight. I watched, mesmerised by their silent splendour. Soon a different, unforgettable, scene unfolded. A shaft of bright white light fell from under a huge cloud, towards a tree on the horizon. I was overawed by the heavenly look and feel, and found myself enveloped in warmth. I took one photograph and then it was gone. I had my sign.

I knew that I'd be late getting out of the park if I didn't leave then. I was on my way when I came across 15 crowned cranes at the roadside – extraordinarily beautiful birds, with stunning grey plumage, bright red wattles and yellow crowns. Drawings of them had adorned Andy's funeral service sheet. I accepted it, unquestioningly, as another sign.

During the days that followed, I spent time with Lol and other friends and then, when it was time for Lol to leave for Andy's memorial service in Harare, I went to say goodbye to her at Umtshibi. As I drove away sadly in darkness, I suddenly found myself behind the enormous backside of a lone bull elephant. Forced to travel at his chosen speed, the drive took me twice as long as it should have. I didn't mind though, for I derived great pleasure and comfort from his lingering presence. Later, Lol thoughtfully referred to this elephant encounter as having been 'a gift from Andrew'.

My visit had turned into a week of extra-special memories that I knew I'd hold close to my heart forever.

Back in Australia I re-read an e-mail Andy had sent me two weeks before he died. I hadn't replied to it. It was short, as they always were.

'See you in July?' he'd written.

July was just a few months away. I thought it might be too painful to go back so soon after his death. Once the memories became comforting and could bring a smile, I would return.

Ties with my 'African family' had been strengthened, although those of us who loved Andy would never be quite the same again. His death would prove to have a profound impact on many lives, including mine.

Still today, words from Kuki Gallmann's *I Dreamed of Africa* come to mind: 'They had loved him, shared in fun, mischief, adventures. Now they shared the same anguish… contemplating their memories and their loss. This experience would forever live with them, and make them grow, and make them better, wiser.'

Even in death, Andy was still giving.

After I returned to my IT contract in Brisbane, I was invited to join permanent employees at an interstate seminar – one considered to be rather New Age and a little controversial, but designed to enhance leadership skills. More especially, for many of us, it turned out to be a time of bonding and self-discovery.

In a room filled with IT professionals lying on the floor, surrounded by candles, relaxation music and soft voices – feeling cosy and warm with duvets and pillows, in our snowy mountainous surrounds – we listened for three days to a man telling stories. Every story had a message. It was up to us to find that message, confront it, and if we chose to, incorporate its lessons into our personal and professional lives.

For me, the experience was life-changing. It helped me to realise what was important in my life; to believe in my own abilities; to look out for my own welfare; to find a balance between my personal and professional lives; and not to worry unduly about the small stuff. It helped me to accept the things I cannot change; to walk away from negative forces; and to leave life's unnecessary baggage behind. It had a positive and calming influence on my life.

We were told about a survey carried out among a group of 95-year-olds. If they could do it all again, they were asked, what would they do differently?

The responses of these wise elders inspired me:

They would take more risks.

They would take more time for reflection.

And they would leave a legacy...

Special friendships developed during these days and nights together, colleagues bonded by shared experiences. Our journey of self-discovery eventually ended with a song. Hands were joined, swaying in the air, as we listened to Stevie Wonder sing 'A Place In The Sun'. There were tears in our eyes, but we were smiling. Just as the song said, we were all moving on – in one way or another, having grown in mind and spirit.

Soon after this seminar I decided that I *would* return to Hwange in July, just a little more than four months after Andy's death. Sadly Lol and Drew, no longer allowed to live in their National Parks home, had been forced to move from the area. I arranged for them to return to see me and together we visited what we now spoke of as 'Andy's tree'. Lying under its imposing canopy, we gazed up into the branches and marvelled at its magnificence. Andy's body, we knew, was already a part of the leaves.

The repercussions of what had happened were still overwhelming. I offered my support and understanding while Lol tried to put the shattered pieces of her life back together.

Despite the sadness, I revelled in the wildlife, returning to Australia more determined than ever to work full-time with the wild animals in Zimbabwe. I dreamed of working with the elephants I loved. I was undeterred by the fact that I had no formal qualifications in the scientific world. Instead, I took heart in Dr Louis Leakey's early view of Jane Goodall, whose work with the chimpanzees of Gombe is world renowned. 'A mind uncluttered and unbiased by theory, a real desire for knowledge and a sympathetic love and understanding of animals', was considered by the legendary Dr Leakey to be more important than a scientific degree.

It is a view that I share.

PART II

A New Beginning

Arrival in the Hwange Bush

The land-locked country of Zimbabwe (formerly the British colony of Rhodesia) lies in central southern Africa and is bordered by South Africa, Botswana, Zambia and Mozambique. It's about three times the size of England and almost the same size as California. Its most special treasures are the great wilderness regions that cover 13 per cent of its total land mass.

Zimbabwe gained independence and majority rule in 1980, after a 13-year civil war – a prolonged battle to end white rule. Amazingly, the long war did not destroy the economy and at the time of independence, the Zimbabwe dollar was strong – even stronger than the US dollar. The country's future looked rosy.

However, by the time of Andy's death, in March 2000, its once-bright prospects were deteriorating into dark chaos. In the name of land reform (which was meant to give land to land-less blacks) white-owned farms were being invaded, amid violence and general lawlessness.

There were certainly imbalances in land ownership, but the way they were being addressed was cause for serious concern. Farms were being forcibly taken over without monetary compensation, and farmers were being murdered. One of these killings occurred in Matabeleland North – the province in which Hwange National Park is situated – just a few days before I arrived there to live. Instead of being given to the people, as promised, many farms were grabbed by high-level officials and their associates. Land invaders like these were often referred to as 'settlers'.

Zimbabwe's once well-developed farming sector, which had boasted high levels of production, lay in ruins. Confusion, terror and corruption reigned, while the economy rapidly crumbled. Every week thousands of people, black and white, emigrated to escape the situation, stripping Zimbabwe of its skilled workforce. Many things that had been taken for granted – food, fuel and basic commodities – were in short supply.

The value of the Zimbabwe dollar had plummeted in response and Z$50 were now needed to buy just one US$.

The future of the country may have looked grim but I was blissfully naive, and oblivious to many of these goings on. Perhaps I was also a little blinded by grief. I'd pondered long and hard, eventually deciding to leave my safe, comfortable life to make a new home for myself in this troubled country. I was ready to jump into the unknown.

It was Andy's death that had given me the courage to choose this path at a time when so many were fleeing Zimbabwe. There'd been one key lesson for me in his untimely passing, which was not to waste precious time. Andy had been just 38 years of age. I would soon be older than he would ever be. Life could be unpredictably short, and *now* was the time to do the things I really wanted to do.

I was heading to the country of my choice, to be with the animals I loved. I hoped to do some of the things that Andy no longer could. The land where I was to work was land for the wildlife, and for the tourists. It would surely be safe from invasion, I thought.

It was in September 2000 (the year I turned 38, and just six months after Andy's death) that I unexpectedly received the letter granting me approval to work on a full-time voluntary basis with The Presidential Elephants of Zimbabwe. Although attached to a photographic safari company for visa purposes, I would be working with these elephants entirely alone, and I would receive no salary. I'd have to organise everything I needed in order to live and work there, and it would have to be funded from my own savings.

I knew little about this free-roaming clan of elephants, beyond the fact that they were habituated to the presence of people in vehicles, and that their key home range was the Hwange Estate – 140 square kilometres of unfenced land set aside for tourism, adjacent to the national park. In the year before his death, Andy had introduced me to a progressive, conservation-minded man named Lionel Reynolds, who now gave the go-ahead for my voluntary work to proceed. It was my mission to get to know these elephants as individuals, and as family members, so that I could monitor their close-knit lives and report on their wellbeing.

Hwange (formerly known as Wankie) National Park is the largest of Zimbabwe's national parks, covering a vast 14 600 square kilometres – an area roughly the size of Belgium. Declared a game reserve in 1928, it was later accorded national park status. It took its original name from the nearby coal mining town of Wankie, which was itself named after a local chief named Wange, and then renamed Hwange at independence. Many names of places, said to have been corrupted by, or named after, white pioneers, were changed at this time.

Wankie was, originally, sparsely populated by just a few nomadic Bushmen. It was land that had been deemed harsh, waterless and infertile, unsuitable for agriculture. Some wildlife though, lucky to have escaped the big-game hunters, was present in this Kalahari sand region. The first park warden, Ted Davison, began sinking boreholes so that water-dependent species could survive in the long dry season, where up to seven months pass every year without rain. As a result, the wildlife flourished. Today Hwange National Park boasts more than 100 species of mammals and about 400 different types of birds.

The Hwange Estate, which is separated from Hwange National Park only by the Cape to Cairo railway line, came into being in the 1970s when two railway farms were privately bought and combined with state and forestry land to form a wildlife sanctuary. Before this initiative, large-scale slaughter of wildlife was occurring, particularly of the elephant population. With care and nurturing the Hwange Estate had, by the mid-1980s, become a key tourism area, rich in wildlife and famed for its habituated elephants.

Andy had thrown me the key to a door that I didn't know if I could open. I was excited, and also somewhat terrified. There was so much to think about, so much to do, and I wondered, while tossing and turning in my comfy king-sized bed in Brisbane, whether I could *really* go through with it.

Kind e-mails from Julia and others encouraged me and helped me to remember that this was an exciting opportunity and I wasn't crazy (as some, I'm sure, quietly suspected). At the time, Julia was looking after an orphaned bat-eared fox she'd named Batty. Secretly, I wondered if *I* was actually the batty one.

The words of those 95-year-olds echoed in my mind, '*We would take more risks... we would take more risks...*'

This was a risk – one that I needed to take.

So it was that on 5 March 2001 (one day short of the first anniversary of Andy's death) I walked across the tarmac at Victoria Falls airport, feeling that I'd arrived where I was always meant to be.

Julia and other friends were waiting to meet me. We shared a respect for animals and nature, and immediately the special links with my 'African family' were revived. Some friends had been born in Zimbabwe, while others were expatriates, like me. Regardless, we were all bonded by a common choice of life in the African bush and an acute awareness of sharing this privilege with each other.

Before heading home towards Hwange National Park we stopped to marvel at the world-famous Victoria Falls. The rains had been late that year, but when they came, it was with a vengeance. The Zambezi River was full and the falls were spectacular. They are twice the height and one-and-a-half times the width of America's Niagara Falls. So impressive are they that the explorer David Livingstone, who was the first European to stumble upon them, commented that angels in flight must surely gaze down on them.

While enjoying an outdoor lunch in a beautiful spot overlooking the Zambezi National Park we caught a glimpse of elephants in the distance, and I yearned to be among these magnificent giants. It was a surreal feeling knowing that soon I would be.

After lunch we drove south for two hours to Miombo Lodge, where I'd paid for a small cottage to be renovated. It was a concoction of old and new, hand-made bricks and an old thatched roof, with a concrete floor that had been painted, and then polished, red. I had the luxury of electricity, running water and even hot water. A fine net covered my hand-made bed, protecting me from the deadly malarial mosquitos. I needed to buy myself some curtains, a small fridge, a hotplate, a sofa, a coffee table and a grass mat. That was all I needed, I decided, to make it home.

There had, however, been some delays (something I'd have to get used to in Zimbabwe) and my cottage was not quite ready. So for the next three days I revelled in the splendour of Hwange National Park with Julia and other friends.

Everything delighted me. It's difficult to describe what if felt like, but it felt very much like 'coming home'. I'd always found a sweet and satisfying pleasure in the unrestricted freedom and space that is the wild African bush, and these first days back were no different. There's something exceptional about the sights, the sounds, the smells, the air, and the colours. For me, no other place evokes such a deep feeling of contentment.

We slept inside the park on wildlife viewing platforms, tall sturdy structures overlooking busy pans. In wild Africa, a pan is so much more than a mere waterhole. It's an oasis where animals of all species quench their thirst, a place where birdlife abounds. There is always a quiet beauty, a cooling of the air, a magical feeling at sunset.

The moon was exquisitely full. The unmistakeable laugh of hyenas and the rumbles from bull elephants were constant companions throughout the night. The musical voices of throngs of frogs came from the reeds in the pans, some tinkling like wind chimes in the night, others sounding like champagne bubbles bursting.

The contrast between the wet and dry seasons is spectacular in this part of Africa. At this time of year the veld is always lush and green, the bird-life is prolific and animal babies of all types are in abundance. Their attendant predators, the lions, made their presence heard. I absorbed it all, delighting in every detail. Finally, I was living in Africa, the world's largest animal sanctuary.

There was no way I could know the hardships, the hazards and the heartache that lay ahead. For now the only struggle I was aware of was the age-old, ongoing one between animals that have to kill to survive and those that have to avoid being eaten. Life here could be harsh, I knew, but I was certain that the experience of living among the wildlife of Africa would be like no other.

A few days later, before setting off to track hyenas, Julia and I enjoyed sundowners at Makwa pan, beneath billowy clouds touched with evening gold. Within an hour or so, as we watched the comings and goings of the wildlife against a deep pink sky, the sounds of the night began to emerge. It was getting dark and the animal calls around us grew louder. One, in particular, was constant.

'Is that a duck or a frog?' I asked.

'It's a baboon,' Julia replied.

How wrong could I be! This momentary lapse of bush-sense struck us as absolutely hilarious and we laughed much too loudly for two women alone on the back of a 4x4 in the middle of the dusk-shrouded bush. Some superior-looking giraffes approached, demanding that we keep quiet.

Andy and Lol had frequently enjoyed visiting Makwa pan. It now held special, but different, meaning for me too. Chloe had died in September of the previous year, taking with her a small piece of me. She was nearly 18 years old and was loyal and loving to the very end, having shared so much of my life. I remembered my promise to her, that one day she would come with me to Africa. So, on this journey, Chloe came too. I carried her ashes in a small ceramic urn and one day, with Julia, I let the wind carry them over Makwa pan. She deserved to be set free, I thought, in this place of beauty and peace.

At last, my cottage was habitable and I settled in quickly, despite it being rather bare. It's customary in Africa to give things a name. Optimistically, I christened my cottage 'Salaam', meaning peace. I took this name from a majestic male lion I'd spent time with in Uganda. He'd been rescued from poachers in Kenya after his mother was killed.

I, too, was honoured with a local name – Thandeka – an Ndebele name chosen by my African friends, whom I'd already known for a few years.

'What does Thandeka mean?' I'd asked.

'Love nest,' I was told proudly.

I laughed with embarrassment, explaining that these two words conjured up all sorts of 'interesting' images in my mind. I was immediately comforted to hear that my given name also simply means 'much loved'. I felt honoured to be known as Thandeka, a name that remains with me still.

I had no television, and international newspapers were non-existent in the bush. Often the only news came from what we termed 'the bush telegraph' – reading the local news of what had happened in the last 12 hours from the ground beneath your feet. Elephant, hyena, lion, zebra – the spoor of every species is uniquely identifiable. Clearly, elephants were regular night-time visitors to the grounds of my cottage, and lions and buffalos passed by often.

As I walked around my cottage, especially after dark, I was always alert to all sorts of possibilities, not least of all an unwelcome surprise encounter with an elephant, buffalo, lion or snake. And encounters there were, despite my vigilance – some quite memorable and at times a little too close for comfort.

Not long after moving in, Julia and John accompanied me to Bulawayo (known to the Ndebele as 'The City of Kings'), the largest city after the capital, Harare. As well as items for my cottage, I needed to buy a 4x4 and I was pleased to have John and Julia's expert assistance. I had no idea how long I would remain in Zimbabwe and therefore how long my savings needed to last, so I opted to be cautious and decided that I shouldn't spend *too* much money on a vehicle and furnishings.

We were up early on our first morning in Bulawayo. Once described as a handsome city, the streets are wide, the buildings reasonably modern. Now, though, the city looked grubby; littered with rubbish. Everything appeared tired and run-down. There were, nevertheless, a number of small second-hand car dealerships that we planned to visit.

'Buy this!' John urged, while standing over a big old white monstrosity of a vehicle with a black leather roof.

'I'm not going to buy *that*,' I retorted with a frown.

Yet, somewhat apprehensively, and feigning indifference to the constant shaking of our mechanic friend's head, I eventually did.

A 1980 Range Rover. The local word for 'rust bucket' eluded me, so I named her Nicki Mukuru – Nicki after our trusted mechanic friend who had the unenviable job of making her roadworthy, and Mukuru meaning elderly one. As it turned out, it would be many long weeks before Nicki Mukuru's overhaul was complete.

While still in town, John and Julia took me to the auctions, searching for second-hand things that I might buy.

'Buy this!' John urged, pointing to a small coffee table. Above thin, splayed wooden legs was a copper top embossed with elephants, covered with glass.

'I'm not going to buy *that*,' I retorted. 'It might be an elephant, but it's ugly,' I muttered.

Yet when bidding was low, feeling sorry for the ugly elephant table, I bought it.

Julia, I might add, was the complete opposite to John, constantly telling me what I *didn't* need to buy, and I couldn't work out which was worse. Eventually though, I had all that I needed, and some things that I didn't *really* need.

In John's very old Isuzu, pulling a small trailer overloaded with my purchases, the drive back from Bulawayo in drizzling rain took us five hours instead of three. It was a relief to finally get back to the bush.

Occasionally over the next few months when we needed to get to Bulawayo, Julia and I caught a chicken bus. It's called a chicken bus, I was told, because it's likely to have chickens in cages on the rooftop, and indeed inside the bus itself – along, perhaps, with the odd goat. There were often chicken heads popping out of backpacks, others sitting obediently at the feet of their owners and still others clucking their disapproval. These buses are noisy, old, crammed with people and often rather unpleasant smelling. They hurtle along like crabs, with the rear frequently at a scary angle to the front. Somehow, they always delivered us safely to Bulawayo.

We hitch-hiked once, arriving in Bulawayo in a hearse. I kept trying to peek through the blackened back window to see if we were in the company of a coffin, with somebody inside it. I couldn't be sure, and I didn't like to ask. Funeral parlours are many in Africa, and 'Farley' – the one to which our hearse belonged – was one of the better known in Bulawayo. It was so well known, in fact, that the old-age home where Del lived had been branded 'Farley's Takeaway'!

This was all a little too much for me, and I never hitch-hiked again.

Back at my cottage, my least favourite creatures – snakes and spiders – were giving me a hard time. For reasons unknown to me, I have a disproportionate fear of them. It wasn't long before their constant presence became a little irksome, although I joked about them in order to cope. Indeed, I found myself welcoming friends into my cottage with the words, 'Sit back. Relax. Pull up a spider,' or perhaps 'Sit back. Relax. Pull up a snake'.

The day the Mozambique spitting cobra came *inside* my cottage, however, I screamed like a banshee and ran. Hearing the commotion, the gardener came to investigate and to deal with the deadly intruder.

'What did you do with the snake?' I asked him later.

'Out,' he answered in his limited English.

'You put it *outside*?' I exclaimed. Outside! Oh, man. As far as I was concerned that was only remotely better than leaving it inside.

Sensing my unease, John advised me to sprinkle ash around my cottage. It was, he said, a deterrent against snakes. I looked at him sceptically, but at this point I was prepared to try anything. So I gathered ash from our nightly campfires, in the hope that it might also work for spiders (not to mention the scorpions, which looked like they were on steroids). A few months later, for my birthday in May, I received a welcome gift of 'snake flaps' for the bottom edges of my cottage doors, successfully closing off the gaps to the floor. This was a present that I wholeheartedly appreciated.

John had told me rather sheepishly about a time when he'd been awoken from an afternoon nap by a spray of liquid. He'd sleepily told Del to quit spraying him with the water pistol they often playfully used on each other, only to open his eyes and find that he was in fact sharing his bed with a spitting cobra. I named John 'the Snake and Spider King', and always conferred with him on matters of this kind.

I personally was more comfortable around the larger creatures, which was not to say that I always approved of their deeds.

One morning a small bright-eyed boy appeared at my doorstep and grabbed me by the hand. 'Sharon, come! Come!' he pleaded breathlessly. 'I want to show you what the *ndlovus* did to the garden.

They're in *biiggg* trouble.'

He yanked me out of my cottage and hurried me towards the lodge garden. Those *ndlovus* really were in big trouble. What were once tall banana trees had been shorn off at ground level, and there were a few craters where the roots had clearly also been savoured. Then, to rub salt into our wounds, they'd quenched their thirst from the swimming pool, leaving any guests who were so inclined to have to swim with dirt particles and floating banana tree roots.

'Please can't you keep your elephants on a leash?' my young friend's mother asked sarcastically. I could do little but laugh, and then help to clean up the mess.

A few mornings later I accompanied two companions to a nearby rifle range for target practice – something well worth doing when you spend your days in the wilds of Africa. Having previously handled only a revolver, the rifle felt heavy.

'Aim at those tins,' I was instructed. 'Just try.'

I protested feebly, but no one was listening to me, so I eventually took aim.

The .458 Lott shots were as loud as I had anticipated; the recoil was worse. Somewhat to my own surprise I hit the tins – and pretended not to notice the stunned expressions on the faces of my male friends. Days later I was still nursing a sore, bruised inside upper-arm where I'd rested the gun while taking aim. Having made such a good impression on the range, however, I decided to keep that secret to myself.

As time went by I added a touch of myself to my cottage. I hung my wildlife photographs on the walls, and learned to garden the Zimbabwean way.

'Can you move that log over a little to the right please,' I heard myself say one day, 'and put that plant over there.'

It was sinful really. I knew that I should get out there and do it myself, but at least this way I had someone else to blame when the deep Kalahari sand claimed its first victim.

It was not usual to do gardening and household chores yourself, but then, despite having accepted the help of the lodge gardener, I was never very conventional. This was especially true when it came to the type of clothes I wore in the bush. Typically my clothing was dark-coloured, inexpensive and comfortable, meeting my important criteria, and I rarely wore closed shoes. Usually I wore a knee-length black skirt in preference to shorts or long pants. I had never, after all, fancied trying to look like Tarzan's girlfriend, fitted out in designer khaki, and I found it curious that some people seemed to think that I *should* look like Jane of the jungle.

Wildlife Outings

While awaiting Nicki Mukuru's overhaul, I was stranded without a vehicle of my own. Unable to drive myself to the elephants, I filled my time by accompanying other wildlife people on their outings into the bush.

Two of the lion researchers lived near me in the grounds of Miombo Lodge and one afternoon I was invited to join them for a collaring operation. Although radio collars do detract from the wild appearance of animals, they are a valuable research aid. They make it easier to track and therefore locate the wearer for purposes of study and the collection of important home-range data. Collars also identify animals as research subjects, which may help to save their lives should they happen to wander outside the unfenced protected tourism areas onto sport-hunting ranches, where, if their species appears on an approved hunting quota, they can legally be shot as trophies.

We collected a side of decaying meat that was to be used as bait. Snack-sized for the lions, but a heavy lift for a mere man, it was hauled onto the roof rack of a 4x4 for transportation to a chosen spot on the Hwange Estate, close to where the lions had earlier been seen. The bait dripped blood and smelt particularly unpleasant – at least to me. When we reached our destination it was thrown to the ground, tied to the back of the 4x4 and dragged in a wide circle, creating an enticing trail for the lions to follow. It was then chained to a nearby stump where, we hoped, the lions would settle down to feed.

The conditions were ideal. This was a known pride of 17 lions but they had split temporarily and a quick drive just a few kilometres down the vlei confirmed that 12 of them were there, feeding on a fresh wildebeest kill. They would hopefully stay put for the night, so they wouldn't disturb our operation, which was focused on the rest of the pride: Ulaka (the pride male), two adult females and their two cubs.

We stood around the research vehicles as the head lion researcher explained how he intended to collar Ulaka and one of the lionesses. As an extra incentive to the 'drag', a tape recording of a squealing pig was to be played at high volume. A squealing domestic pig, I guessed. I supposed it would sound similar to a distressed warthog, but I wondered how the wild lions would react to such a sound. Eventually we all climbed back into our respective vehicles. The lion researchers sat in the back of an open 4x4. I sat with a girlfriend in the vehicle that had transported the bait, the sound system on the seat in front of me.

'Play the tape,' we were instructed.

My friend pushed the play button, and the loudest hog-squeal that I'd ever heard rang out into the wilderness.

It worked a treat. Ulaka appeared instantly, in all his magnificence, from the dense bush in front of us. The two lionesses also appeared, with a pair of seven-month-old cubs in tow. The descending ball of fire provided a splendid, glowing backdrop, creating a magical moment.

Ulaka came close, less than five metres from our 4x4. He sat and stared at us, and the reality suddenly hit me. I was sitting in a vehicle that smelt deliciously of blood and rotting meat. Ulaka had just heard the sound of an appetising squealing pig coming from where I sat. He'd arrived so promptly that the power-window closest to him was still fully open, and moving to close it now was not a great idea.

Did Ulaka think that I was the tasty squealing pig? It certainly looked like he might have. I decided somewhat nervously that it was wise not to keep eye contact with him for too long. As I sat perfectly still, listening to the beat of my own heart, I had visions of him leaping onto our vehicle and diving in through the open window.

A towering elephant – the *true* king of the jungle – approached, causing all five lions to run a little further away in the direction of the other vehicle. I breathed more easily. Then Ulaka marked his territory in the exact spot where we'd earlier relieved ourselves. Thinking back now, Ulaka had undoubtedly *watched* us relieve ourselves!

Given the rapid appearance of the lions, there'd been no time for the researchers to pull down the canvas sides of the open 4x4 in which they sat. Ulaka approached them now, too close for comfort. A quick flash of torchlight directed at his eyes chased him off. Uninterested after that in the bait that lay nearby, all five lions headed off in the direction of the other 12.

We took advantage of this opportunity to quickly rearrange ourselves. The windows of our vehicle were closed, the canvas sides of the other one were pulled down, and the dart gun was readied. Then the signal was given to replay the pig tape.

The ear-piercing din of the squealing pig once again rang out into the still night. Within seconds the five lions returned, this time striding straight towards the bait before crouching down to feed greedily. The head lion researcher aimed and fired. Ulaka was the first to be darted, followed by the two lionesses. The cubs were left to feed in peace. Twenty minutes later the drugs had taken effect and all three lions were fully sedated.

It was a warm evening. Stars filled the sky. The lights from the nearby Hwange Safari Lodge silhouetted the trees as we climbed out of our vehicles and walked among the lions that lay motionless on the ground. The cubs scattered but, curious, they stayed close by throughout the night.

I stroked Ulaka's long black mane. He was huge and magnificent.

Apart from a few tense moments when the spotlight picked up nearby eyes that could have belonged to the other pride members coming to investigate our presence, and those heart-stopping moments when sedated Ulaka let out an unexpected deep groan, everything went like clockwork. Data was collected and Ulaka and one lioness were collared.

The air became cold in the wee hours of the morning while we sat watching and waiting for the lions to recover from the drugs, making certain that nothing attacked them while in their sleepy state. All in all it had been an exciting and successful night in the veld.

Before going to live in Zimbabwe I'd helped to secure a dart rifle for the Animal Rescue team (also based at Miombo Lodge), which was formed to fill just one of the gaps that Andy had left. They responded to reports of snared animals. Poachers' snares were a constant reality. Times were tough in Zimbabwe. Some people were poor and hungry, although others, as I eventually came to know first-hand, were simply greedy and uncaring. In any case, the fact remains that the sight of an animal carrying a deeply embedded wire snare, often around its neck or leg, is a horrific one.

Fortunately the callout on this day was a false alarm. We arrived in the field to find that a zebra had indeed been snared. The wound around her neck was red and gruesome, but there was no wire. The Animal Rescue team had darted this same zebra just a few weeks earlier and had already removed the snare. Although it would be a lengthy road to recovery, she was feeding well and looked likely to survive.

Before long, we saw a second zebra with a wire around her neck. Soon after being darted, she galloped off. We drove off too, searching for her. She'd collapsed with her head caught in the fork of a small tree. Fortunately, she hadn't hurt herself, and within seconds of the tight wire being cut, she bolted off at high speed, freed from the deadly trap.

That was one saved, but there were many more to go, like the noble sable antelope bull, with massive curved horns, that was suffering the debilitating effect of a tight wire snare around his leg. He fled into dense, impenetrable bush immediately the dart hit his rump. It wasn't possible to drive in after him, which left us with no choice but to walk in, relying on the impressive skills of an African tracker. The ground was hard in places and covered with leaf-litter, yet the tracker expertly followed the indistinct spoor and managed to locate the sable. This had taken some time and the drug was already wearing off. It took three men to hold the sable down while a 'top-up' was administered. The tight wire around his leg was successfully removed and yet another animal was spared what could potentially have been a protracted and painful death.

Darting could be a risky business for reasons unrelated to the recipients, as I came to know personally. I accompanied the Animal Rescue team on a callout to yet another snared zebra. This one was heavily pregnant. She was successfully immobilised and the snare removed, however she got to her feet before all of the 'reversal' drug could be administered and started to gallop away. With the chances of her relapsing into immobility now high, it was decided to dart her again with the remainder of the reversal drug, using a non-barbed dart this time. The drug would automatically be injected on contact with her body and the dart would fall to the ground. It wouldn't be necessary to pull it from her rump, obviating the need for more human contact. But something went wrong.

The dart was prepared as usual. It wasn't human error; it was pure mischance. The dart exploded and the liquid drug sprayed all over us.

'Oh sh*t!' we gasped in unison, knowing the deadly danger of an accident like this.

We were lucky. Had it been the *immobilisation* drug in that dart our lives would have suddenly hung in the balance. Without the antidote, death is only minutes away if this drug is absorbed into the human body via cuts on the skin. The antidote is always at hand, with people who know how to use it, however it was a frightening reminder of the potential risks involved in saving an animal's life.

There were other hazards associated with snare removal, though fortunately most were not as life threatening. Despite a serious goring while walking in the bush with friends many years earlier, John held no grudges against buffalos. One day, while a snare was being removed from one of these fearsome animals, he thoughtfully took off his shirt and placed it over the buffalo's head, to protect its eyes from the glaring sun. The snare was soon off and the buffalo was up and running into the bush quicker than expected, shirt around its horns. John panicked. His house keys were in the pocket! Luckily, the buffalo eventually tossed off John's shirt, and everyone chuckled their relief.

Early another morning Julia and I were driving on the main tar road towards the Hwange Safari Lodge when we came upon three painted hunting dogs by the roadside. The dogs, which are among the most endangered species in Africa, have stunning patterned coats and white-tipped tails. But this was a tragic scene. Another dog lay on the other side of the road, alert, but struggling to get up. Humans pose the biggest threat to these animals. Considered vermin by some, they are persecuted relentlessly. This particular dog hadn't managed to escape the all-too-frequent recklessness of man. It had been hit by a vehicle and was seriously injured.

From the nearby Hwange Safari Lodge I tried to call the painted dog research team and finally reached the Animal Rescue team instead. They responded quickly. A blanket was thrown over the dog and it was carefully placed in the back of a vehicle. A drip was attached and it was driven the three-hour journey to a vet in Bulawayo. However, the trip was in vain. The dog's spine had been severed and there was nothing that could be done to save its life. Humans had tried to undo the damage that other humans had caused; a tragic scenario that I was already coming across too often.

Thankfully, other encounters with the dogs were less heart-rending. One afternoon, six puppies lay together in the shade of a tree inside Hwange National Park – an exhausted heap of painted dogs. The Ndebele call them *'iganyana'*, which means 'cruelty to another animal' – because they disembowel their live prey. These puppies certainly looked endearing enough, quite unlike ruthless predators. Indeed they were just adorable, playful and mischievous like all domestic pups. When the adults returned from their hunting foray there was pandemonium as food was regurgitated to the accompaniment of the usual (and rather surprising) puppy sounds – not unlike those of twittering birds and barking baboons.

Later that evening we cooked pasta over an open fire and slept under the stars. It was definitely not a five-star hotel. It was, in fact, a five-billion-star hotel. It was tempting to stay awake until dawn, so as not to miss out on the beauty and activity of the African night.

Before falling asleep we found ourselves reminiscing about an incident that had happened a few years before, which I couldn't help breaking into hoots of laughter about for many years after. Before moving permanently to Zimbabwe, I was in the dog team's 4x4 one evening as rain tumbled from dark skies. We pulled up at a lodge where I, and the team member who'd been driving, opened our doors against the pelting rain and raced to take cover under the thatched reception area just a few metres ahead of us. We already had a drink in hand when the guy who'd been riding in the covered back – an Englishman in his 30s – finally appeared, looking more than a little frazzled; his face pale, his body wet, and part of his curly head of hair literally standing on end.

'What on earth happened to you?' I blurted with an involuntary giggle.

There was a brief pause, as if he couldn't believe what had happened to him.

'I...walked...into...the...electric...fence...' he muttered slowly, clearly bewildered.

It really wasn't funny. It was raining and the electric fence, designed to keep elephants and other animals at bay, was switched on. Yet we all rolled around in fits of uncontrollable laughter at the sight and sound of him, managing to ask if he really was okay and listening to his story while he, good naturedly, chortled along with us.

He'd become disorientated after heaving open the heavy rear door of the 4x4 and inadvertently set off in the wrong direction. Thinking it unusually dark, but still not convinced that he needed to change direction, he extended his arms in front of his body, like a sleepwalker in a movie, trying to feel his way. The first thing his fingers had touched was the electric fence...

There was still no sign of my 4x4. I checked on its progress regularly, but it remained in Bulawayo, awaiting parts. Fortunately there were plenty more wildlife-related activities to occupy my time while I waited impatiently for its repair.

I was keen to observe hyena youngsters, so one evening I accompanied Julia to the den she was monitoring inside the national park. Hyena cubs don't really look like hyenas at all; to me they look like little cuddly brown bears, with backsides a bit like those of koalas. This den was a big old fallen tree, the hollow interior of which was a communal refuge, housing two different sets of cubs. We watched the smallest of the cubs play, racing around and around a circle of bushes, biting the ears of the much bigger cubs. Displaying surprising tolerance, the older cubs didn't mind at all and seemed to relish some fun.

The moon shed just enough light for us to be able to see. A myriad of stars were above, the cries of hyenas and jackals piercing the silence.

'Nothing beats a night in the star-studded African veld,' I mused contentedly to myself.

I had to be careful not to break into hoots of laughter around Julia too. There'd recently been another incident that, after making sure she was okay, caused us all to giggle wildly. Julia had been asked to manage Miombo Lodge for a few days while the owners were away. She was always the perfect hostess, chatting enthusiastically with the guests before dinner. One guest had a particular interest in the stars, and I watched as he and Julia gazed high above their heads, pointing to various constellations as they wandered slowly across the lawn, keeping a keen eye on the heavens above. All of a sudden there was an almighty splash. Fully clothed, shoes and all, Julia had accidentally stepped (backwards) into the pool.

Back on solid ground – smiling as always and no worse for wear – Julia was keen to find a second active hyena den, but she'd been having no success. One morning we walked, with an armed scout, through thick bush. Spoor indicated that hyenas had indeed padded along our path just hours before, but we didn't manage to find them.

We had better luck, though, on a collaring expedition soon after. We filled Julia's 4x4 with field equipment and supplies, and waited in the bush until nightfall. When finally the sedation dart hit its target, the stunned hyena raced off. Without the light of a full moon we couldn't be sure exactly where it had succumbed to the drug. There were a few tense minutes as we drove slowly off-road, searching with spotlights. We eventually found the hyena lying in long grass, its coat blending in perfectly with the surroundings. Julia wasted no time in recording the important data she needed, and attaching the collar. Soon the hyena was back with its clan, seemingly unconcerned about its new 'necklace'. I listened again that night to the contagious giggles of these curious animals, bewitched as always with Africa's wildlife.

The wildlife activity never ceased. It was a cold night on a game-viewing platform inside the park named Nyamandlovu (*Nyama* meaning meat; *ndlovu* meaning elephant – forming a rather disturbing name: *meat of the elephant*). Julia and I had warmed ourselves with a glass of Amarula (a Baileys-like cream liqueur, made from the small yellow fruit of the marula tree so loved by the elephants), before retiring to our sleeping bags. The call of a male lion – an incredibly wild sound that reverberates through your body to the very tips of your toes – disturbed our deep slumber. In fact, I sat bolt upright in utter fright. The loud guttural bellows were so close that I wondered if this *shumba* was actually on the platform with us. Although the platform is high, we normally placed chairs at the top of the wooden stairs to give us some (albeit false) sense of security against roaming animals – since I had, in the past, seen hyenas bound up these stairs. That night we hadn't even taken this feeble precaution. Pointlessly, I rallied to correct the situation, shuffling along like a penguin with my sleeping bag around my ankles. The lion called again, shattering the still night. Fortunately, he wasn't on the platform with us, but he was indeed *very* close.

'Sharon, look!' whispered Julia urgently, pointing towards the sandy road below us.

By moonlight she'd spotted the magnificent male lion just a few metres from the edge of the platform, walking down the road.

His mate, on the other side of the pan, called back to him. It is an unforgettable, soul-shaking sound in the still of the African night. It is, though, hardly a 'roar'. More precisely, there are grunts and bellows and moans. I ultimately decided, somewhat irreverently, that the call a lion makes sounds like something between constipation and climax. Instead of a roar, I hear a low and powerful constipation-like grunt mixed with the rather pleasurable sound effects of an orgasm!

Eventually, Julia and I retired to our sleeping bags, listening to the wild conversations of the lions that continued into the early hours of the morning.

Soon full moon was with us once again, the phases of the moon always influencing our night-time activities. While spending the night with another friend on the same game-viewing platform (this time with chairs placed strategically at the top of the stairs), we were rewarded with the company of three white rhinos, massive and prehistoric-looking. It is, tragically, no longer a common sight. Elephant herds arrived in the twilight, bringing a smile to my face. Shaking their huge heads, they trumpeted at the sight of their rhino companions. We enjoyed the extraordinary wildlife theatre under the light of the full moon, the rumbles of the elephants eventually lulling us into a sound, peaceful sleep. We awoke in the morning to the breathtaking sight of the dew-spangled veld, refreshed and ready to face another day.

While the moon was still full, another male lion was collared. He was part of a mating pair, full of testosterone and rather unhappy about wasting his time with us when more urgent matters clearly beckoned. There was neither aromatic bait nor squealing pig needed this time round; the lion close enough to dart without encouragement. The researchers collared him by the light of the moon. Even bigger than Ulaka, this *shumba* had a remarkably soft mane. His girlfriend waited patiently in the veld just a couple of hundred metres away. It was another splendid night in the African bush, man and beast bathed in moonlight.

Some of the lion and painted hunting dog researchers were now learning to fly, so they could track their radio-collared animals from a microlight. I felt a degree of nervousness for them, and was adamant that it would take a long time before I was comfortable climbing on board another small aircraft.

I eventually relented though, and enjoyed an experience not unlike one of the memorable scenes from the Academy Award-winning *Out of Africa* (the motion picture based on the Danish Baroness Karen Blixen's book of the same name), which I've watched countless times.

It was when the flying instructor was present that I forced myself to face my renewed aversion to light aircraft, and decided that taking the plunge with this highly experienced pilot was the best thing for me to do. It was good for my soul. The air was calm and the ride was remarkably smooth and quiet. That feeling of unbounded freedom and space hit me hard.

It was a flight tinged with sadness as I remembered my last flight, before that fateful day the previous March, when I flew in an adjoining area with Andy and Lol. Now, I crossed a barrier into a new world. There was time to pause, and once again take in the splendour of Africa as seen through the eyes of a pilot.

Soon after, I went radio-tracking on the vlei with one of the lion researchers. The sky was clear, the grass long and green. As it turned out, we didn't need the tracking equipment after all. The many photographic safari vehicles, all parked together, indicated that the lions were there. Fourteen members of the pride lounged close to the road, enjoying the late afternoon sunshine. Collared Ulaka and one female were missing that day, perhaps off together mating. Also missing was one cub, presumed dead, permanently reducing the number in this pride to 16.

The safari vehicles eventually moved off, allowing us to enjoy the spectacle alone. One by one the four lionesses moved off too, leaving the cubs behind. The cubs intuitively knew that they must stay put. The adults, their muscular bodies golden in the late afternoon light, strode purposefully across the vlei. Soon they were out of sight, but clearly they were on a mission. These are predators that must kill to survive, like it or not. It wasn't long before the loud bleating of an unfortunate victim rang into the still afternoon.

The 10 cubs listened intently, seemingly knowing that their mothers had successfully organised dinner, but they didn't move from the spot where they'd been left, a couple of hundred metres from the fresh kill. Instead, they waited impatiently. A few minutes passed before their mothers called them to join the dinner table. I didn't hear a thing, but the cubs obviously did, because all of a sudden they raced off together in single file across the vlei.

We followed too. The lions were now deep in the bush, but fortunately there was a track in. We found all 14 gorging ravenously on an adult kudu. There were guttural growls and mean-faced snarls, and the swatting of huge paws. Blood and sand covered their upper bodies. 'These guys have terrible table manners,' my companion commented with a smile, and I had to agree. With their dinner rapidly disappearing, we left them to squabble over who could bury their head deepest in the carcass, and returned home for some supper of our own. Thankfully, kudu wasn't on the menu.

Easter Sunday found Julia and me on the Hwange Estate with one of the painted dog researchers, tracking the dogs. We tracked from the ground for hours and hours with no result, and in desperation were tempted to wind down the windows and sing. Perhaps, we jested, this might bring the dogs out of hiding. Acknowledging our combined limited singing abilities, it was suggested that we play the dogs some music instead. 'Bach, perhaps?' offered Julia with a grin. In the spirit of the moment we rolled our eyes and emitted playful little doggy barks, and we laughed and laughed.

I contemplated my days in the African bush. No day was ever the same, every one of them bringing something new and unexpected. I smiled to myself, and wondered how my family and friends Down Under had spent their Easter Sunday. Not with lions and painted hunting dogs, that was certain.

I decided that if the 'Easter bilby' (an animal native to Australia, vaguely similar to the introduced bunny) is the official egg-bearer in Australia, then its equivalent in these parts must surely be an 'Easter springhare', a pint-sized animal that you have to be alert enough not to run over after dark. Some unfortunate ones don't make it. That, I concluded playfully, must be why Easter eggs in Zimbabwe are always in such short supply.

Meeting the Elephants

The day finally came when Nicki Mukuru was deemed roadworthy, and was ready for collection in Bulawayo. 'I've been trying to make custard out of cow dung,' my mechanic friend declared with a disturbingly straight face. I managed a grin, convinced she must surely be a better vehicle than that. *Elephant* dung at least, I decided. And I would strangle John, I secretly vowed, if she wasn't!

Our partnership didn't begin well. With Julia and one of the lion researchers for company, I drove Nicki Mukuru back from Bulawayo. We were chatting enthusiastically, enjoying the leafy country drive, when there was an almighty explosion. I struggled to keep control. It all happened so quickly, yet it also seemed to unfold in slow motion. Within seconds we were on gravel and sand, off the other side of the road close to the tree line, facing in the opposite direction. I was astounded that we didn't roll, or at least end up on our side.

Since the moment of the explosion, there'd been complete silence inside Nicki Mukuru. 'Is everybody okay?' I asked with concern once we were stationary, amazed that they'd kept their cool without even one murmur of alarm. Thankfully, we were all fine.

We soon discovered the cause of the explosion. One of the tyres had blown out in the most extraordinary fashion. The force of the blast had even damaged the body of the vehicle above the tyre! The mud flap behind the wheel was shredded and my newly fitted exhaust system was deeply dented.

I'd been travelling at just under 100 km/h on open road. Many here drive much faster. That very day a cabinet minister and his driver had been killed instantly in an accident caused, so we were told, by a rear blowout similar to ours. I was a little shaken, determined now to travel considerably slower.

Aside from the blowout – cow dung or not – Nicki Mukuru proved to be extremely dependable. Large windows all around and a sliding roof meant that she was ideal for elephant observations. I did have one problem though, but it wasn't of her making. Due to the worsening economic climate, fuel was regularly in short supply, which curtailed my fieldwork.

Still, I had a vehicle of my own and at least now I could spend my time with the elephants on the Hwange Estate, getting to know them as individuals. Those that comprised the Presidential Elephants were unusually habituated to people and vehicles, with many approaching to greet you. This unfenced estate was, indisputably, one of the best places in the world to have close-up encounters with wild, free-ranging elephants.

The extraordinary feeling when standing up through the roof of Nicki Mukuru, with a six-tonne Mr *Loxodonta Africana* approaching close enough to put his trunk just centimetres from your hand, is something not easy to put into words. There is an unmistakable touch of fairy dust and animal magic about it all.

It wasn't long before the bonnet of Nicki Mukuru was riddled with dents and scratches caused by the occasional elephant rubbing its tusks, but I valued these tokens of familiarity. I felt enormously privileged to spend time around the pans on this estate, at one with the wildlife, warmed by the rumbles of the elephants.

I watched them move, majestic and free across the vlei, looking out for a flap of ears to help me identify who was calling. I repeatedly got a kick out of two discoveries made in Amboseli National Park in Kenya. Firstly, female elephants use many more and varied vocalisations than males do. The ladies clearly like to natter. And even more typical, the males have been proven to talk primarily of supremacy and sex!

Yet I knew that what I could hear was only a smattering. Many elephant vocalisations are of such low frequency that they are inaudible to humans, yet it has also been proven that their extraordinary infrasound ability is so effective they can communicate with each other over as far as 10 kilometres.

Elephants can be silent in all ways if they wish to be. There are times when you won't hear them until they appear, seemingly from nowhere. At other times it's the snap of a twig, the flap of a huge ear or the thud of a dung ball as it hits the ground that alerts you to their presence. So often you smell them before you actually see them. It's a smell that has been described as the most evocative in Africa: the sweet, straw-like fragrance of fresh elephant dung.

While out in the field, sharp acacia thorns, often hidden in elephant dung, regularly pierced my tyres. Sometimes I found myself with three flat tyres in two days – frequently with a herd of elephants in front of me and, as luck would have it, a herd of buffalos behind me. This was, I guess, Murphy's Law. It certainly did seem to me that Murphy was alive and well, and living on the Hwange Estate.

Given that there was no roadside-service to call, I needed to practise using a hi-lift jack and asked John for his help. I was promptly subjected to what felt like army training. In John's front yard (a tall electric fence, which didn't work, separating his dilapidated home from the untamed bush), I took off the heavy tyre and put it back on.

'You must never be stuck in the bush just because of a flat tyre,' John barked at me. 'Do it again.' Under his watchful eye, I once again took off the tyre and put it back on.

Nicki Mukuru was not really designed for a hi-lift jack, and the crooked grin on John's otherwise impassive face couldn't hide the fact that he was getting perverse enjoyment out of watching me struggle in the heat of the day.

Now he tightened the wheel nuts, making them *very* tight, and gave me a hollow metal length of pipe to assist with leverage when removing them.

'Do it again!' John bellowed, with a cheeky grin. By this time I was laughing so much that I could barely lift the tyre. 'Do it again!' he insisted.

With a furrow in my brow, now sitting on the dry, bare ground with wheel spanner and metal pipe in hand, I looked up at him towering above me, and all of a sudden it seemed perfectly clear to me why, all those years before, that buffalo had gored him...

Africa, for many, is a desolate place, filled with poverty and unrest.

I was fortunate, I knew, to be seeing and living another face of Africa. My Africa was filled with an abundance of free-roaming wildlife, native bush, splendid sunsets and friendly people (and some just a little nutty, like John). During the day, I shared my solitude with elephants. Who better to spend time with?

I was lucky, I often thought. Africa had been kind to me. It was the perfect place to rejuvenate my soul; it held the promise of an unforgettable journey.

In the months and years ahead, expert now at changing tyres (and enjoying the feeling of independence that this brought), I spent countless hours working on an elephant identification library. Making sense of thousands of notations and photographs was a time-consuming task. I no longer looked at my pictures just from a photographic point of view. It was no longer merely a photograph of an elephant; now it was a photograph of a *particular* elephant. I studied the tusks. Was the elephant left- or right-tusked? Just as we are left- or right-handed, elephants favour the use of one tusk. This master tusk becomes more worn, often shorter than the other, and sometimes develops a groove in its tip where the constant action of pulling branches across it wears a furrow in the ivory. I looked at the length and circumference of these oversized incisor teeth, marvelling at this quirk of nature. I also studied the elephants' massive ears, noting all the holes, nicks and rips. More so than the tusks, the ears are uniquely identifiable, or at least they're supposed to be. I rolled my eyes at those elephants that seemed to have walked into the same thorny bush, sustaining almost identical ear injuries.

I organised my photographs into family groups. Who were the great matriarchs – the wise adult females who each lead a different family? Who was the mother of whom? Who belonged to what family – a family that, in the case of females, they would remain with all their lives, for up to 65 years? Which young males were no longer with their family? Nature dictates that males leave their natal family when they're sexually mature, usually around the age of 14, when their adult female relations become less tolerant of them. They gradually embark on life as independent bulls. Some mature males choose to tag along with other family groups, while others prefer to join small all-male groups, or wander alone. To be able to figure out their 'social structure', I needed to get to know the elephants both individually and in a family context, before determining and recording events such as births, deaths, matings, calving intervals, and age and sex ratios. These are all keys to understanding the population dynamics of the Presidential Elephants and are therefore important inputs to elephant management plans.

To make identification easier, I assigned a letter of the alphabet to each family group, and gave each elephant within the family a name beginning with that letter. Although some easily identifiable elephants could be singled out as early as the 1970s and 1980s, useful monitoring efforts had only started around 1993 when complete family groups were more accurately identified and documented. No photographic library existed however, nor a formal naming structure. So I began these tasks from scratch, with just a few of the easily recognisable elephants retaining their original, arbitrary names.

There were now, for example, the Ls. Every elephant in the L family, as the naming convention dictates, was given a name beginning with that letter. I could not yet know that the matriarch of this family, named Lady, would eventually grant me a most extraordinary place in her world.

Then there was Skew Tusk, the matriarch of what was now the S family, who'd been named many years before by the photographic safari guides on the Hwange Estate. It's possible that her tusk, when damaged or infected, became loosened in its socket, rotated, and then continued to grow in an abnormal direction. There was no need to look at her ears; her skewed tusk made her uniquely identifiable.

Skew Tusk was one of a small group of 22 frightened elephants that formed the nucleus of what eventually became The Presidential Elephants of Zimbabwe. They were the only ones left roaming the Hwange Estate following a period of relentless slaughter. Nurtured initially by photographic safari owner Alan Elliott, these elephants gradually became habituated to people and vehicles and in 1990, on Alan's recommendation, President Robert Mugabe issued them a 'special protection decree', as a symbol of Zimbabwe's commitment to responsible wildlife management. This decree, it is said, provides for the perpetual safety of these elephants – now numbering around 400 – that spend the majority of their time during the dry season on the Hwange Estate. Based on Skew Tusk's estimated age in the 1970s, she is believed to be more than 50 years old now and is no longer the shy, aggressive teenager Alan first met.

The oldest of the original 22 elephants was a tuskless cow named Inkosikazi (an Ndebele name, sometimes used to refer to the wife of a king). Like Skew Tusk, she was named in the 1970s and is estimated to be at least 55 now. Although she will always be known as Inkosikazi, I categorised her as a high-ranking member of the 'A' family. (Finding sufficient 'I' names for all the members of her family was simply too difficult a task.) Longer-term observations eventually proved that she does in fact head her own smaller sub-family, which simply chooses to spend much of its time in association with a larger bond group of elephants.

In time I grew particularly attached to the tuskless elephants such as Inkosikazi because to me, they represent an end to the slaughter and greed of the corrupt ivory war. There is Alisha (Inkosikazi's daughter), Debbie and Delight, Cathy, Echo, Precious, Zelda and others. They are all favourite elephants.

Tusklessness is said to be hereditary and, like tusk size, is believed to be the result of selective sport-hunting and poaching of large males with the heaviest ivory, resulting in the disappearance of the genes responsible for large tusks, and indeed any tusks at all. The majority of the Hwange elephants (the migratory bulls always sport-hunted relentlessly) are endowed with relatively small tusks.

My data collection became increasingly meaningful the more I got to know the elephant families. I noted changes in group size and composition, and constructed family trees. I became familiar with individual interactions, both within the family groups and between different families. There was much to be learned, and comparative analysis with studies in other countries – in other ecosystems – was expected to yield interesting results.

It is well worth noting that the expansion of what was, in 1974, a group of only 22 Hwange Estate elephants to around 400 today, did not come about purely as a result of births. During the 16 years to 1990, when the presidential decree was obtained, various elephant families clearly found peace and calm on the Hwange Estate, adopting it as an important and preferred part of their dry season home range. There was now no hunting of any kind allowed here, making it a safe haven for elephant families.

There are elephants of similar age, and some even older than Inkosikazi, that today form part of the Presidential Elephants, proof that not all the elephants are the offspring of the original 22. It is likely, too, that between previous data collections and my arrival in 2001, some additional elephant families also found refuge on the Hwange Estate. So, for the purposes of my work with them and in the absence of prior, clearly identifiable, photographic records of family groups, the Presidential Elephants are defined by me as those families that, based on my sightings during 2001, spent the majority of the dry season on this estate. Although not all are related by birth, the families that constitute the Presidential Elephants *do* form a cohesive clan, visible at certain times of the year in one large gathering.

The work I was doing could earn degrees, but academic advancement didn't interest me. This didn't lessen my desire to gather and share information though. My first priority was to help the snared elephants, and to take part in other anti-poaching and conservation-related activities that aided *all* the wildlife. My next priority was to learn more about the lives of the elephant families in this unique ecosystem, and to share this privilege with others.

Conservation of elephants can only be done successfully with a thorough understanding of the animals themselves. I subscribe to the widely held view that, should the elephants disappear, other species will also disappear and biodiversity as we know it will forever be impoverished. Recognising the importance of knowing as much as possible about elephants, in as many different habitats and countries as possible, I valued the opportunity I had to contribute to this.

The elephants were fast becoming like family to me. I looked forward to their visits and was thrilled when I easily recognised members of a family. They were no longer just great lumps of endearing grey. They were individuals – members of close-knit families – and I was privileged to have the chance, in time, to get to know them intimately. Curious, they moved close to my vehicle. Rarely threatening in any way, they came simply to say hello, rumbling their contact calls. I revelled in my close-up view of the finer details – eyelashes to die for, a hairy lower lip that you wouldn't wish on your worst enemy and huge tough-looking toenails. They came close enough for me to count their tail hairs. At times, however, they came a little too close for comfort. When one cheeky sub-adult put his huge foot on my front bumper, John, who was sitting in the passenger seat beside me, cringed. 'I think you'd better put foot,' he urged. So I did. I put my foot on the accelerator and got out of there. I learned though, in due course, that this elephant was just being friendly.

My fascination with elephant language continued to deepen. There is always a symphony of rumbles as elephants greet, call, comfort, coordinate and converse with each other. There are long soft rumbles, loud throaty rumbles, slow deep rumbles, low purring rumbles, short gurgling rumbles – and these are just some of those that are audible to humans.

Not all elephant noises indicate a conversation in progress, mind you.

'Was *that* an elephant rumble?' a friend asked one day when we went out to meet the Presidential jumbos.

'Actually that was elephant flatulence,' I replied…

After spending just a few months with the elephants, I wrote one day in my field notes: 'Why do the elephants lift one foot and move it in a circling motion above bare ground? Is this another communication mechanism? Are they sensing distant vibrations?' It has since been proven that elephants do, indeed, use the ground as another way of communicating with each other. They can detect, and distinguish, different types of seismic vibrations generated by their own kind. Incredibly, they can 'hear' through their feet.

Not unlike human children, I also found it incredible that one so comparatively small could make *so* much noise. Resorting to a temper tantrum when his mother didn't stand still long enough to allow him to suckle, one young elephant screamed in protest. A chilling high-pitched scream, it had the desired effect, stopping his mother in her tracks. Another youngster, standing alone, bellowed a call of distress. He'd lost his mother, or at least he believed he had. He bellowed relentlessly, a loud harsh call that echoed around the veld. His mother ran towards him and when she reached him, wrapped her trunk around his belly, caressing and comforting him.

Just like any toddler, the baby elephants seek constant attention, and not unlike human families, close bonds between family members are strikingly evident.

I learned various lessons about close encounters of the elephant kind. One day I was observing a small family group when two more families arrived. Now there were more than 50 elephants surrounding me. Everything was peaceful until a dominant bull approached, his rumbles audible. Excited by his arrival, the members of the family groups jostled. One huge female found herself, unintentionally, pushed up against the side of Nicki Mukuru, which I'd parked on a slight incline.

'Holy sh*t', I mumbled to myself in fright. I continued to mutter expletives, carefully climbing down from my rooftop, as several tonnes of elephant threatened to tip my vehicle. Thankfully she managed to regain her balance and right herself, leaving three rather large dents and no side mirror as a constant reminder of that memorable day.

Being almost sat on by an elephant was definitely a new experience (and I quickly learned not to park on inclines), but I was out in the field doing what I loved most – unravelling the secret lives of The Presidential Elephants of Zimbabwe.

They continued to provide endless pleasure as I delved further and further into their fascinating lives. They loved to play around the deep excavations that they made while seeking minerals in the open calcrete areas. Using their tusks, heads deep in the excavations and huge backsides in the air, the adult elephants break off large chunks of salty earth that crumble to the ground. The youngsters steal what they can. It certainly doesn't look particularly appetising, but for the elephants – and often for pregnant African ladies who also crave it as a dietary supplement packed with calcium and potassium – it's clearly a special treat.

I quickly learned that elephants do very human things. They greet, they caress, they protect, they communicate – alert to everything going on around them. And they are better at it, I eventually decided, than many humans.

I often sat on the rooftop of Nicki Mukuru as the sun set, savouring the elephant spectacle that surrounded me. As the twilight deepened, the elephant families disappeared into darkness and the star-studded night sky magically appeared. There was always a short space of time when I was unable to see around me. During these dim moments, I delighted in the familiar sound of leather against bark as the elephants scratched themselves against tree trunks, and in the equally memorable sound of mineral-dust being inhaled. When the moon was full it rose like a distant campfire aglow on the horizon, a gigantic single hot coal soon resplendent in the night sky. On these round moon nights everything around me gradually became luminous as the bright orange ball crept higher and higher. Piercing play screams often echoed in the still night as the moonlight gradually turned bright and silvery, enabling me to once again make out the bulky shapes surrounding me.

How privileged I always felt to be part of the elephants' world.

2001 *at a Close*

When terrorists attacked the United States on 11 September, resulting in the explosion and collapse of The World Trade Center's iconic Twin Towers, I felt far removed from the appalling tragedy. The wild Africa that I knew seemed comparatively peaceful and I was happy to lose myself in the bush. Land reform was by now causing terrible chaos throughout Zimbabwe, yet I intentionally remained oblivious to a lot of what was going on, both here and around the world. Events taking place were shocking but some of us, I believed, needed to stay focused on the welfare of the wildlife.

Although my world *seemed* at peace, I was already beginning to feel distressed by the number of snared animals that I encountered and was especially tormented by the sight of elephants with lethal snare wounds.

It was of no comfort, but the poachers didn't mean to snare the elephants. An elephant won't usually die immediately from a snare wound, so there's little chance of the poacher being rewarded with meat, hide or tusks. Similarly, the poachers had probably not meant to snare the four lions that we found strangled. One lioness had been caught around the waist in a snare meant for a buffalo, her agony unimaginable. Ultimately, death for these tawny cats must have been merciful. Not all locals eat zebra meat, so many of the snared zebras that I came across were likely to be pathetic 'mistakes' too. But snares are as indiscriminate as landmines. They will maim, if not kill, whatever they catch.

Darting an elephant is often not an easy task. Elephants don't always stay in an open area for long, and locating a snared one in thick bush can be difficult and dangerous. When the snared elephant forms part of a family group, the difficulties increase. It's a challenge dealing with an entire family of concerned jumbos all wanting to assist their fallen comrade – especially when no helicopter or light plane is available to assist with herding them away. Despite these obstacles, I desperately hoped that we would eventually be able to help all the suffering elephants, injured so cruelly at the hands of humans.

By now I was making plans to help support an anti-poaching/snare-destruction team, which I believed was essential to assemble. These men would be employed, paid and fed by one of the photographic safari companies that operated on the Hwange Estate. It was my task to elicit donations of overalls, boots, hats, jackets, warm jumpers, tents, bedrolls, sleeping bags and water bottles. I would also help to deploy the men into the field. The animals deserved to have more people on their side.

There was still more distressing news to end 2001. Ulaka, the magnificent male lion radio-collared earlier in the year, was no longer with his pride. I'd been given his collar to return to the head lion researcher. Ulaka was dead. He was shot, legally, on a nearby sport-hunting ranch.

I remembered the night he was collared. I remembered his magnificence. I remembered stroking his mane. And I could not understand anyone's desire to want his head on a wall of their home.

I decided to give my troubled mind a rest and so, once again, I went to join friends inside Hwange National Park. I spent a week on a sort of working holiday, travelling the remote regions with Julia and one of the French impala researchers, Mathieu. Assisting with game counts and hyena calling, in an effort to determine population densities, we had an average of four hours sleep each night. It didn't matter though given the many memorable moments.

From the hyena-calling equipment, perched on top of Julia's 4x4, came deafening sounds of wildebeest bleating and hyena whooping. It sounded like something out of *Star Wars* gone wrong. Regardless, it worked a treat. One night we were surrounded by 14 hyenas, ranging in size from large to small. On another night there wasn't a hyena in sight, but we did witness one dreadfully confused hippo retreating rapidly to his watery home, away from all the strange noises.

'Shame!' we all chorused, and then speculated about what he'd do next. Someone suggested that he would remain deep in the pan for many hours, hiding, breathing through a straw.

On the other side of our vehicle, five lionesses came to check out this bizarrely appealing sound. They lay down to rest some 20 metres from us while I walked freely around our vehicle enjoying a nightcap. One eye on the breathtaking full-moon sky. One eye on the lions. Someone else's eye, I hoped, on the pan – just in case the hippo was bolder than we thought.

The days were hot. From a fresh lion kill, one of the scouts collected the tail of an unlucky wildebeest. Its purpose? To swat the many irritating (although sting-less) mopani bees, which seek moisture from around human eyes. Another scout collected three impressively large piles of dry elephant dung and placed them in the shade of a tree. Their purpose? Stacked on top of each other, they made a seat to rest on. These men were unpolluted by the sophistication of the Western World. It was refreshing.

After continuous night work, we were often tired by mid-afternoon and usually made camp early, by a waterhole if we were lucky. On one such occasion, we revelled in the continuous stream of elephants that started at three o'clock in the afternoon and didn't stop until nine the next morning. They trumpeted and screamed in the night, raucously at play. Brilliant moonlight shimmered on the surface of the pan. The sky was filled with stars. It was difficult to sleep and yet, soothed by the rumbles of the elephants, I eventually drifted off and had one of the most restful night's sleep I'd ever experienced.

We were in two 4x4s, travelling together in these remote parts, for safety sake. Although not always in convoy, we met up each night at a prearranged rendezvous. One evening, Mathieu – who was to have collected our water supplies for the next day – didn't arrive as expected. Flat tyres. A breakdown. Anything could have happened. That would not normally have been too much of a dilemma, except that Julia's 4x4 had developed electrical problems. We were not going anywhere in her vehicle as it needed to be pull-started. We tried to raise somebody – anybody – on our two-way radio, but there was no response. The situation didn't look bright.

As the hours ticked by, we became increasingly concerned. To make matters worse, our water supply was indeed very low. The next day we would have to collect some from one of the pans, we decided. If it was good enough for the elephants to drink, it was good enough for us. We would simply have to boil it. Who would walk the 12 kilometres, through the thick bush, to collect this water the next morning? How much ammunition did we have? How many flares? How much radio battery power was left? How much food was there? How far were we from the nearest human?

There was plenty to think about.

Two inquisitive elephants had walked up to our camp earlier that afternoon, stopping less than 10 metres from us. When the sun sat low in the sky, the scout patrolled the surrounding area. '*Shumba*,' he announced on his return.

'No, surely, not *shumba*,' I sighed. Lions were all we needed. The scout dragged dry tree branches around us in a makeshift boma, seemingly flimsy protection from the lions that he expected to visit us during the night. That done, we retired to our sleeping bags, as there was little else we could do for the time being.

Thankfully, Mathieu arrived late that night. The proposed water collection point, a pumped pan, had not been working. He'd travelled another five hours to collect fresh water. Everything was fine and no *shumba* appeared either, which was a great relief.

We eventually headed back to Main Camp a day early, Julia's 4x4 still with electrical problems and Mathieu's, after suffering many punctures, with no spare tyres. The 4x4s had different-sized wheels, so it was not possible to interchange. 'It's okay,' declared one of the scouts, 'in the bush it fits.' That was usually true, but not this time.

A few weeks later, it was time for Mathieu and his fellow impala researchers to get their overalls on. The impala breeding season had started and there were newborn babies to ear-tag, in an attempt to determine mortality rates. This tagging is best done during the first week after birth, since it's only then that the mothers leave them to sleep alone at night, perhaps under a bush or a fallen tree. The impala herd is nowhere to be seen, the young fawn safer from predators when it sleeps on its own.

Using a spotlight, distant eyes are picked up. Then binoculars are used to check whether these glinting eyes belong to an impala fawn. Sometimes, though, it's difficult to tell. 'I'm not sure,' said Mathieu hesitantly as he sat on the roof of his 4x4, straining to see through his binoculars.

Bounce... bounce... bounce...

'Now I'm sure!' he laughed, as we watched the eyes of the springhare disappear into the darkness. Springhares – Africa's equivalent of miniature kangaroos. Sometimes in almost plague proportions, they ensured that we remained alert.

As we set off into the park again the next evening, hoping to successfully tag large numbers of impala fawns, I turned to Mathieu and made a flippant request. 'Tonight I would like to see an aardwolf please,' I said. I'd never met this relative of the hyena before, and knew that the chance of such an encounter was unlikely at best.

It turned out to be a long night. Early on, our spotlight picked up many sets of eyes all bunched together. 'We have 15 problems,' moaned Mathieu in response. A well-known pack of 15 painted hunting dogs was resting on the vlei (or perhaps it was 14, if the report of a crocodile having grabbed one of the dogs earlier that day was accurate). These are formidable predators, and so we saw very few impala eyes about. We feared that the fawns were also getting wise to us by now, and perhaps even had 'the springhare hop' down pat, just to confuse us!

Only two were caught that night, jumped on by Mathieu. Walking purposefully towards each of these fawns with spotlight in hand, the impala researchers (dressed in their overalls) had looked not unlike the ghostbusters of movie fame. Weighing and ear-tagging the babies was quick. They were soon released unharmed.

Although we came across so few impala fawns that night, we enjoyed some incredible wildlife sightings – and had a flat tyre a few minutes after midnight, just to make certain that everyone was awake. We encountered two huge eagle owls at a pan; a pennant-winged nightjar, his long wing-streamers spectacular in flight; a bat-eared fox family; a monstrous crocodile relaxing grandly in the middle of the veld; hyenas feasting on the remains of a kudu kill that the painted hunting dogs had made earlier that day – and, just as we were about to leave the park at 2am... an aardwolf! It was an extraordinary sighting. The elusive aardwolf walked slowly, unconcerned, within three metres of our vehicle, the vertical stripes on its body and thick-haired mane on its sloping back, clearly visible.

I was awestruck.

Mathieu turned to me, eyes wide. 'Please, next time, won't you ask me for baby impalas?' he begged.

The days were passing rapidly and the fawns were getting older. Many now, at over one week old, had joined the herds in their night-time wanderings, but Mathieu decided to try to catch them anyway. A different strategy was formulated. We would drive swiftly up to the herd, and then the men would jump out and race after the fleeing babies on foot.

On one occasion there were four babies in one group and five men were running around like lunatics chasing three of them. Where was the fourth one? It was chasing the five men. Confused by the spotlight, this little impala must have thought that those running legs belonged to its mother. Through hysterical laughter, convulsed with mirth while desperately trying to hold the spotlight still, I managed to yell, 'Behind you! Behind you!'

Mathieu turned in mid-step, stunned, to find an impala baby running straight for him. He lunged at the fawn, but it took swift evasive action and he hit the ground hard with an armful of nothing. Within seconds another team member, standing close to Mathieu, had repeated the exact same performance. They didn't give up however, and the youngster was eventually caught, tagged and released unharmed.

There'd been no less than 11 successful captures during the course of that night. Things were definitely improving, but running around in the African bush in darkness can be quite disconcerting. You sometimes find yourself flat on your face with one foot in a springhare hole. 'I'm broken!' groaned Mathieu at one point, as he lay spread-eagle on the ground – which was a significant improvement on the previous year when he'd been stalked by inquisitive lions.

There were some tense moments, but mostly there were a lot of laughs. The animals had the last laugh, though. Covered in red lumps, it turned out that Mathieu – the head impala researcher – was allergic to impalas.

The next night we stopped at Nyamandlovu platform to have a midnight snack. Frogs were perched precariously on the wooden beams above us. Just the week before one had leapt onto my head, landing with a loud plop (followed by an involuntary shriek from me), and promptly became tangled in my hair. Now, as we stood eating our open sandwiches, Julia said warily, 'Watch out that a frog doesn't land on your sandwich.'

'I don't mind,' replied Mathieu, 'I'm French!' I wondered then, while enjoying my snack, if his earlier comment, 'hhhmmm, foie gras' – muttered as we gazed at a pair of Egyptian geese – had indeed been in jest.

Dinks was no longer managing the Main Camp restaurant, however she and another friend returned to visit Julia and me just before Christmas. We hung decorations on a broken branch of a tree, which we pushed into the soft earth. In the wilds of Africa you make do. There was, though, no need to do without. We had stimulating company, tasty food and sinfully delicious drink – and a beauty salon in the bush to boot. We were four women with brightly coloured masks on our faces, our feet soaking in basins, revelling in the throaty rumbles of passing elephants. We really must have looked a sight when an afternoon thunderstorm sent us scurrying across the sandy ground to shelter. Luckily only the elephants were witness to this bizarre scene. They're my friends, I reasoned. Surely they wouldn't tell anybody.

Father Christmas entwined with Mother Nature... Nothing beats celebrating the festive season in the African bush. A few days later, I spent Christmas Eve and Christmas Day among the wildlife in Hwange National Park with Julia, Mathieu and others. We enjoyed French cuisine one day and a taste of Aussie cuisine the next.

Then, after saying my goodbyes to the elephants, I boarded a plane bound for Australia. I planned to be away for two or three months, and already I longed for my return to Africa. Sitting on the plane, awaiting take-off, I recalled the heartfelt words written by Ernest Hemingway, 'All I wanted to do was get back to Africa. We had not left it yet, but when I would wake in the night I would lie, listening, homesick for it already.'

Well, I reflected, Hemingway and I certainly had one thing in common.

Homeland of Choice

Soon after stepping off the plane in Australia I experienced a very real culture shock. It was odd returning to the Western World and I was struck by the luxury of many different things.

There was always electricity, water and working telephones, fax machines and photocopiers. There were no fuel queues; no streams of people 'footing' along the roadside; no one trying to sell you curios. Faces looked familiar, yet they were faces I didn't know. It took me some time to figure out that this feeling of familiarity among strangers was because I was once again in the midst of so many *white* faces.

There seemed to be an incredible number of food and clothing shops, offering endless varieties of brands and styles. My own walk-in wardrobe was overflowing with clothes. Why had I ever thought I needed so much clothing? Everywhere, there was so much 'stuff'. I walked around somewhat bewildered – it all now seemed to be rather excessive.

When I'd left for Zimbabwe 10 months before, I had kept my Brisbane home and all my things. Although it was now glaringly obvious to me that I'd lived in a very materialistic world, it was, nonetheless, a tough decision to sell my most valuable possessions and completely pack up my life to date. Regardless of what the future held though, I knew with comforting certainty that I could never live quite like this again. It had once been an all-consuming and rewarding part of my life, but I couldn't pretend to miss my former career and the lifestyle that had ensued.

The most difficult time was the lead-up to my decision to sell. Once I'd finally reached a decision, a sense of relief set in and I felt more at ease. I couldn't bring myself to sell absolutely everything however. I'd sell my car, my home and its furniture, but I couldn't yet bring myself to dispose of *all* of its contents. And so, boxes and boxes of 'things' were destined to sit in a rented storage room, no doubt gathering moths and mildew and growing even more redundant. My world of material possessions would not yet be completely gone; some things would just be hidden from view.

It was an enormous job packing up my double-storey home, which I did on my own. As I sorted, wrapped and packed, I thought about the elephants. I still had no idea how long I'd stay with them, but I knew in my heart that their home was where I wanted to be. My family was relatively quiet, perhaps a little disbelieving, while close friends encouraged me. Many of these friends had enjoyed living vicariously through my adventures in the wilds of Africa, and they looked forward to this continuing.

Days passed, and then weeks. Eventually I looked around the empty house that was no longer mine. I walked silently from room to room, switching off the lights. Then I gently closed the front door behind me and, without looking back, drove away from my past life. I tucked all the memories away carefully in a corner of my heart, knowing that my imminent return to the wilds of Africa would soothe any buried anxieties.

I'd chosen to cut most of my material ties with my homeland and to make Zimbabwe my homeland of choice. Australia had become a little like a stranger to me, and me to her. Soon, I was back home among the elephants of Africa. Back where I belonged. Back where I felt certain that I was always meant to be.

Julia was there to greet me. Her cottage inside Hwange National Park had just been robbed, and she was feeling a little rattled. I, too, had a problem to solve. I needed to find somewhere to live. My old cottage, Salaam – which I'd paid handsomely to renovate – was no longer mine to live in. Although I (foolishly) had nothing in writing, in return for me paying to renovate the cottage, I'd been told I could live there rent-free on an ongoing basis. Yet, now that it was fixed up, when someone offered a high US dollar rental for it (at a time when local rentals were the equivalent of just a few dollars a month), greed won out.

My trust in and respect for those involved was forever injured. This was my first real taste of the greed and self-interest that so often plagues the African continent.

'What goes around, comes around,' said a friend in consolation. 'Karma takes care of people like that. These men will get their just desserts.' And over the next few years, as fate would have it, they did.

Today, Miombo Lodge is owned and operated by others, with only a few familiar African faces still to be seen among the people working in the grounds. Despite the hurt and inconvenience, it felt good and right to start afresh and I soon found myself a new home that was to serve me well for many years.

Immediately on my return, I was eager to drive around the Hwange Estate and re-acquaint myself with the bush. My soul craved some peace and quiet. I wanted to see *everything*. In fact, I wanted to see *two* of everything! Most of all, I wanted to see the elephants. I knew that I might be gone an hour – or a week and a half. Such is the uncertainty of wildlife viewing in Africa. It's not unlike a *Forrest Gump* box of chocolates; you never know what you're going to get.

I looked and marvelled. Everything was as I remembered it, yet everything was different, as it is every moment in the African bush – wild, beautiful and mystical; a complex web of life. I didn't try to hold back my tears, for this is the emotional effect it has on me.

The elephant giants were there to greet me, natural gardeners as always – cutting, clearing, fertilising and sowing seeds. My heart pounded with the thrill of my first re-encounter with these wonderfully bizarre looking animals. I'd missed them terribly. Oversized teeth, an oversized nose and oversized ears – we could well be ostracised if we looked like that. On them, however, it looks magnificent. They are a masterpiece of nature.

Africa was in my blood, of this there was no doubt. I recalled a remark that an Aussie friend had made to me just a few weeks before. 'You're like a leopard,' he'd said, fully acknowledging my bond with wild Africa at last, and finally conceding that I might never return to Australia to live. I'd smiled at his observation, remembering how he'd once had difficulty differentiating between a leopard and a cheetah.

A leopard. A cheetah. It didn't really matter, for he was right. In Australia I wore high-heeled shoes and designer suits, and I rarely saw the sunset. After a year in Africa of wearing no shoes, my feet had widened. Those old shoes no longer fitted – and it wasn't just the shoes.

Family and friends around the world wondered how I could ever choose to return to Zimbabwe. How could I live there with all the instability and uncertainty that continued to be reported in the Western World's media? I looked around me. I saw the elephants. How could I not?

I was thrilled to be back in the Hwange bush with the elephants, and I delighted in their company. Although I was most often alone in the field, John still occasionally joined me on elephant outings, a grey beard on his chin and an *akubra* on his head. '*Mushi* hat,' John had muttered in thanks, when I presented him with this legendary hat of the Australian outback. It was, indeed, a really nice hat.

The night sky was as enchanting as ever. Full moon, I believe, is only outdone by the African new moon lying on her back, and I'd returned to a new moon. It must surely be true, I mused to my elephant friends, that you can see further while out in the wilds at night than any other place on earth, and the stars are far brighter.

My friends Down Under had asked about the dangers, expressing concern for my safety, given that I was so often in the field alone. I'd assured them that the Presidential Elephants were habituated to the presence of people – a relationship based on mutual trust. I was forever conscious that I was an intruder in their environment; careful always to respect this, continually reminding myself never to take it for granted and moving off when a situation felt like it might become awkward.

I was also often asked, 'Don't you get lonely?' and 'Aren't you afraid of getting lost in the bush?' It was true that I was often alone, but no one who loves untamed Africa with a passion is ever lonely in it for long. Indeed, I treasured my wild aloneness. And getting lost in the wilderness was unlikely. I carried a compass, although I rarely had reason to use it. I didn't always want to know where I was going after all.

After months away, and with the annual wet season now at a close, there were newborn elephants to add to the family trees that I was compiling. It was always exciting to see these brand new little bundles of joy, and to decide on suitable names.

Driving through the veld I noticed elephants in musth, important data that I also needed to record. Musth is a period of heightened sexual activity, which periodically grips males over 30 years of age. Musth males are easily recognisable by their head-held-high posture and constant dribbling of urine, combined with swollen and streaming temporal glands (which are located just behind the eyes). As they have extremely high levels of testosterone during this period, some musth bulls can be particularly aggressive. Most on the Hwange Estate though, were quiet gentlemen. The most dominant of these, usually those over 40, win the right to mate with females in oestrus.

Oestrous females are not so easily recognisable, but they come into this state most often during and just after the rainy season when environmental conditions are more favourable and they're in good condition. I returned to females temporarily wandering with only their youngest calves, as elephants in oestrus do, eventually attracting both musth and non-musth bulls. They preferred to stay close to a musth bull, who protected them from the unwelcome advances of the smaller, less desirable males.

I took out my notebook and enthusiastically recorded all of the oestrous females, musth males, and matings that I saw.

PART III

Mandlovu

Kanondo: A Place of
Timeless Peace

When I arrived in Zimbabwe in early 2001 all of the Hwange Estate's 12 pans always held water. Those responsible ensured that enough was pumped year-round (in this area devoid of rivers, streams and dams), which resulted in abundant wildlife.

There are pans on the Khatshana side of the estate – Mpofu pan, Mtaka pan, Foster's pan (which is named after John), Mandebele pan and Khatshana pan. Among others, there is Sable pan and Windmill pan on the vlei. There is also a small pan in Acacia Grove within a cathedral of *Acacia eriolobas* – their branches meeting in exquisite archways overhead, dwarfing the elephants as they come to drink. Of all the pans though, it is one named Kanondo that was most favoured by the Presidential Elephants.

Everything the elephants needed was at Kanondo: fresh water for drinking (the pumped water running first into a round concrete trough before entering the main pan); a large clear body of water where they could bathe as well as drink; a mud-bathing area to wallow in; and the natural mineral licks that they loved. The surrounding vegetation provided both food and shade.

During July, Kanondo hosted what I termed 'reunion month'. For some reason unknown, this was the month when the largest number of family groups regularly mingled in the middle of the day, creating an unforgettable spectacle. Several hundred Presidential Elephants revelled in the mud-bathing area and took advantage of the nearby mineral licks and surrounding vegetation, regularly returning to the pan to drink and splash around playfully in the cool water. These memorable displays were made even more special for me because I knew *who* the elephants were, and was able to interpret their interactions with one another.

Kanondo was indeed the Presidential Elephants' favourite playground and, in my opinion, was perhaps *the* best place in Africa for tourists to experience the magic of close-up encounters with wild, free-roaming giants.

Given that this was one of the few places where I could be sure of lengthy, unobscured (and therefore unambiguous) sightings of the Presidential Elephants, particularly important when monitoring individuals as I was, Kanondo became my office – a far cry from the skyscrapers around the world where I used to spend my time. I spent many hours there every day.

Now and then while sitting in my vehicle beside Kanondo pan I reflected on my past, pondering just how different my life was now. Years before, people appeared unexpectedly in my high-rise city office: all were unafraid, some were entertaining, some spoke enthusiastically, some raced around frantically, some wanted to mate... while still others swallowed their subordinates whole. All had their favourite drinking places. And I would smile to myself – perhaps it wasn't so very different after all. As I drove a little further down the road though, my sense of reason always prevailed. Zebra crossings were *really* zebras crossing, and families of lumbering elephants formed the only traffic jams. Similarities were, in actual fact, few and far between.

Sometimes, as I drove home from Kanondo in the midst of the early evening glow, I pulled over beside a huge steel power-line structure. Baboons regularly sat silhouetted high on its diamond-shaped crossbars, playfully leaping from one side of this V-shaped monstrosity to the other. Their dark agile outlines, arms outstretched with tails up while in mid-flight, always looked stunning against the backdrop of blazing orange. Here the baboon troop would spend the approaching night, their elevated positions ensuring safety from predators.

Kanondo was where I so often took my joys and my grief. The wildlife there was always a delight, and many times it was a welcome hiatus. It was extraordinary what I saw in a short space of time, when

I just sat silently and watched, especially in the wet season when a greater variety of birds and smaller creatures were about. There were always many *little* things going on, so easy to overlook.

Typically nocturnal, two honey badgers, a short stocky duo of black and white, sometimes came to drink from Kanondo pan in broad daylight. I always thought they looked so well dressed, as if they were going out to dinner (which, whenever I saw them, they no doubt were). When it was mating season for the monitor lizards these giant reptiles raced through the elephants' mud-bathing pond emerging grey and muddy, still chasing each other frantically. The turkey-sized ground hornbills were always particularly entertaining, one singing the first few bars of a well rehearsed call, and another, with bright red throat sac inflated, always providing the same last few notes. This they repeated over and over, in harmony, like a concert duet. The smaller ground-birds chattered in alarm whenever a mongoose family skulked past their nests in search of eggs. And of course there were the larger animals: waterbucks, roan and sable antelope, impalas, kudus, zebras, giraffes, warthogs, and the occasional rhino, as well as the carnivores: jackals, cheetahs, lions and sometimes painted hunting dogs.

After just a few months of living in the Zimbabwean bush I could feel myself becoming more attuned to my surroundings. I no longer tripped over things without really seeing them, everything suddenly taking on a clarity and an intensity that I hadn't detected before. Some say that there are no distinct seasons in Zimbabwe; just the wet season and the dry season. Yet if you take the time to look closely, the changing months reveal a multitude of wonders, dazzling and unique. Summer, autumn, winter and spring each bring changing colours and patterns to the veld, and all are greatly affected by annual summer rainfall.

Every year in the wet season, African jacanas (also known as lily-trotters), crowned cranes, white-faced ducks and Egyptian and spur-winged geese raised their babies at Kanondo. Occasionally, there was also a stunning saddlebill stork pair wandering around the pan.

It was Julia who taught me how to tell the male saddlebill stork from the female. Only one of them has bright yellow 'tear drops' hanging from the base of its sizeable red-and-black bill.

'*He* is the one with the tear drops,' she said. 'Just remember that *he* is the one who is crying... because he's not female!'

Delivered in Julia's quick-witted style, it was a quirky lesson which I've never forgotten.

Sometimes, when there were no elephants in sight, I sat on the edge of one of the mineral-lick excavations (created by the elephants), imagining that the surface of the moon might look something like this. At one time it was flat ground, but now there were numerous excavations up to one metre deep in this earth – which seems at first glance to be as hard as rock. The edges of one particular excavation, which formed a large semicircle, had been smoothed by the gentle rubbing of the elephants' legs. Certain jumbos had also opted to sit on these edges, to massage their enormous rear-ends, ensuring some particularly smooth spots. Rounded rocks of mineralised earth, small and large, sculpted by the elephants' giant feet, lay scattered. Footprints abounded in the fine, soft sand, allowing me to note the 'shoe size' of the elephants that had visited recently. Dried elephant dung was strewn, like dark brown straw, over the surrounds. When the rains came, excavations like this one stored life-giving water.

I enjoyed sitting there with my legs dangling over the edge where an elephant would soon come to dig for minerals. It had a kind of primitive feel. I was fascinated, as always, but I was also alert for any creatures that might steal up behind me.

It was the quiet, peaceful times at Kanondo pan that helped me to keep things in perspective. Spending time among the wildlife there always prompted me to recall just how much beauty there is in the world. It was there, too, that I so often remembered that small things *do* make big things bearable.

One evening, I sat on the rooftop of Nicki Mukuru with a G&T in hand. (When you manage to buy tonic in Zimbabwe, you must truly enjoy that G&T.) I heard the familiar honking of Egyptian geese. I turned around, gazing now into the deep orange sky, full of billowy clouds tinged pink and gold by the setting sun. To my delight, nine geese were flying low, straight towards me. I was so proud of 'my geese'. I'd watched these seven goslings, daily, since they were tiny. Now they could fly! They flew in formation with their parents, right above me, elegant in the air, landing at the far side of the pan. Within minutes they took to the sky again, returning to where they'd come from. Even if the flyover had not been in my honour, I was thrilled. The seven goslings had grown up. They were regal now and self-assured. They had made it.

The G&T was indescribably good. The sunset was dramatic and the tranquil surroundings allowed me the freedom to dream – to *dare* to dream.

Five days later the gaggle of geese was gone for good and I felt a, perhaps illogical, sense of loss. Kanondo felt empty without them, but I knew that the parents would return at the beginning of the next wet season, as they did every year, to raise another family.

Sometimes I didn't leave Kanondo, choosing instead to sleep on the back seat of Nicki Mukuru. Brimming with contentment I would watch the resident grey heron, silhouetted against a deep yellow sky, fly off into the night. I wondered where he would spend the night before returning, as he always did, the next morning.

A light breeze sometimes made ripples on the glassy surface of Kanondo pan, the water shimmering in the moonlight. As I lay on the back seat I could usually hear the waterbucks enjoying their dinner, and the soothing rumbles of elephants. In among the tall reeds two adult male lily-trotters and their young had already made their beds. Fireflies often danced with dreams and desires, extending an invitation to follow their light. If I were able to follow, I thought that I'd arrive, perhaps, at some place magical. But I stayed where I was. I was already at a magical place.

Guarded by a big old *Acacia erioloba* behind the pan, I came to know Kanondo as a place of abundant wildlife, and a place of timeless peace.

And, over time, I felt that something of myself lingered there with the animals.

My Friends the Elephants

There is a timelessness about watching majestic elephants stride across the plains. They are creatures of supreme dignity, undoubtedly belonging to this land. They have a mighty form, yet it's one delicate enough to take an acacia pod from a human's hand. While sitting watching these magnificent beasts I am forever overwhelmed by a strong sense of what is precious.

My desire to be out among these grey giants was unquenchable. One day while at Kanondo pan, surrounded by more than 300 of them, one of the safari guides drove towards me. He stopped and smiled, remarking on what a spectacle surrounded me, and how relaxed these jumbos were in my close presence.

'We will have to call you *Mandlovu* (Mother Elephant),' he said thoughtfully.

I grinned. 'They already do,' I replied. My African friends had embellished my local name. Now they called me *Thandeka Mandlovu* – but often just *Mandlovu* or simply *Mandlo*.

Elephant families appeared regularly around me, doing their familiar 'floppy run' as they approached the pan, their loose relaxed movements, heads swaying to an age-old rhythm, always bringing a smile to my face. I loved watching them mud-bathing in the sloppy mud, their delight revealed in unusually bright pink eyes rolling around in their massive heads, making them appear possessed.

Of course all of the wildlife is wonderful, but for me it's the elephants that consistently outshine the other animals. They have a way of making themselves appear infinitely superior to everything else around them, even when they're clowning around in the mud. Many of the gracious ladies in particular, I often thought, deserved to rank highly in 'elephantdom', as they led their loved ones through good times and bad, always delighting in the company of their offspring.

I frequently witnessed one or other of these elephant children racing around like a lunatic, high-pitched squeal-like trumpeting filling the air as the youngster ran giddily backwards and forwards. Who was he chasing, I wondered? Or who was chasing him? No other elephants were running with him. It was just a game, and he certainly appeared to be loving it.

It must be true, I decided. There must surely be some thought process going on in that comical little mind. Perhaps the young elephant has an imaginary friend, or possibly foe. Or must we really believe that elephants are, as some suggest, simply genetically programmed to behave in this bizarre way? I personally don't believe so.

I believe that elephants often simply *choose* to have some fun... and I hear loud protests of anthropomorphism (attributing human characteristics to things that are not human) echoing around me! Am I guilty of this sin? Yes, certainly, I'm guilty as charged. With good reason though – I've been on the receiving end (more than once) of an elephant's sense of humour. But science rejects many interpretations of what animals do and feel, frowning on statements that have not been *proven* to be true.

Are mine purely emotional interpretations? I often wonder why it is that humans are allowed to experience so many different emotions, yet elephants are not. If my observations are in any way typical, then I suspect that many elephant researchers suppress certain of their own observations and interpretations – for fear of the wrath of science.

I sit among a playful family group and wonder if all of those in the scientific world will ever be broad-minded enough to formally concede more about these highly intelligent beings, finally leaving conservative interpretations behind.

The wild free-roaming Presidential Elephants regularly exercised their sense of humour at my expense. They were elephants just being elephants. Adorable. Silly. Intelligent. Downright naughty sometimes!

One summer's day, with the smell of grass seeds burning on my radiator, I pulled up within two metres of a bull elephant that was standing at a water seepage by the roadside. He wasn't really thirsty;

he was playing. As he brought his trunk up in front of his face, he squeezed together the two fingers at its end so that water sprayed skyward, falling in all different directions. He appeared to take great pleasure in his ability to create his very own fountain, causing me to smile with pleasure too. I delighted in the glint of sunlight on his tusks, the sun shining through thick foliage, coating him in a mottled light.

The tip of his trunk returned to the puddle and without delay he siphoned up more of the murky water. Then he turned his head just slightly, looking at me now. My focus changed from the glint of sunlight on his tusks to the cheeky glint in his eyes. He twisted his trunk towards me, still holding it low but upturned. He pinched those two fingers together and, in a split second, the inevitable happened. Millions of fine droplets of dirty water sprayed all over me, and Nicki Mukuru. I sat with my eyes closed, muddy water all over my face and body, a grimace on my lips.

'That ... wasn't ... funny,' was the eventual extent of my feeble response.

On another day there wasn't a grey elephant in sight. Instead there were brown ones, black ones, red ones, and even two-tone black-and-red ones. They'd been revelling in the various consistencies and colours of mud and dust around Mpofu pan.

It was here that I played a game of 'catch' with a youngster from the M family. Not yet two years old, he was still without tusks. He stood a few metres from my vehicle, and used his trunk to investigate a small log on the ground. Then he picked up the log and hurled it towards me. It hit hard against the door of my vehicle. He looked quite pleased with himself and, although stunned by his cheekiness, I admired his fiery spirit. I opened my door with a smile, bent down and picked up the log. I threw it back to him. Tentatively, he smelt the log and, deciding that it was okay, promptly picked it up and hurled it back to me. This time it landed hard on my bonnet with a loud thud.

By now I was having no end of fun, but everyone seemed to want to join in. There was quite a commotion, with elephants appearing from everywhere, rumbles filling the air. I decided that it was best for me to move off. This young elephant was the son of Mertle and I subsequently named him 'Mettle', in celebration of his daring.

Soon after, I was sitting in Acacia Grove trying to sort out the mother-calf relationships within the E family. Who were the offspring of Emily, Eileen, Evonne, Edith, Eve and Elaine? An adolescent bull was feeding close to my vehicle. It was lunchtime and I was hungry too. With my head down, I fidgeted in my cooler-bag, trying to find a yoghurt. Eventually I located and opened one. I was straightening myself back up in the driver's seat, still focused on my lunch, when finally I looked up – to find a colossal grey face only centimetres from my own, looking straight into my eyes. My heart skipped two beats, and I jumped 20 centimetres. My yoghurt got the biggest fright. It jumped 30 centimetres, straight up and out of its container, landing all over me, and everything around me.

The fact that there was a windscreen safely between my face and that of the playful 'jelly-pants' did little to lessen the effect. My heart racing, I was at the time totally unaware of the windscreen. Utterly nonchalant, that cheeky grey lump simply walked away. I swear he was smiling! I sat there smiling too, wondering whether elephants giggle in infrasound.

One morning a huge bull elephant stood face-on to me, just a few metres away, down a small incline at the edge of Mpofu pan. He was about to have a mud bath. I was standing up through the open roof of Nicki Mukuru, admiring his magnificence, when he took his first trunkful of gooey red mud. He threw his trunk skyward, in that incredible way that elephants do, so that thousands of mud particles snake in an 'S' shape high in the air.

Then everything, suddenly, appeared to unfold in slow motion. Through my camera lens I saw the mud globules starting to snake, but something went wrong. They were surely meant to go over his massive head and back. Perhaps he blew them out of that long nose of his too soon, too eager for the pleasurable muddy sensation on his body, or perhaps it was that 'elephant humour' which I was becoming so accustomed to. Separated and snaking, the mud particles came hurtling straight towards *me*, and there was nothing I could do about it.

In a split second I had what felt like mud the size of a dung-pile right on top of my head, dripping down into my eyes. I could barely see the skin on my left arm, which was now almost completely covered in red mud. I stood, stunned, in total disbelief that there could possibly be this much mud in one trunkful. That wasn't all. My camera, despite an attempt to shield it behind my back, was splattered with mud. I could barely tell that my 4x4 soft-top was black. I could scarcely read the instruments on my dashboard. There were layers of mud over everything.

Ignoring the close-by elephant family, I put my head out the window and tipped my bottle of drinking water into my hair, the ice cubes an unwelcome addition. Red water dripped to the ground. I had no towel; nothing to wipe myself with. Reluctantly, I decided that I'd better return home early, as there was plenty of cleaning up to do.

'What on earth happened to you?' asked a colleague – his mouth gaping in astonishment and his eyes bulging like some sort of crazed bug – as I emerged bedraggled from my mud-splattered vehicle.

'Don't even ask,' was all that I could reply.

That was lesson number 854 in the African bush: stay further away from mud-bathing elephants.

Frequently, while driving in the field, I stopped to study the fresh wrinkled spoor and cannonball droppings of an elephant family that I'd missed seeing. Elephant dung always reminds me of the first elephant project that I ever participated in, which focused on their importance as seed dispersal agents in Hwange National Park. One day in 1997 we'd painstakingly counted an astonishing 5 689 acacia seeds in just one dung pile. It was tedious work, and a new record.

I still recall the nonchalant words of a female colleague, who was busy extracting seeds from yet another dung pile: 'Just one more pile of poo to do,' she shouted into the late-morning breeze, 'and then we'll be in for lunch.'

Picking through elephant dung was surprisingly inoffensive, so much so that we decided not to wear the surgical gloves provided. That was lesson number 126 in the African bush. For days nothing could mask the smell that, hours later, began to emanate from our hands.

One afternoon we came across a bull elephant that had recently feasted on the sweet fruit of a manketti tree. The nut-like seeds in the fruit had been swallowed whole, their hard, woody shell ensuring that they remained untouched by his digestive system. A pile of these nuts had passed through the elephant completely intact, and we dutifully collected them. The next day we enjoyed freshly baked 'manketti nut cake', while pondering just how many others had relished such a treat – the key ingredient having been collected from a pile of elephant dung.

Especially during the months of April and May, adult elephants – with relentless vigour and tenacity – shake *Acacia eriolobas* for pods; a task often left to the high-ranking males. Large velvety grey seed pods shower to the ground, like a blizzard from the sky. The sound of hundreds of pods hitting the ground is a special one, always bringing a smile to my face. The members of nearby elephant families react enthusiastically to this sound too, running to share in the rewards. It's a battle of the fittest. Although sometimes amid screaming and jostling, sub-adult males are simply not tolerated.

One evening I was both delighted and saddened to watch a snare victim attempt to join the feast. A wire snare had ripped off the lower section of this elephant's trunk and, having lost the functional 'fingers' at its tip, he could no longer pick up a pod easily. He bent his head in order to get his trunk to the ground, and then manoeuvred a pod with his foot, pushing it against the flat surface of his severed trunk. He then bent his knee, and brought his foot off the ground, carefully balancing the pod between foot and trunk. Higher and higher his foot and trunk were raised until eventually the pod somehow made it to his mouth. He managed just one pod to the others' five or six. Scenes like this one always stirred me deeply, the snared elephants forced to adapt to the limitations of their maimed bodies. It is a sad fact that those elephants that have endured trunk injuries are often the last to leave a feeding or drinking area. Having to work much harder to obtain the same amount of food and water, they often lag behind the others in their family.

During 'reunion month' (July) at Kanondo pan there were often hundreds of elephants around at midday. I could never be certain why the families chose to combine so regularly at this particular time of year. Just when vegetation was becoming less plentiful, and you'd expect them to disperse to maintain foraging efficiency, there they all were together, not only in their complete family groups, but in their socially cohesive bond groups and even larger clan. Perhaps the pull of the Kanondo water source was too great. Perhaps they were preparing for the lean months ahead, their bodies in need of the Kanondo minerals at this particular time of year. Or maybe, I liked to think, this was a ceremony of some sort, held prior to the elephants splitting once again into smaller groups – a ceremony they were called to by their friends and extended family members; a ceremony which they *chose* to attend. The dizzying magnitude of 'reunion month' could not, I knew, be mere coincidence. Whatever the reason for their gathering, all of the Presidential Elephant families would mingle, in a peaceful, leisurely fashion, and I would revel in their presence.

There was no doubt that the elephants were very aware of my presence, and also of my absence. Hearing my voice again after some time apart, those elephants I knew well would break from their normal routine to pass close by my vehicle, rumbling, returning later to spend extended time beside my door.

It was indeed a humbling relationship between (wo)man and free-roaming beast.

Seeing the elephants in large gatherings always triggered my imagination. I watched and imagined them, together again, hungry for conversation after their long time apart. I imagined them without acid judgement, more respectful of each other than many humans are. I imagined them alone under a full moon, dancing in celebration of their reunion, their trunks and bodies fluid with the exquisite music of the dawn and dusk symphonies.

I imagined them roaming this earth forever.

Lady of the Estate

Lady, the great matriarch of the L family, is undoubtedly the friendliest elephant on the Hwange Estate. I believe her to be just a few years younger than me. She's an enormous pachyderm, with a longer left tusk and a distinctive hole in her left ear. Born wild and living wild, she's free to roam with her family wherever she desires. Yet we enjoyed an increasingly special bond.

I was the first human to gain her complete trust.

When I initially arrived on the Hwange Estate, Lady was simply one of the many habituated elephants that were unafraid of the safari vehicles. As was the case with most of the elephants, she would approach only to within a few metres.

In the early days I saw Lady and her family several times every week and occasionally, at Acacia Grove, I would throw her some previously collected acacia pods. It wasn't something I did with many of the elephants and it wasn't something I did often, but gradually over the next year she came closer and closer to my vehicle, eventually using her trunk to accept a pod from my hand. I did this only occasionally, fearful of over-habituating her.

I'd once read *Coming of Age with Elephants* by Joyce Poole, a respected elephant expert based in Kenya, who sang to one of the elephants in her study group. At the time of reading, this struck me as nothing short of bizarre. Yet while looking at Lady one day, many years after first reading Joyce's book, I started to sing. And singing is definitely not my strong point. At first Lady gave me a sideways glance and just kept on walking. Eventually though, she actually seemed to enjoy it.

Sometimes when Lady was only centimetres from my vehicle, I sang 'Amazing Grace' and she would stand and listen, opening and closing

Perhaps my future life in Zimbabwe was predestined; I learned at an early age, on my parents' farm in Australia, to get down and dirty.

In the late-1980s and 1990s I led a high-flying life. With me here is Chloe, who shared my life for nearly 18 years. Her ashes came with me to Africa.

Andy's death in the year 2000, when he was just 38 years old, greatly impacted my life.

Andy's wife Lol, and their son Drew, the year that he died so tragically.

Carol and Miriam, my American friends who both lived in Harare.

Julia, who studied hyenas in Hwange National Park, shared many memorable times with me.

John was something of a legend in the area; the happy hermit of the Hwange bush.

The 'Rrah Rrah Sisters' – Dinks, me and Shaynie in 2007.

Dinks and Shaynie in the Matopo Hills. We often went there to relax, while enjoying the spectacular rocky outcrops.

Nyamandlovu game-viewing platform – where I sometimes slept overnight – inside Hwange National Park.

Sunset at Makwa pan – inside Hwange National Park – where I scattered Chloe's ashes.

Ulaka, shot by licensed sport-hunters.

When I arrived on the Hwange Estate in 2001, Kanondo pan was a lush oasis.

By late 2005, Kanondo pan – once the busiest waterhole on the estate – had been left to deteriorate to this.

The W family at Kanondo pan, in the good old days. Whole is on the front left.

Lady, a wild, free-roaming giant, eventually granted me a most extraordinary place in her world.

Inkosikazi – known since the 1970s – with baby Inky.

Vervet monkeys regularly entertained me with their antics. Sometimes we watched the sunrise together.

Lady comes to me when I call her, like a familiar friend.

Lady accepts an Acacia erioloba *pod from my hand, while members of her family enjoy the Kanondo water trough.*

Misty at Kanondo in 2001 (the calf close to her is not her own).

In time, Misty allowed me to place my hand on her trunk (I'm seated inside my 4x4; camera in my other hand).

Whole with her son, Wholesome in 2001.

Wholesome with his sister, Whosit – they were inseparable.

After Wholesome was killed by a wire snare (his body in the water behind), everything about Whole spelt intense grief.

After the settlers butchered Wholesome's body, clan members lifted their hind feet over his remains, in a chilling gesture of awareness.

Eketahuna looks on as his mother Eileen is mated.

In 2005, Lady gave birth to a tiny baby girl. I was as thrilled as a surrogate mother would be! Carol named her Libby.

'Greeting ceremonies' are among the most special things you can witness in the wild. Here Whole and her mother Wendy reunite after a short time apart.

The rock dassie (also known as a rock hyrax) is the closest living relative of the elephant. They love the rocks in the Matopo Hills.

Willa, who practically sat on Shaynie's lap.

her eyes so very slowly. Completely relaxed, she would cross her back legs and rest her trunk on the ground. I sang the first verse of this hymn over and over, until she got bored (or perhaps couldn't stand my incredibly bad singing for a second longer), at which time she'd wander off.

Then one day, when Lady was right next to my vehicle, I leaned out of the window and very tentatively placed my hand on her tusk. She didn't flinch or react in any obvious way, and I left my hand there for several minutes. This brief connection left me feeling warmed, my spirit replenished, for now I truly had friends in wild places.

After that, Lady always went out of her way to come and stand beside my vehicle, trunk swinging like a pendulum as she hurried my way. Then she would rumble. Was she talking to *me* I wondered? I would look up into her amber-coloured eyes, and place my hand on her tusk. She was an incredibly gentle giant, with an extra special quality that always caused me to pause, and to breathe in the magic surrounding me.

Perhaps another year of special encounters passed, and then one day, through the window of my vehicle, I placed my hand, so very tentatively, against her trunk. It felt warm as the Kalahari sand, much rougher than I thought it would be, and deeply grooved. Lady tensed just a little at first, not knowing what this strange human appendage was against her skin, but she didn't try to escape my tender touch. In that moment, time stood still. A rush of adrenalin shot through me as we two creatures – such unlikely friends – momentarily blended; holding each other's gaze, placing our trust in one another.

As my hand rested against her trunk, close to the base of her tusks, I felt as if I was dreaming. Imagine! Such trust from a wild elephant. The reality slowly began to sink in and tears sprang to my eyes as I struggled to comprehend the enormity of the privilege.

More months passed, and eventually – incredibly – I could rub my hand up and down her trunk. In time, I could apply as much pressure as my own strength allowed. She revelled in it, as did I.

I knew that Lady was a wild, free-roaming jumbo who could have killed me with one swipe of that mighty trunk, but instead she graciously accepted me into her world. I continually reminded myself that this was a truly wild elephant and, always trying to read her mood, I never pushed her level of tolerance.

Ultimately, Lady's eldest daughter Lesley, about nine years old at the time, boldly approached the window of my vehicle. I decided to offer her an acacia pod, although she'd never taken one from my hand. She let the tip of her trunk snake within centimetres of my outstretched hand, but then snatched it away quickly, not yet ready to make such contact. She wandered away, but soon returned to the door of my vehicle. She turned side-on to me, and opened her mouth.

Eyes wide, I laughed. 'You expect me to put this pod *in your mouth*?' I asked her.

This too was a wild elephant. Putting my hand so very close to her open mouth was nerve-racking. Lesley had reversed our roles. Now it was *me* who was snatching my hand away quickly. I fed her only three pods in this way, amused by the playful expression in her eye facing me, before deciding that this was crazy.

We never tried it again. Lesley came to the door of my vehicle frequently after that, just for a pat on her long grey nose, so very smooth and soft compared to her mother's. Clearly she'd learned from Lady that I was a trusted friend. I was, though, always a little wary of Lesley. Playful and energetic, she liked to butt like a billygoat.

Human friends were with me in the field one morning to witness Lady and Lesley greeting me. They were speechless.

Later, still awestruck, they told me that they'd felt incredibly privileged to observe such extraordinary interactions with wild elephants; that they'd experienced a deep sense of wonder – and, at the time, felt a little like intruders to a very intimate scene. They suspected that Lady, wild and free, had bestowed on me the status of *'honorary elephant'*. I was moved beyond words.

By this time the Ls were no longer one of my 'focal families', about which I recorded more detailed behavioural data. Instead, I studied those whose behaviour didn't alter so much in my presence. Still though, I recorded details of L family oestrous sessions, matings, births and interactions with other elephants.

I was with Lady one day when she was in oestrus. As elephants in oestrus have been proven to do, she would have sent out pheromones and an infrasound call to broadcast her readiness to mate. Bulls responded enthusiastically. Soon, she was guarded by Andrew – the highest-ranking bull currently in musth, with 14 lower-ranking suitors forced to keep their distance. As is typical, Lady clearly wanted only 'the best of the best' to father her calf and Andrew had won the right to mate. He was a big old bull, wide between the tusks, with layers of fat around his neck. Dribbling urine and secreting from his temporal glands, testosterone levels soaring, he picked up a stick and tapped it persistently against one of his short thick tusks. What did *that* mean I wondered? Impatience, perhaps!

Males in musth are undoubtedly males in lust.

For the first time ever, I felt a little nervous with Lady so close to me. She explored the door of my 4x4, the corrugated appearance of her trunk clearly discernible. Not keen on becoming the victim of a musth bull's jealous rage, I was wary of her close presence and didn't attempt to touch her. Andrew showed little interest in me but I kept one eye on him just the same.

As I crooned to Lady and looked up into her long-lashed eyes, her temporal glands erupted with liquid. It wasn't a trickle, but more like a bubble of liquid that sprung up from within, before streaming down the sides of her face. Given that temporal gland secretion is said not to increase during oestrus, but rather is known to occur when females are excited or agitated, I took it as a sign of excitement. It seemed to me that both Lady and I thoroughly enjoyed our encounters with each other.

It was a delight to watch the L family grow in numbers, and to watch the progress of the youngsters. As well as Lady and Lesley, there was Leanne (the most dominant adult after Lady), Lucky and Louise, and their offspring, Lee, Lucy, Loopy, Levi, Leroy, Limp, Lazarus and Lol. In time the family was to increase in size, with some extra special little ones to enjoy and observe.

One day, some years after I first met Lady, she and her family were on the vlei. I raced to fetch the resident safari guide, keen for him to be able to identify her, so he could share her special majesty with photographic safari guests.

By the time we returned to the vlei, Lady had wandered some distance away and was hidden behind bushes peppered with fresh buds.

'Lady, Lady. Come on girl,' I called.

'She'll come right here?' the safari guide asked in disbelief.

'Come on Lady. Come here my girl,' I called again.

Before he knew it she was beside his door, flaunting her infinite charm.

'She knows her name,' he stated, shaking his head.

I'd decided that she probably didn't know her name, but rather knew the sound of a friendly voice; the sound and smell of a friendly vehicle. Yet I found myself wondering once again if perhaps she did know her name, this 40-something-year-old wild elephant. Could it be true, I mused to myself?

I regularly pressed for and tried to assist with tourism publicity, believing that the Presidential Elephants provided a wonderfully unique wildlife experience, and eventually Lady became a star of local television. A film crew had arrived at the Hwange Safari Lodge, wanting to meet the Presidential Elephants – to feature them on TV – and it was their lucky day. I could see the L family drinking at the lodge pan and we drove to meet up with them.

With a grin I watched the interviewer (seated behind the cameraman in another 4x4) as he held his breath nervously while the elephants mingled around them. Then the cameraman joined me in my vehicle, hoping for an even closer encounter.

Soon the tip of Lady's trunk was exploring the lens of his rolling movie camera.

'I think that's enough,' he eventually whispered to me, more than a little anxiously. Lady's trunk had snaked inside the window and was exploring his lap. I couldn't suppress the giggle that found itself flowing from my lips. It can indeed be an overwhelming experience for a first-time visitor. Nevertheless, he had excellent footage of the tip of Lady's trunk right up against the lens of his camera, of the entire relaxed family, and of Lady interacting with me.

Later, when I asked the cameraman if he now believed me (as I'd earlier said on film), that there was perhaps no better place in the world to have close-up encounters with wild, free-ranging elephants, he could only smile and nod.

'She was *this* far away from you,' I enthused, my fingers spread to show the distance.

'It was then I was thinking this isn't so good anymore,' he confided with a cheeky grin.

It was a unique adventure which, once it was over, caused both young men to exhale long deep breaths and to laugh at themselves. It was an adventure that they would not forget in a hurry; one that many an elephant-lover would sell their soul for.

My Home in the Hwange Bush

My new home turned out to be a small rondavel – a common sight in rural Zimbabwe – located in the grounds of the Hwange Safari Lodge. A rondavel is circular in shape and mine, instead of being made of mud, had a concrete outer wall and floor, two windows, one door, and a tall conical thatched roof. I loved living under thatch, which is so evocative of the African veld, its cooling properties being particularly welcome. Around my rondavel a tall fence, also thatched, ensured that I had some privacy.

Inside, a three-quarter-height concrete partition separated my shower, hand basin and toilet from the five- by four metre living area. With my fridge, coffee tables, sofa bed, cupboards and tin storage trunks placed around its edges, I had just three metres by two metres of free space.

Beside my fridge, I cooked (now and then) on a two-plate hotplate that sat on top of one of the coffee tables, cardboard boxes of utensils beneath – *my kitchen*. I ate while sitting on my sofa – *my dining room*. I sat on the floor on my grass mat with my computer on my lap and my printer on the floor beside me – *my office*. I lazed on my sofa to read a book – *my living room*. Every night I unfolded the sofa and made up my bed, tucking the edges of a mosquito net under the foam mattress – *my bedroom*. It's incredible what you can do in three metres by two metres of space.

I washed my clothes in the small hand basin on the other side of the partition, and hung them outside to dry on a length of yellow rope tied between two trees. Many folk spoke of putzi fly, warning that clothes needed to be ironed to rid them of this fly's eggs, otherwise they'd hatch beneath your skin. Despite this gruesome warning, I never even owned an iron, and no putzi fly larva ever metamorphosed under my skin.

My rondavel walls were adorned with photo enlargements of more than a hundred of my feathered and leathered friends. Among these photos there were beetle shells, butterfly wings, porcupine quills, snake skins, pressed flowers, seed pods, feathers, leaves and stems of dried grass, all of which I picked up in the veld. I had, it seemed, turned into an Australian bowerbird.

I painstakingly established the garden, transplanting succulents and more succulents, which are less attractive to the bushbucks and impalas, as well as the baboons, vervet monkeys, porcupines and elephants, all of which came regularly to visit. I also planted succulent cuttings, and successfully grew many others from leaf. In winter these succulents flowered profusely, splashes of purple, pink, red, yellow and orange brightening my small piece of Africa. In time bougainvillea climbed, in tangled thorny profusion, over my thatched fence. In summer it bloomed lavishly, deep purple, while the raggedy white flowers of a neighbouring bauhinia glowed under the full moon. When there was a breeze, a wind-chime made of wood (a gift from Julia), which hung from a beam supporting my thatched roof, tinkled sweetly. Five birdbaths attracted incredible numbers and varieties of birds, and also watered the four-legged animals that frequented my garden. At the sight of a dainty bushbuck drinking from one of them, I always caught my breath in wonder.

In the early mornings of spring, dozens of shimmering sunbirds with quivering wings probed the masses of white flower-balls on a nearby combretum bush with their curved beaks. Paradise flycatchers, with silky bluish-grey faces, always arrived in pairs a few weeks later. During the rains, a brown-headed kingfisher darted from his perch high in the magnificent teak tree overhanging my home, feasting on flying ants skilfully plucked from the moist air. Every summer this teak tree flowered profusely, stunning pinkish-mauve blooms on long stems, the nectar attracting vervet monkeys. In winter the sound of its golden-brown velvety pods exploding disturbed the still nights. It is nature's way of ensuring that the seeds are well dispersed.

Every morning a pair of hornbills, with huge curved yellow bills, waited on the branch of a smaller tree for a feast of bugs from my dustpan. Butterflies and giant bees often flitted about. I mistakenly thought the gigantic black and white bees were bumblebees. When I discovered one excavating a tunnel in an old carved wooden giraffe in my garden I turned to my reference books. I learned that they were in fact carpenter bees – an apt name, I thought – and the tunnels that were being hollowed in my wooden giraffe would be used to store a mixture of honey and pollen to feed young soon to be born.

I was content in my new home (the deadly puffadder, though, had to go) and I excitedly e-mailed a digital image to friends and family across the sea.

'Dare I point out that this structure looks rather like an outhouse,' took the prize for the cruellest comment.

'A can of baked beans with a pointy roof,' came a close second.

I had to laugh. What else could I do but lovingly name my new home 'The Can'.

I was now Thandeka Mandlovu who lived in The Can!

Africa after dark is a place full of wildlife, the nights filled with creatures big and small, known and unknown, singing their own unique songs. The sounds were truly magnificent – and close. I was always pleased to be tucked up safe and sound inside my new home, especially when the guttural bellows of lions were a little too close for comfort.

Close was one thing, but continuous was unquestionably another matter.

'Shut Uuuuup!' I couldn't help blurting out into the darkness whenever these noisy lions woke me up repeatedly, night after night.

If it was not the call of the lions, it was the whooping of the hyenas, the cries of the jackals, the rutting sounds of the impalas or perhaps it was the bark of a zebra that was echoing down the nearby vlei. Or it might have been the huge bull elephant that loved to come at night and feast right beside my thatched fence. He had bad table manners – and bad flatulence. Often there was anonymous scurrying just outside my door and I'd sit up sleepily in bed, listening, wishing that all these creatures would just go to sleep!

If I was lucky I awoke at dawn to sweet birdsong, but more frequently it was to the less pleasing raucous outburst of the red-billed francolins. Clearly ecstatic about something unknown, these tone-deaf feathered visitors regularly shattered the peaceful morning with their boisterous racket, right outside my door.

One morning I awoke to an incredibly well-pronounced 'go away' coming from a tree in my garden. It was the first time I'd heard the grey lourie (the go-away bird) call so very clearly. I walked sleepily outside, listening to his repetitive call, which went on and on.

'Go away? ... *You* go away,' I told him playfully. 'This is *my* house.'

Spiders remained my constant room-mates, and in time I learned to live with the harmless, less intimidating ones. The 'daddy-long-legs' and the flat 'wall spiders' became my friends, and I left them in peace, webs adorning my roof and walls. The huge, hairy baboon spiders though, I simply refused to commune with. When Doom insect killing spray disappeared from the shops – as so many things did eventually – I resorted to using Mortein. Recalling the catchy commercial on Australian television, I had little remorse for 'poor dead Louie' – who wasn't a fly after all, but more regularly a mosquito, a spider, a scorpion, a centipede or a wasp.

I frequently glimpsed snakes in my garden, and on two memorable occasions had one inside my rondavel. The long thin one behind my toilet cistern one morning – after I'd awoken to the melodious croaking of copious frogs and the pleasing call of the crowned crane – was very definitely unwelcome. My mouth was instantly dry and my heart thumped uncontrollably. Little or big, poisonous or harmless, a snake in my tiny rondavel was my very worst nightmare. I'd slept with this one for at least one night, only metres away. Too early to call on neighbours, I dealt with the situation completely mechanically.

Outwardly I was strangely calm, but inside my blood raced like rapids through my veins. I reflect now on the uncanny daring of terror and trepidation. In my wildest dreams I could never have done what I did, and still today I feel somewhat mortified about it. I grabbed, of all things, my long bread knife...

Unable to deal with the aftermath, I sat on my doorstep waiting and waiting for someone to wake from their Sunday morning slumber. It was rather strange, I suppose, for me to feel that I needed assistance now.

'*Nyoka!*' I cried out to Josias (whose job it was to wash the safari vehicles), when I saw him arrive on duty. He reacted immediately, racing to find a suitable weapon, before I could enlighten him further. 'No, no Josias,' I muttered, the moment I saw him reappear, 'the *nyoka* is dead.' But Josias didn't understand me. He was making his way, very cautiously, into my rondavel, weapon in hand. 'Josias, it's okay,' I said, trying once again to explain but still failing to make myself understood. 'Josias, the *nyoka* is late!' I finally blurted out, probably a little louder than was necessary, but at least Josias now understood. Dead is not a word that you hear often in Zimbabwe. Perhaps it sounds too final. 'Late' is the less harsh euphemism.

Josias was visibly confused, and more than a little amused, when he saw the dead snake. He was clearly wondering why on earth he'd been called – although my phobia of snakes, even late ones, was well known. For weeks afterwards I rounded the partition to my bathroom area warily, fearful of what I might find. This incident also brought about a new nightly ritual – tucking my mosquito net *securely* around and under my sofa bed on the floor. It was no longer only deadly mosquitos that I feared. I was already sprinkling Dettol disinfectant on my doorstep (a tip from a new friend), the smell said to be highly offensive to snakes, but after episodes like this one I was somewhat sceptical. Even so, I always kept a bottle of Dettol on hand as it did make me feel just a wee bit safer.

Dormice threw regular all-night parties in my rondavel, racing in and out of my dreams until dawn. Whoever invented the phrase 'quiet as a mouse' clearly had never met a dormouse. They are attractive little creatures, with bushy squirrel-like tails, but they ate my clothes – and I didn't have many. They climbed up the outside wall of my rondavel, under my thatched roof, and down the wall on the inside. I often switched on the light in the middle of the night and watched them racing about on top of the concrete partition, or on my curtain rods.

Dormice are insectivores and their arrival coincided with an invasion of stinkbugs that lasted for 10 months. Insectivores they may be, but as well as nibbling at my clothes they also liked to chew through the plastic encasing my kalamata olives, not to mention clearly enjoying a feed of paw-paw and the dregs from a glass of Amarula!

One day, on entering my rondavel after two weeks away, I noticed two nearly empty plastic bags lying where they shouldn't be, each decidedly ragged at one end. In these large plastic bags had been handfuls of feathers, gathered from predator kills in the veld. The feathers were soft and beautifully patterned, and were to be used as decorations on greeting cards and boxes. I immediately consulted my mammal reference book to check if dormice made soft, comfy nests, but there was no breeding data to be found. So I gathered up what remained of my bags of feathers and gave it no further thought.

It wasn't until late that night, when I unfolded my sofa to prepare for sleep, that I again remembered the dormice. When the foam of my bed hit the floor, a few exquisite feathers floated high into the cool air. I could see a few more feathers wedged between blanket and duvet. Hesitantly, I flicked up the edge of my blanket, its silky border tattered by industrious teeth. There lay thousands upon thousands of small feathers, so very neatly placed. I stood stunned, feeling a mixture of admiration and horror. Something had surely been lying there, a gentle form having smoothed many of the feathers into a soft cosy cup.

Cautiously, in case something scary remained beneath the pile, I gathered the feathers into a plastic bag. Would a dormouse do this, I wondered? Or did I have yet another visitor? Had young already been born?

I went to sleep that night having tucked my mosquito net in tightly around me, my mind filled with fanciful thoughts, wondering if my uninvited guest would return to finish what had been started.

And return a dormouse did, waking me with loud, frantic, high-pitched chatter. Entry to the nesting site was now blocked by my mosquito net, and the wee creature was clearly hysterical about the whole situation. I must admit that I felt rather the same way.

Later, having relayed this tale to my family in Australia, bemused words from my niece took wing across the ocean, 'A dormouse in your *bed!*' she wrote teasingly. 'Well at least you're not lonely.'

My most unexpected guest was, one spring afternoon, a metre-and-a-half-long monitor lizard. There was definitely not room for him in *my* house. His massive head and front legs were already inside my open door when I saw him. Both of us were clearly startled. He turned and raced, like one possessed, to my thatched fence, where he clung upright to a wooden pole for a prolonged rest, before scurrying off.

The vervet monkeys were as mischievous as ever, performing their destructive acrobatics on my thatched roof and in the towering teak and other smaller trees in my garden, eating my flowers and drinking all the water from my birdbaths, yet I couldn't help but take pleasure in them. I often walked out into my garden and sat among them. Sometimes we watched the sunrise together. Although the powder blue and bright red genitalia of the males was fascinating, I preferred to watch the pretty faces of the youngsters, their shy eyes shining below bushy white brows. They often played 'peek-a-boo' with me from behind a tree stump, making me laugh out loud. They also entertained themselves (never failing to amuse me too), with a series of other playful head movements, inviting me to copy them. Sitting on a log in my garden, one would look my way and bounce his fury face three times to the right, and I would do the same. Then twice up and down, and I would copy. Once around in a circle, and then around again, pleased that I never lost interest in their game. Towards the end of each year there were always cute new babies, each clinging tightly to its mother's belly.

The baboons visited too, although they were somewhat less welcome. His dental weaponry and her bright pink rump (used to excite the males) were not particularly attractive – at least not to me.

The big daddy baboon that occasionally appeared from nowhere at my open door, to sit for a while, was particularly unwelcome. Sometimes he dashed inside to steal scarce bread, or an egg left unguarded on a table. The day he stole a whole packet of potatoes (a recent gift from a friend), I took after him, intent on recovering some of my produce – which I eventually did, albeit in a rather undignified manner. I have to admit though, that he ended up with more potatoes than I did. One day, I feared, he would give me a heart attack. I regularly eyeballed him, recalling with a grin the evening of happy debauchery when an African man had offered the male colleague by my side (believing him to be my husband), a payment of three baboons for one night with me. Playfully, I'd pretended to be most indignant. A night with me was surely worth more than *three* baboons!

It was the baboons that I blamed for the 'skylight' that eventually appeared in my thatched roof. I walked into my rondavel one winter's morning, after some days in Bulawayo, and I could see the sky. They'd been busy in my absence. Perhaps attracted, like the dormice, to the tasty bugs in my roof, they'd taken advantage of the rotting thatch, striping it off layer by layer to get to the tasty treats. The thatch was said to be more than 10 years old and it was time to replace it, a particularly messy job that I'd been putting off for months. Now I had no choice. Everything I owned was laboriously moved out and stored elsewhere for the week of work, which ended up taking three. And I'd really rather forget about the newly deceased rat that fell out of my sofa bed as it was lifted outside.

On the exterior circular wall of my rondavel, beneath the lip of the thatched roof, lived a battalion of bats, with cute little faces and big ears.

There was life, not always particularly welcome, everywhere I looked. I always tried hard to ignore the less welcome critters, relishing the relative solitude and quietly celebrating the surrounding beauty.

There was no carport near my rondavel to provide shelter for Nicki Mukuru, and after years of sitting in the relentless African sun, her black leather roof became stiff and brittle. The eventual tears and holes only really posed a problem in the wet season, when rain poured in from all angles.

'I'll make a hat for your 4x4,' offered one of the maintenance men, having seen me sitting drenched in the driver's seat. 'It won't cost you too much.' So it was that Nicki Mukuru had studs riveted into the frame of her roof, and a frog-green heavy plastic 'hat' ready to be securely attached when summer brought welcome rain to the veld. She was once again watertight (as was my newly thatched roof), but still I had other vehicle problems.

Her clutch caused me trouble for about a year, until I finally managed to source the replacement part required. One evening, before that happened, I was driving uphill in deep, soft sand when she asked to go down a gear. To my dismay, I discovered that I had no clutch. Nicki Mukuru conked out and, in those merciless conditions, simply refused to start again without the luxury of a clutch, leaving me stranded in silence. I was reasonably close to my rondavel, but it wasn't sensible to walk in the dark.

I'd thought about spending a night out again soon, but a *planned* one was more to my liking. Now I had no choice, so I decided to make the most of it. I smothered myself with insect repellent, opened the roof wide, and lay down on my comfy back seat. With a cushion, blanket, water and food always kept in my 4x4, I was well prepared. I had dried apricots, tinned ruby grapefruit, water crackers and a chocolate bar. It was a veritable feast! As I dined, thousands of sparkling stars, like diamonds, studded the night sky. Acacia trees stood silhouetted, dark and contorted, the glowing jewels clearly visible through a maze of twisted branches.

It was beautiful, and it was quiet. Early the next morning I was awoken by a game-drive vehicle, on which I cadged a lift back to my rondavel.

A supply run meant driving Nicki Mukuru two hours return to the closest town of Hwange, or six hours return to Bulawayo. So, with fuel always in short supply and becoming more and more expensive, I made these trips very seldom, surviving, when my other supplies ran low, on stocks of tinned fruit and three-minute noodles. My inquisitive friends Down Under couldn't figure out why they were *three*-minute noodles, since they are *two*-minute noodles there. I explained, with a grin, that things *always* tended to take time in Zimbabwe.

I drenched these bland noodles in sweet chilli sauce, sometimes adding stir-fried vegetables, cheese or perhaps a boiled egg. The perishables I kept in my small fridge were regularly depleted though, so I often had to settle for just noodles and sweet chilli sauce. This sauce was usually unavailable in town, but I was fortunate to have kind friends who came back from their sojourns in South Africa laden with it. These same cheeky friends always cut me off mid-sentence. 'Yes, yes, we *know*,' they'd say. 'The brand is *"All Gold"*. It is *sweet* chilli sauce, not chilli sauce. It is *mild*, not hot.'

One day, I liked to scheme, I would make them all eat noodles with *hot chilli* sauce at every meal for a month. Only then would they fully appreciate the consequences of getting it wrong.

When tinned peaches and pineapple became impossible to find, I devoured tins of ruby grapefruit, fruit cocktail and litchis (or 'lychees' as I knew them). My salads also came out of tins: beetroot, peas, potatoes and ham – and asparagus too, if I was very lucky. When they were available and not too expensive, I bought containers of smoked mussels, cucumber relish, sun-dried tomatoes and cocktail onions to eat on water crackers, as well as olives, which I needed to hide from the dormice. I learned to eat shrivelled fruit and vegetables, the likes of which, in the First World, would be picked up gingerly and tossed hastily into the nearest bin. Whenever my fridge contained fruit, cheese, yoghurt or eggs, I felt like I had a feast fit for a queen. Occasionally, if flour was available, I made myself pancakes, and opened a tin of dessert cream as an extra special treat.

The 'use by' dates printed on the tins always made me grin. Supposedly still at its best for another eight months, I once inspected a can of grapefruit beginning to contort – bulging and bending like some sort of weird sea creature. I took it outside, can opener in hand, nervously anticipating an explosion. Ever since the tomato paste, from a perfectly cylindrical can with 'use by' date still pending, sprayed my thatched roof like a burst aorta, I made it a habit to open *all* cans facing away from me, outside.

Although there was no room in my rondavel for them to stay with me, Lol and Drew sometimes came to visit. This happened much too infrequently, since they now lived on the other side of the country. Drew was growing tall, like his father, and in his eyes I could once again see Andy. When they arrived, I'd always make a cup of tea, Lol graciously turning a blind eye to the stale teabags and lumpy milk. Sometimes, we sat on wooden benches in my garden, looking at photographs. Then we drove out and spent time among the elephants, and I introduced them to the various families.

'Why do you give the elephants names?' Drew once asked. 'My daddy wouldn't like you giving them names.' Drew, then six years old, was sitting out through the window of Nicki Mukuru watching the mud-bathing elephants. His question took me by surprise and I couldn't help but raise my eyebrows and smile, knowing that he was quite right. Andy wouldn't really have approved of so many elephants having names.

I gazed at Lol and her son holding hands across the front seat of Nicki Mukuru, jointly delighting in the performance put on by these playful elephants (which was now an extra special treat for them), and I knew that my brief explanation was already forgotten.

Drew's question, though, prompted me to think again about my use of names. Identification of individual elephants was, I reflected, crucial to my study and when dealing with so many jumbos I knew at once that I would find it easier to remember a name, rather than a boring old number preferred by many in the scientific community. Andy, I hoped, would understand.

Lol missed the sights, sounds and smells of the bush, all of which remained such an important part of her being. She breathed in the bush air, soaking everything up like parched ground.

When the three of us, spurred on by a grinning Lol, clowned around in the elephants' mud-bathing pool once they'd moved off, I was delighted – and more than a little afraid of being caught, by person or crocodile. Their lives had changed forever, but the Searle mischief lived on.

Still we laughed, and we cried.

PART IV

An Adopted
Child of Africa

Company in Paradise

The two largest ethnic groups in Zimbabwe are the Shona and the Ndebele. The Shona people live mostly in the central and eastern districts, with the Ndebele dominating the Matabeleland province in the west, where I lived. Although Sindebele is widely spoken, English remains the official language. I can't speak Sindebele, so everyone conversed with me in English.

It was Gladys who first honoured me with the Ndebele name Thandeka. She worked at Miombo Lodge and I'd known her since my days as a tourist. Always cheerful and smiling, with a charming gap between her front teeth, she tried to teach me to carry a bucket of water on my head – to no avail. Unlike the African ladies, I couldn't even carry a small parcel on my head, let alone a bucket filled with water. Forever pleased to see me, Gladys regularly swept me up in her arms and I would always emit a little squeal of apprehension as she tried to lift me off the ground.

Three mechanics – Nicko, Wezi and Domiso – all helped with the onsite servicing of Nicki Mukuru at one time or another, exercising their superb bush skills. I became convinced that, with a piece of wire, they could fix almost anything. Nicko was the head mechanic, always polite, and always with a smile on his lips. Once, he interrupted the servicing of Nicki Mukuru to dispatch a deadly puffadder from my doorstep. Full of mischief, he then ran after me with its long body dangling from a stick, enjoying my terror. But Nicko looked increasingly unwell. After his last bout in hospital I came upon him, driving in the field. 'Are you fine Nicko?' I asked, concerned.

'Yes, yes. I am fine,' he assured me, nodding his head heartily and smiling. Yet he did not look well.

It was Wezi who broke the news to me while I was on my way home from Bulawayo, less than a week later. We were changing vehicles, halfway home, when he appeared at my side. 'Maam...' he addressed me hesitantly.

'Hi Wezi,' I said, offering him my hand, and wishing that he wouldn't call me that. A shortened version of Mama, it always made me feel so old. It was, I knew though, a term of respect.

'It's Nicko, Maam. He's late.' So it was that I found out Nicko had left this earth. In Africa, I quickly learned, death is never far away. It felt strange to go to the workshop and not find him there. In time, Wezi took over as head mechanic.

About two years later, when Domiso was helping me with a problem with Nicki Mukuru, he asked, 'How much would a man have to pay for you in Australia?'

'Men don't pay for their wives in Australia,' I replied.

'Do you know how much a man would have to pay here for someone like you? Twenty cattle! Imagine. Twenty head of cattle.' Domiso was shaking his head.

I later pondered this rather odd observation, and questioned him the next day. 'That was a strange question you asked me yesterday. What were you thinking?'

'Our cultures are very different,' Domiso replied.

'Twenty cattle?' I asked.

But overnight I'd lost value, not unlike the Zimbabwean dollar. 'Well, at least six or seven,' he said, still shaking his head.

A number of people helped mend Nicki Mukuru's many punctures. Of them, Lovemore – always friendly and polite – was the most efficient. When the hotel filling station, like many filling stations in Zimbabwe, closed down because of lack of fuel, Lovemore left his post as petrol attendant and began working in room service. It was odd to see him always smartly dressed and I teased him about looking so dapper. He never asked me for anything, which was uncommon. I was thankful for his presence, and trusted his quiet and undemanding ways.

Another man, named Champion, demonstrated a genuine interest in and concern for the wildlife. He sometimes used a panga to cut the grass around my rondavel. One day, while he was working in my garden, I noticed Lady and her family passing by on the other side of the electric fence, which ran quite close to my home. 'Come!' I called to Champion. His lithe form scurried into my vehicle beside me, and we drove to meet up with the Ls.

He was thrilled with his encounter with Lady, and later bragged (quite rightly) about having touched a truly wild elephant. Yet Champion, like so many others, was no longer content with life in Zimbabwe, regularly insisting that he would work very hard if I took him with me to live in Australia. More and more often, it seemed to me, people were trying to flee Zimbabwe. Most, I knew though, had no choice but to stay forever.

Andrew worked for an onsite tour company, and was the opposition representative for the area. He sometimes shook his head and spoke of 'these people,' and we laughed whenever I reminded him that 'these are *your* people, Andrew!' He had the maturity of an elder, and a ready willingness to help if he could.

Jabulani, a tall, fit young man with enviable bush skills, headed up the anti-poaching/snare-destruction team, which was now based and operating on the Hwange Estate. When given adequate support, Jabulani proved to be reliable and hard working with a sheer determination to catch poachers. He regularly appeared on my doorstep to show me the hundreds of snares that he and his team had successfully destroyed.

Faith, who was one of my neighbours in the early days, occasionally accompanied me into the field to watch the elephants. Like Champion, she wasn't scared when the elephants came very close. 'I trust you, and I know that you will not put me in danger,' she once said to me.

To celebrate her interest, the matriarch of the F family was named Faith, and this matriarch's son, at Faith's request, was named Freddie. Faith thought her elephant encounters were fantastic, and so in time Freddie's new brother was named Fantastic. Just before Faith and her husband left the area for the city (taking their treasured photographic enlargement of Faith, Freddie and Fantastic with them), we transplanted some of her well-tended pot plants into my garden, so she would never be very far away.

Whenever I sat in the Hwange Safari Lodge reservations office, trying to send an e-mail, Busi and I would chat. We spoke of our families, and of life in Zimbabwe. Busi was well-spoken and level-headed, with a very responsible and professional manner that I found, in this bush environment, somewhat unusual and certainly refreshing. She was a comfort to me during the days when my eldest niece in Australia was battling cancer, always asking after her.

One New Year's Eve Busi placed a small white package, tied up with tape, in the palm of my hand. 'It's nothing. Don't get too excited,' she said.

This was so special, so unexpected.

I walked back to my rondavel, holding my white paper package and shaking it from time to time, deciding eventually that there were jelly beans inside. It was a tiny package that had lifted my spirit. Once inside my rondavel, I peeled away the paper and gasped with surprise. Inside a camera film box was a silver bracelet – eight exquisite elephants all chained together. It was divine. The perfect gift for Mandlo. I raced back to the lodge, excused myself to the client Busi was assisting, and squealed with delight. It was a special gift that touched my heart.

Most of my African companions held many mysterious beliefs, foreign to my Western mind. Almost without exception they believed in the *tokoloshe*, a mean little gremlin-like man sometimes said to be only 10 centimetres tall. It's widely believed that an *inyanga* can, for a fee, craft a *tokoloshe*. This (often bearded) little creature will then, it is said, execute dastardly deeds as instructed by its master.

The *tokoloshe* is feared, as is the chameleon. I always swerved abruptly to avoid running over these miniature slow-moving dragons. Sometimes green, at other times brown, white or occasionally even orange, I find them adorable, a view not shared by many of my African friends, who consider them bad luck. Whenever I saw one on my drives through the veld I climbed out of my 4x4, usually to witness one foreleg suspended motionless in mid-air. I always picked up the chameleon, enjoying the prickling sensation of its tiny feet as it ran up my arm. I was enchanted by their changing colours and swivelling eyes, and always placed them out of harm's way.

Occasionally, to celebrate a birthday or a special holiday, I took a trip with a group of friends to a different part of the country, revelling in a fresh slice of Zimbabwean paradise. I felt at ease in the countryside and cherished the opportunity to explore.

On one of these trips there were, among others, Julia, Dinks and an American named Carol McCammon. I first met Carol (a former school teacher) at Umtshibi when she volunteered part-time with the painted dog project. Carol lived in Harare, and in time became a loyal friend and supporter.

Together we drove north from Harare to Mana Pools, a World Heritage site at the far north of the country, where the Zambezi River separates Zimbabwe from Zambia. We anticipated a memorable wildlife and wilderness experience, and we weren't disappointed. In this national park you can walk around, if you choose, unescorted. On arrival we were met with a sign that read 'Driving off-road is strictly prohibited, especially up to lion kills... Leaving your vehicle and walking is permitted.'

Well, this was the special sort of African logic that I never quite got used to!

One evening when we were sitting outdoors for dinner we heard loud munching sounds close by. It was clear that someone else was enjoying their dinner; someone whose table manners left much to be desired. Inquisitive, I needed to confirm what I suspected. Using a red filter on a spotlight, to limit any negative effect on the nocturnal wildlife, I spotted a hippopotamus just over five metres away, grazing contentedly. Hippos, I'd been told, kill more people in Africa than any other animal. He walked on towards the riverbank, the metres between us dwindling rapidly. My friends sat and watched, chatting loudly, casually, in the still of the African night, while I began to wonder somewhat nervously if perhaps 'holy sh*t – *close* hippo' might well be the last words I ever uttered.

The hippo passed by, as if wandering nonchalantly under star-filled skies, so very close to his two-legged friends, was perfectly normal behaviour. Maybe it was for him.

The night before we'd all wandered – unwisely in hindsight – just the few metres to the edge of the riverbank after dark. I'd felt uneasy, the fear of the unknown too overwhelming. My whispers then about the likelihood of coming face-to-face with an unhappy hippo, or some other dangerous beast, soon came back to haunt me – although I figured at the time that I didn't need to be able to run fast; just faster than the others I was with! The next evening my fears were justified beyond all doubt. There in front of us, in the place where we'd taken our walk the evening before, was a buffalo. A sitting buffalo. My heart still skips a beat when I recall that we had, unknowingly, been walking in darkness in a buffalo's bedroom.

The resident vervet monkeys were not nearly as hazardous, but they were as mischievous as only monkeys can be. 'What on earth was *that*?' I blurted out, startled.

Carol and I had been standing around the outside freezer (which refused to freeze), our minds perhaps preoccupied with the wonder and magic of life in the African bush. From under our noses, a long-limbed form stole a whole loaf of bread, whisking it away high into the treetops. Our jeers and glares did nothing to entice the monkey to return it, and able to do little else, we hoped that he at least ended up with a bellyache.

Early next morning an avocado was more to his cheeky liking. I interrupted him sitting on our dining room table, like King Vervet, enjoying his stolen treat. I'm not sure who got the bigger fright – the vervet or a friend in her bed, only partially clad, who was rudely awoken when the monkey hurtled past her at high speed (with me in hot pursuit), and then leapt out of the bedroom window next to her, avocado in hand.

The vervet had bread, and avocado. I wondered if he would return for the salt and pepper, and the Worcestershire sauce.

We drank G&Ts, watching the crimson sun set over the shimmering water, basking in the peaceful evening beauty. The G&Ts were strictly for medicinal purposes of course. It's a sound local theory that the quinine in the tonic helps to ward off malaria, and with all this water around, Dinks and I decided, we definitely needed two or three.

One Christmas I drove to the Eastern Highlands with Dinks and a new-found friend named Charmain Beswick, whom I came to know as Shaynie. Like Dinks, Shaynie is gifted with kindness and goodness. We sat three-abreast, taking turns to drive, and singing songs (not often in tune) to the great outdoors.

En route to the spectacular Vumba Mountains we passed areas of boulder-topped koppies and the gnarled, bulbous trunks of baobab trees. When we arrived, we meandered cautiously up winding roads. I was amazed by the seemingly endless vistas of rolling green hills, cloaked in patches of forest, that offered glimpses into neighbouring Mozambique. It was an entirely different world from the one I'd come to know so well in Hwange.

Our cabin was nestled high up in the Vumba, where we were quickly immersed in 'the mountains of the mist'. Mist rolled in tangibly over the hills and soon the rain began to fall. We sat in front of a crackling log fire, listening to the peaceful tinkling of the numerous frogs.

We awoke on the morning of Christmas Eve to the sparkle of raindrops suspended from the tips of pine needles, the soaring pine trees dwarfing our cabin. A Livingstone's lourie – green with red underwing – flitted graciously among the trees. It seemed fitting to see these 'Christmas colours' in the sky. Yellow flame lilies (Zimbabwe's national flower) were abundant, as were the stunning large blue flower-clusters of the hydrangeas.

The samango monkey is at home in these misty forests. Found in Zimbabwe only in the Vumba area, the chubby silvery-faced samango, with its dark grey body, is a delight. A troop of these elusive canopy-dwelling creatures allowed us a glimpse into their world on Christmas Day. We stood quietly and watched as they swung swiftly through rain-sodden branches. We also encountered the beautiful emperor swallowtail butterfly, with sizeable wings and distinctive clubbed tail, found in Zimbabwe only on this eastern border.

The new moon was suspended in a crystal clear Vumba night sky. Around the log fire we toasted marshmallows, enjoying good South African wine, a treat for our often-deprived palates. Pine cones burned, and a firefly appeared, flashing its bright light just above my head, willing me to make a festive season wish.

We took a trip northward to Nyanga the next morning, and found the mountains to be more rugged. Pine forests dominated the landscape and there were sparkling waterways and waterfalls. The return journey was shrouded in mist, our Vumba log fire beckoning to us once again.

Some days the mist and rain were with us all day, which was a welcome respite from the Hwange heat. We wandered around in the mist, collecting pine cones for the fire and admiring the over-sized toadstools, snails, slugs and frogs. We relaxed around the log fire playing Scrabble, laughing and inventing new words, while enjoying endless cups of hot Milo.

We ate mushrooms freshly picked from the Vumba forest floor, and survived. We ate berries growing by the roadside, and survived. We visited a well-known coffee shop, and barely survived the shock of the prices. A slice of cake was the same price you'd have paid for a roadworthy vehicle just a few years before. Zimbabwe's economy was in free fall. None of us was prepared to pay *that* much for a piece of cake, but Dinks and Shaynie, unable to resist, ordered a very expensive hot drink while I sat and watched them savour every mouthful.

From the Vumba we headed south-west to Great Zimbabwe, a World Heritage site (close to the town of Masvingo, where Shaynie once lived), said to have been a royal capital of a Shona community. The ruins exhibit extraordinary workmanship, a maze of well-finished stone block walls, astonishingly wide and tall, built without mortar. They're considered the most spectacular ruins south of the Sahara.

Back in Bulawayo, we welcomed in the New Year watching videos, while struggling to adjust to the high temperatures. Separated by just seven hours' drive, but seemingly another world, log fires were definitely not needed here. Dinks expertly made sadza, the maize meal staple of Zimbabwe, white and bland and somewhat of an acquired taste. With the smell of the accompanying relish tantalising our taste buds, we tucked in, eating it in the traditional way, with our fingers.

We celebrated New Year's Day among the spectacular rocky outcrops of yet another World Heritage site – the Matopo Hills – a 20-minute drive south of Bulawayo. This is 3 000 square kilometres of some of the most spectacular granite scenery on earth, superbly sculpted by nature over hundreds of thousands of years, resulting in extraordinary castles of balancing rocks. It's a place of bushman rock art where, in bygone days, these hunter-gatherers used caves and crevices as canvases.

There is an overwhelming sense of power and grandeur here and a profound atmosphere of spirituality, which left us feeling awed and humbled. The lime-green, rust and grey lichen on the huge granite boulders resembled splashes of paint – an unexpected smattering of colour among the leafy trees and the breathtaking towers of stone.

The unmistakeable call of the African fish eagle echoed hauntingly, but it is the larger black eagle that is the master of the skies here. On terra firma, rhinos roam, leopards have their lairs, and rock dassies (also known as rock hyraxes) scamper over the boulders. Small and guinea-pig-like, the dassie has been proven to genetically be the closest living relative of the elephant.

With a glass of wine in hand, while watching the sun sink behind the boulders of smooth rock, we drank in the overpowering ambience and mystique of these timeless rocky hills – Dinks's favourite place on earth.

Victoria Falls is another World Heritage site in the north-west of the country, a two-hour drive from my rondavel. It was the closest international airport to me and so my visits there were usually of necessity. Occasionally though, when collecting friends from the airport, or when being picked up myself, we spent a few hours basking in the glory of the Falls.

Generally in April, which is the end of the wet season, they're at their most spectacular and we would stroll through the thick misty spray generated by the force of the falling water (which, from a distance, looks like smoke), listening to the continuous thundering roar of the vast volumes of water plunging over the cliffs. Wandering around, our hair and clothes drenched by the spray, we fully appreciated the African name 'Mosi-oa-Tunya' – 'The smoke that thunders'. We delighted, too, in the habituated bushbuck, with their delicate white spots, that live in the surrounding rainforest.

With all these spectacular landscapes and natural wonders to behold, you'd imagine that tourists would flock to Zimbabwe. And before the year 2000 – the year that the farm invasions began – they did. Tourism used to be one of Zimbabwe's biggest industries. Yet we always found ourselves among only a handful of tourists, if any at all. We cherished the experience of having entire wilderness areas to ourselves, for this was a joy in itself, but without the tourists bringing much-needed foreign currency into the country, Zimbabwe's decline only worsened.

Wildlife conservation work remained critical, I believed, to help preserve its priceless natural heritage.

Favourite Ladies,
Endangered Offspring

Back on the Hwange Estate it was the Ws, the Ms and the Es (in addition to Lady and her family), that I stumbled upon most frequently. The Es and the Ms often spent time in each other's company, distant relations perhaps or maybe just close friends, while the Ws and the Ls usually chose to wander alone.

Like Lady, Whole, Misty and Eileen are all particularly gentle giants, though unlike her, none are matriarchs. Whole was so named because of a distinctive hole in the middle of her left ear, but belonging to the W family, the word hole needed to be prefixed with a 'W'. Misty is easily recognisable with two small pieces of skin dangling from her right ear, and Eileen's right ear is uniquely indented with two deep notches. Yet all can be recognised, even from a distance, just by the way they look and how they walk.

Eventually I could place my hand on Whole's tusk, although she would usually swing her trunk towards my outstretched hand in greeting, not quite making contact. Eileen preferred to stay a metre or so away. Misty enjoyed closer contact and the comfort of my door, sometimes standing within centimetres of my arm for over an hour. In time, Misty allowed me to place my hand on her trunk, just below her eyes. It was only Lady who liked me to rub her trunk really hard.

I don't know why it was that I was initially attracted to these elephants more than to others in their families. Once singled out, I talked to them more often than I talked to the others, and in return they responded affectionately. Ultimately they approached me, rather than me approaching them, and they brought their babies with them.

Naturally there were others, in these and every family, who were special too. Indeed, I often found that there were times in the field when I had little desire to collect data, but wanted simply to spend time with the elephants because they'd become my friends.

Wendy, who I believed to be Whole's mother, was a high-ranking female in the W family. She was an enormous lady with relatively short legs, particularly large ears and an air of great dignity. When the grass around the pans was long and lush, the elephants spent hours feasting on it, fanning themselves with huge ears in the heat of the day. This ear flapping chills the blood in the surface veins, which helps to keep them cool. I observed with interest how the elephants foraged on the grass. They would wrap their trunks around a clump of grass and then, using one of their front feet, they'd kick it loose from the ground. They clearly didn't like to eat too much soil, so before stuffing the grass into their bewhiskered mouths, they typically flicked it between their forelegs to rid it of dirt. Not Wendy though. She always brought the clump up to her ear and flicked it there.

Wilma is another high-ranking member of the W family. Her baby was just hours old when Carol and I stumbled upon mother and child in October 2002. Wilma was still dripping blood, and the little baby girl was struggling to stay upright on wobbly legs. Because she was very swollen where the umbilical cord was attached and walked strangely, with a bulky lump hanging low between her legs, Carol named Wilma's baby Worry. As it turned out, Worry was only a worry for a few months, and grew up to be strong and healthy.

Why is the name of another adult female in the W family. She was injured a year after I first met her, and whenever I saw her, I wondered why. It looked as though her right hip was dislocated; her right back leg now dragging. I thought she may have been injured while mating, but when she gave birth within 10 months of her injury I realised she'd already been pregnant at the time of her mishap. Why managed well with her disability, and is a kind and caring mother.

The M family is a particularly relaxed group, which often lolled around my vehicle. Along with Misty, there is Mertle (the matriarch) and Mettle, Marj, Marmite, Marion, Melody, Magic, Mandy, Marianne,

Moholi, Moi, Marvellous, Moon and others. The youngsters loved to climb all over each other, building elephant castles, reaching for the sky. Sooner or later they toppled off, and would playfully rebuild them yet again. Mertle often rested her trunk on the open passenger-side window of my vehicle, opening and closing her eyes so very slowly. 'Amazing Grace' regularly found itself on my lips, and I would sing softly to my elephant friends, the sky around me a gentle pink.

It was moments like these that caused me to reflect just how intricately I was caught up in the lives of these elephants.

Emily, who at one time had a tusk configuration similar to Lady's but who is very different in looks and body shape, leads the E family. Whenever I came upon this family I always searched first for Eileen, and then for her youngest calf, Eumundi, and his siblings Eketahuna and Echo. (Some elephants, named after or by special friends, just had a little extra special something about them.) Echo is a young tuskless female, yet there are no other tuskless elephants in the E family, from whom she could have inherited this gene. I often, therefore, sat wondering what Echo's father looked like; which family he'd once belonged to and who was tuskless in that family, a family from which he'd long since been ousted, as nature dictates.

One day, when Eileen was in oestrus, she arrived at my 4x4 accompanied by a huge old musth bull. He was clearly dominant to everyone around him, and just a little bit grumpy. Numerous younger males tagged along too. An oestrous female might have five amorous bulls in tow one day, and 20 the next – the elephants' communication ability never ceasing to amaze me.

Because I was focused on the Ms feeding behind my vehicle, I didn't notice Eileen – her cushioned feet allowing her to walk with silence – until she was just one metre from my front bumper. It was in fact the deep rumble of the musth bull that prompted me to look around.

I got the distinct impression that Eileen had come to me for comfort and protection of some sort. She seemed tired of all these pesky males! Yet what she'd done, inadvertently, was bring this huge musth bull right up to my stationary vehicle. Now I was definitely intimidated. I climbed down from my rooftop, with slow and confident movements, keen to make myself smaller than he was, so as not to appear a threat.

He held his head high and spread his ears, making himself look as imposing as possible. His legs touched my front bumper, his head no longer visible from where I now sat behind the steering wheel. Looking up through the windscreen, I could see only his huge trunk and neck. His head towered, unseen, somewhere above my 4x4. A male elephant by age 18 is typically taller than every female in a population and, unlike the females, who reach their full height at around age 25, the males continue to grow in height throughout their lives. A musth bull like this one, aged over 45, dwarfs every adult female – elephant and human.

By now my heart was pounding, but I knew to keep low and not to switch on my engine – something that he would probably interpret as a threat. I had to sit it out, and those few minutes felt like an eternity. I silently begged Eileen to move away from me, knowing that her enamoured bull would move with her. Looking around, I realised that I was parked in a position where I could only reverse and I knew, too, that I couldn't escape in reverse from a moody musth bull. So I stayed put.

He walked a few paces away from my vehicle, the air strong with his musth scent, and then he turned around, centimetres from my vehicle once again, kicking the sand and glowering at me threateningly. He repeated this performance again and again.

'Come on Eileen, move off,' I whispered. She eventually did, but it was another few minutes before I felt confident enough to start my vehicle. I didn't particularly like being almost sat on by a huge testosterone-filled musth bull, and Eileen, I thought, really should have better taste.

The musth bull did his duty over the course of the next few days. Whenever I watched matings such as these, at very close range, the male's private appendage – one metre or more long, thicker than a person's thigh, and in an 's' shape – always looked more like some sort of eager sea monster. Taking no further part in the family process, as is always the case, the bull soon moved on to greener pastures.

Each of the elephants, I learned, have very different personalities. To the trained eye, they also look very different from one another.

There are those distinguishing features that are associated with age: long in body length and thin, as opposed to being short in body length and round; a trunk that is wide between the tusks, instead of narrow; sunken below the eyes as opposed to being fleshy and more filled out; a tusk thick, rather than thin, at its base. Individual elephants have, in fact, even more distinguishing features than these. It is the way they walk, the way they hold their head and their mouth, the size of their ears, the configuration of their tusks. It's these features that I always notice first, before peering at the ear notches to confirm the elephant's identity.

It was a tragedy of the times that I felt it necessary to check for snares every time I saw an elephant, or indeed any animal. It had been decreed that the Presidential Elephants should never be hunted or culled, but regrettably this sanction didn't protect them from the horrific effects of snaring, which they suffered from relentlessly.

I regularly drove the sandy roads wondering what gruesome wound I'd have to face that day. Would it be a trunk not long enough to reach the mouth with water? Bloodied flesh dangling hideously from a leg? A wire wrapped tightly under a chin, up to the ear, culminating in a disgusting bow of wire on top of the head? Water spraying out of a sliced trunk? A thick cable around a neck?

One day when I pulled up at Kanondo pan an elephant family arrived soon after me. It was the Ws, and with them was a teenage bull, his trunk severed to tusk length. The horror was crushing. He was yet another elephant that had been caught in a wire snare. He was no longer a proboscidean giant; he no longer even had a trunk. He'd been cruelly – hideously – stripped of his dexterity, at the hands of humans. I knew that he couldn't possibly survive. And he didn't.

The human-inflicted suffering just seemed to go on and on.

Over the course of a few tortured weeks I watched a little four-year-old calf from the V family, debilitated by a tight wire embedded deep in his right back leg. He and his family had been drinking regularly at Kanondo pan. A small family of only eight, including three adult females, they had not wandered far from the pan, the snared calf clearly unable to walk long distances.

Finally, there was an opportunity to dart.

There were many different elephant families around on the day of the darting; too many, I feared, although I knew that some would soon move off. I knew, too, that none had close ties to the V family. The snared elephant kept his foot in the air and swung it backwards and forwards at every opportunity. It was very swollen, very infected and clearly very painful.

A darter arrived, as did extra back-up. From the back of an open 4x4 the darter took aim with the first dart. It was a tranquilliser directed at the snared calf's mother who, with a distinctive 'v' injury in her right ear, I'd named Vee. Not one of the very habituated and better-known Presidential Elephants, she could potentially be the biggest threat to us. The snared elephant was her youngest calf, still suckling, and she was likely to be particularly protective of him.

Rather than bringing her down completely the darter decided he would tranquillise her so that she'd continue to stand, albeit in a sedated state. The dart hit, and a pink, feathered needle now protruded from her rump. Shocked by the sting of the dart, she ran a few paces and then continued to move off slowly. More tranquilliser was needed. A second dart had already been prepared. It was a perfect hit once again, and now Vee had two pink, feathered darts protruding from her rump. She moved off further into the bush, while we did some bush-bashing to keep up with her. Her family moved with her, the snared calf at her heels.

We waited. Although she was clearly feeling the effects of the tranquilliser, a third dart was fired from ground level (with armed support standing by), just to be sure that she was properly sedated. Although she was vocalising, the family members stayed a short distance away.

It was time now to administer the immobilising drug to the calf. Fired once again from ground level, it was another perfect hit. In no time at all, the calf was down.

It was a little disconcerting working on an injured calf with his mother standing just metres away – although everything was going well. Armed supporters kept guard while multiple strands of hideously thick, twisted wire were removed from deep in the calf's leg. Vast amounts of antibiotics were injected, while I constantly sprayed water on and under the calf's ears to keep him cool.

Working quickly, the darter soon administered the reversal to the calf and – after a long deep snort – he scrambled to his feet and walked straight over to his mother's side.

We felt joy, relief and pride. We smiled. We hugged. The sweet smell of success.

The darter walking up to Vee to remove the three pink darts from her rump and to administer her reversal, all by hand, was definitely not in the original game plan. Thankfully, he's still around to tell the story.

Perhaps he'd been lucky to get the three sedation darts into Vee without her running off. Perhaps we'd also been lucky that she had not, in her sedated state, fallen over into a life-threatening position. There were moments when she leaned heavily to one side, and then leaned heavily forward. If she'd fallen forward onto her chest, she could have suffered severe respiratory distress. There was still much to learn.

Later, I became concerned when the de-snared calf didn't stay with his still drowsy mother, walking off by himself into the bush. With the deep, open wound on his leg, he would be particularly vulnerable to lions. The other family members were nowhere in sight. I stayed until nightfall, the family still split.

Back in my rondavel I had a restless night's sleep, wondering if the calf had eventually returned to the safety of his mother.

The next day, I searched and waited. Finally I saw the family of eight drinking once again from Kanondo pan. It was confirmation of success. They were all back together and the calf was putting more weight on his injured leg. They showed no signs of agitation at my close presence, despite their recent ordeal.

I breathed a deep sigh of relief and whispered a quiet thank-you.

Weeks passed without me seeing this family again. Although I considered it to be a good sign, believing that the de-snared calf was no longer inhibiting the wanderings of the group, I longed to know for certain that he was still okay. Then one evening, as I was driving home after a full day in the field, I caught sight of a small family in the bush by the roadside, and I hit the brakes. Out of the corner of my eye I'd seen Vee. I reversed, somewhat anxiously. And there they all were, all eight members of the family. The de-snared calf was at Vee's side. His little leg had healed so well. It was clear there would be no permanent injury.

Belonging as he did to the V family, I named him Victory. Any such victory deserved to be celebrated, for they were few and far between.

Occasionally, there were successes without any human intervention. The story of Max's snare removal surely confirms the intelligence of these grey giants, and highlights the notion of 'conscious thought'.

A cable snare, in contrast to a thinner wire, sometimes works to the advantage of an elephant. It's unlikely that any other animal could break a cable snare; they would be trapped unmercifully, their tragic fate sealed. But a strong elephant, having broken the cable, escapes, and is left with a snare that is sometimes not knotted too tightly, since the thickness of the cable can prevent this. The elephant's dexterity comes into play now, assuming that the snare is not around the trunk.

I'd been spending considerable time with the M family, after seeing adolescent Max with a cable snare around his leg. Max, having made the cable slippery while having a mud bath, managed to slide the snare around his leg, using his trunk. This worsened the wound a little, but the knot was now accessible at the front of his leg. I watched him manoeuvre this cable – and it's difficult to believe that he did it without purpose. He seemed to endure the pain that it must have caused him, anticipating relief. Now he could more effectively use his trunk to try to loosen the knot, which he immediately attempted to do.

That day, and the next, he worked on it, fraying the hanging cable ends into separate wires and managing to break some of them off. The family group didn't wander far, seemingly aware of its injured member. I was ready to call for darting assistance, but Max was making progress, his wound not much worse. I wanted to give him a chance first, hopeful that we might not have to subject him, and his family, to the trauma of immobilisation.

Joyfully, the next day, there was Max with no snare. His wound was not serious enough to require antibiotics, so no human intervention was necessary. The following day the family group had moved off, Max once again able to cope with their wanderings.

I could only wonder: Did Max know what he was doing when he got out of the mud bath? Did he, perhaps, know what he was going to do when he got *into* the mud bath?

Certainly Adelaide, 10-year-old daughter of Adele, knew exactly what she was going to do. I watched her arrive at Kanondo pan with a two-wire snare around the lower portion of her right front leg. She fidgeted with the snare as she drank, while I tried to ascertain just how tight it was. It was definitely very firm around her leg, although fortunately it hadn't yet broken the skin. The knot was quite large and a length of wire stood upright from it. Adelaide pulled on this length of wire, which I feared would only serve to tighten the snare. I then took out my video camera and, as I filmed, Adelaide lifted her snared leg off the ground and held it there. She reached down and used her trunk to feel all around the wire that had entrapped her. Eventually, after having touched it in many different places, multiple times, she used the fingers of her trunk to grasp the wire that remained firmly around her leg. She pulled. The wire slid through the knot, loosening the snare just slightly. Then, within seconds, she had the end of her trunk underneath this wire and curled around it. She pulled again, with the wire now firmly between the fingers of her trunk. Then she pulled again. Incredibly, she had loosened it enough for it to fall to the ground.

It's a sad fact that animal management practices rarely take sufficient account of the high intelligence levels of elephants, nor the close bonds that exist between family members.

My heart was in my mouth every time I saw an elephant snared, but it was always worse for me when it was one of those I knew best. One little fellow, with no visible tusks, was just over two years old. He should have been cavorting around like all the others his age, but instead he wandered around dejectedly without any playmates. His snared leg was a gruesome sight. It was the worst snare wound I'd ever seen, and to make matters even more heartbreaking, he was part of Lady's family. Swollen and infected from the tight wire, his little leg had literally burst, with raw, bloodied flesh dangling hideously. The wire had snapped and was thankfully now off, but the aftermath was sickening. It was time for human intervention. It was not desirable to alarm Lady's family by bringing down one of their own unless it was absolutely necessary. So the darter took the opportunity to administer antibiotics in non-barbed darts that would, by design, fall from the elephant's hide once automatically injected on impact. Although it was relatively small amounts, we hoped that these antibiotics would aid his recovery a little. It was pleasing to try to do something positive to help, but distressing to witness the cruel and merciless acts that humans were capable of. After his snare injury, still unable to walk properly, I named this young elephant Limp.

One day not long after, Limp's young mother, Louise, was on her own in the distant bushes. Limp was closer to me on my right, packing his injured leg with sand. On my left, I spotted two lions, and I could taste the adrenalin.

I heard in my mind the words often spoken by National Parks employees: 'Do not interfere; let nature take its course'. I did not interfere, but I was *ready* to interfere. How many times had humans already interfered, with rifles and snares? Limp's injury was a human-inflicted one; it was not nature's doing. He'd surely been through enough, and to now be tackled by lions was simply too cruel a scenario. To my great relief, the lions showed little interest and Limp eventually returned to the protection of his rumbling mother.

Days later I watched him take great pleasure in a mud bath. He was having fun. For the first time in a long while he was enjoying being a baby elephant. The moment was, however, bittersweet.

Few things are as distressing to me as the sight of a snared elephant. The struggle to assist these suffering animals continued. Despite the heartache, I couldn't give up, for somehow, I knew now, my soul was wrapped up in the endeavour to help save them.

Tragically, Lady's family was struck again just one year later. This time it was her own son, Loopy, who had a deadly wire wrapped tightly around his head and neck. The moment I saw him, there was an aching numbness in my chest. My spirit was stricken. I'd been waiting for the ghastly day when another of the L family fell victim to the poachers. I remembered christening Loopy, so named because of his cheeky, irrepressible nature. Now, unless we could remove this wire, it seemed certain that he would die an agonising death.

I watched Loopy in disbelief, his spirit also stricken. I talked to him, willing him to somehow break the snare before it killed him. The three thin strands of wire were acting like a sharp knife, slicing his innocent little face and neck.

Lady was the only adult present that day. Except when mating, I'd never encountered her without another adult female from her family close by. Was it so distressing for the family group that she chose to bear this burden alone? I closed the door of my 4x4, trying to shut out this tragic sight, and hurried to arrange the approvals necessary to be able to remove the snare. The next day, helpless and distraught, I saw the partial family group again, but there was no one available to do the darting.

Exhausted by the emotions of this awful discovery, I continued to search for Lady's family, in the heartfelt hope that we would not be too late.

Three weeks crawled by. The anguish I'd felt since first seeing Loopy's snare had been hard to endure. I'd searched for him constantly, seen him occasionally, and each time the snare wound was worse. There was never anyone available to dart. I'd lost patience, and was losing heart. But sweet reprieve eventually came. The approvals to remove the snare had long been in place and radio communications, previously unavailable, were now operational.

I'd seen Lady's family two days before, and once again I waited impatiently, on a calculated guess (despite elephant spoor suggesting otherwise), that Lady and her family would return to Kanondo pan. They arrived just before 1pm. With a knot in my stomach, I radioed for assistance. Fortunately, a darter was able to come immediately, although it would take him 20 minutes to get to me. Meanwhile, the resident safari operations manager hurried to collect the required National Parks scout.

Things did not start out too well. Lady's family drank from the concrete trough, and within five minutes were starting to move off into thick bush, in the direction they'd come from. Fortunately, I'd anticipated that this might happen. Help was still 15 minutes away, with another 15 minutes needed to prepare the required darts. I'd brought bags of acacia pods along – those natural food treats so loved by the elephants. Reversing slowly for several hundred metres, I enticed Lady and her family of 12, metre by metre, up the road, by throwing pods just in front of my bonnet. With Lady in the lead, all family members followed, picking up pods as they lumbered my way. I thought that if I could get them to the open mineral-lick area they would feed there, at least for a while, and thankfully, I was right.

There'd been some conflict over how this darting should best be done. Some darters believe that it's *always* necessary to dart the mother elephant as well as the calf. This assumes that they can in fact instantly and accurately identify the mother of the calf, which in 'unknown' families is not always as simple as it may sound, since young elephants will often mingle with their cousins beside an aunt. An isolated observation of an adult female close to or even suckling a calf doesn't mean that this calf is necessarily hers. Over time I came to believe, especially with well-known elephants, that every immobilisation scenario is different, and *all* the known facts need to be taken into account before deciding on a plan of action.

I knew Lady well, and did not want her darted, a recommendation that was rejected by some members of this particular darting team. Except for viewing pleasure, these men had spent no significant time with elephants, yet initially chose to consider my input irrelevant. This was something I was getting used to. To some I was just a lone, unqualified woman without the right letters after my name. But I knew well, as they did not, that Lady was suckling a younger calf, and that she'd recently mated. She had three calves, one younger than Loopy and one older, and perhaps an unborn baby, dependent on her for their very survival. Lady was one of the best known and most habituated Presidential Elephants. Darting always carries some risks, and I didn't want to jeopardise Lady's life, and therefore the lives of her other offspring, unnecessarily.

Somewhat reluctantly, my input still dismissed by some of the team, it was eventually agreed that only Loopy would be darted. A reversal could quickly be administered in the event that this scenario turned dangerous, and I was prepared to be the only one out of the vehicle attending to Loopy, if need be.

While the darts were being prepared, Lady, Loopy and the rest of the family enjoyed the mineral lick. But time was running out. Once again, the family was preparing to move off into thick bush. A few more acacia pods for Lady encouraged her, with Loopy by her side, to stay for a few minutes longer while the darter finally took aim. Just metres from the edge of the bush, the dart (its content determined weeks earlier based on Loopy's approximate age and weight) hit his rump with precision.

As I'd anticipated and hoped, Lady was preoccupied with looking after her youngest daughter, and the other family members simply followed her away into the bush. The most habituated family in the Presidential Herd, they were not thrown into panic. When Loopy went down, two family members came to help him, but as we approached in two vehicles they also moved off towards Lady. Now we were alone with Loopy.

He'd gone down face forward onto his chest (a potentially deadly position) and so, without a moment's hesitation, all 500+ kilograms of him was quickly rolled over so that he was lying on his side, the position vital to ensure no respiratory distress. I was thankful then that he wasn't a full grown many-tonne elephant. With armed support standing guard, the snare was quickly cut and removed, the wound washed, and antibiotics injected. It was a scene that had repeated itself endlessly in my mind for weeks, day and night. Thankfully no elephants bothered us, but the unpredictability of the environment that we were working in never left my mind. It was not Lady who concerned me so much, although I was always on the lookout for her and especially for her sister Leanne who, in these earlier years, could sometimes be a little more aggressive than the others.

Standing now in my 4x4, I waited anxiously for the reversal drug to take effect. Still lying on his side, Loopy took a trunkful of sand to dust his wound, and eventually got to his feet. Loopy knew my voice well. Before being snared he often stood for long periods, and sometimes slept, right beside the door of my vehicle. I crooned to him while he stood placidly between our two vehicles, dusting himself. I suppose there was a comforting familiarity there.

He rumbled constantly, with family members answering him. I wondered, as I do so often, what the elephants were saying to each other in their secret conversation of rumbles. Loopy made no attempt to move off, content to stay where he was. In the end, we moved off before he did. Louise with son Limp in tow were the relatives nearest to him. Loopy joined them in the shade of a tree. The other vehicles and helpers left, and I sat alone with the elephants. Within half an hour they'd moved off into thick bush, and I could no longer see or follow them.

The operation had gone extremely well, but I'm never content until I know for certain that the entire family has reunited. The next day at 10am I returned to Kanondo. It was important to confirm that Loopy and Lady were back together.

Unusually for this time of the morning, there were already close to 100 elephants around the pan. Searching nervously, I found Lady, but there was no Loopy close by. My heart sank. Although not his normal behaviour, Loopy had rarely left his mother's side while the tight head snare had been debilitating him. I switched off my vehicle and watched Lady and her family walk off in front of me, after first stopping by my door to say hello.

There was no Loopy.

While begging whoever was listening to let Loopy be there, he suddenly appeared from the mass of elephants, hurrying towards my vehicle. I was so relieved, and Loopy's own relief was obvious. Everything about him suggested that he was already feeling remarkably better. He clearly no longer felt a need to stay right beside his mother. He held his head higher than he had during the past three weeks and happily ventured his little trunk towards my outstretched hand, before running off playfully to catch up with his family.

This scene triggered delight and gave me encouragement. It strengthened my resolve to keep working with these elephants. My heart filled with a peace that I hadn't felt in months. Having been so distressed and preoccupied by all the tragic snaring that I'd recently encountered, it was only now that I realised just how tired I was.

The snare wound was deep on the top of Loopy's head and nasty on the side of his face and under his neck, but as long as further infection didn't set in, I believed he would survive. And survive he did.

While we were rescuing Loopy, Jabulani and the rest of the anti-poaching unit were sitting out an ambush. Three days later the poachers – a man and his wife – were caught. They were clean, well dressed and obviously healthy. He was employed. I felt no sympathy. I looked at their snares before he was ordered to destroy them. They were set at a height just right to snare an antelope – or the head of another young elephant. They were poachers, and they were breaking the law. They deserved whatever punishment the authorities deemed appropriate. I knew that the sentences were always much too light, but at least there was the added shame of being a convicted poacher.

Elephants are to me the essence of wild freedom. I was adamant that they didn't deserve such agony and disturbance at the hands of humans. Obviously though, not everyone agreed with me.

Animal Antics

The snaring situation ensured that there were taxing periods filled with frustration and worry. Light relief came when my favourite elephant friends wandered by to say hello; when the elephants clowned around playfully; and when animals of various species entertained me with their antics.

One night, a gerbil became my room-mate. A friend assured me that it was good luck to have a gerbil drop in to visit – that a gerbil was a clean little rodent and I should feel special that he'd chosen my rondavel to live in. Although I simply rolled my eyes at my friend, I happily christened my gerbil visitor Gerry.

He had a little pink nose, pink inside his ears, a tufted grey tail, and he leapt like a kangaroo. He was really quite cute, but he kept me awake at night and munched on every packet of biscuits that I owned. Gerry, I decided reluctantly, had to go. I couldn't, however, bring myself to exterminate him. It had to be a live relocation, even though I was under no illusions that this would be easy since I didn't own a live trap.

One morning I had Gerry in my hands, having surprised him while he was still half asleep beside a biscuit packet inside a dark cupboard. Then the little rascal bit me, and I dropped him.

A few nights later he was rattling around much too loudly inside a biscuit box at 2am. I fumbled for the light switch, and grabbed the box. How he got inside I couldn't fathom, as both ends were still closed. I didn't choose to look inside.

Poor Gerry – at least I hoped that it was Gerry – spent the rest of the night, with his biscuit box, inside my small kitchen garbage bin, lid secured, and placed outside. I would have relocated him straight away, but there'd been a long slithery reptile outside my door that very evening. 'Don't worry, the snake's gone now,' I'd been assured.

But gone *where?* I'd wondered with foreboding...

As I wasn't about to venture out into the darkness of the early hours, I could only hope that Gerry wouldn't suffocate. I slept fitfully until dawn, anxious about his wellbeing. At first light, I peered into the bin. There was Gerry, looking ever so cute, beside the now chewed biscuit box. We then took a ride, Gerry and I.

When I decided that we were far enough away, I switched off my engine and walked into the bush, garbage bin in hand – hoping that there were no lions around. I opened the lid and tilted the container but Gerry, clearly confused, just sat there. After I managed to tip him onto the ground he promptly scurried straight back towards my 4x4 and took refuge underneath. I threw a few small stones at him, but still he stayed put. Eventually, I climbed in and switched on the engine, hoping to scare him into the bush. My vehicle rolled back a few centimetres.

'Oh no,' I lamented. Had I run over him? Hesitantly, I looked beneath my vehicle. Gerry was still there, thank goodness, agonisingly close to a tyre. I revved my engine, and looked again. Now there was no Gerry.

I looked into the bush, but still I couldn't see him. 'Oh dear!' I lamented again. 'Where's Gerry?'

Slowly, I drove back to my rondavel, hoping that Gerry hadn't hitched a ride, somewhere under my vehicle, back home with me. There was no further sign of him so I presumed that he was enjoying life, fat from biscuits, somewhere in the bush where I'd left him. I liked to think so anyway.

Spiders were still far from being my favourite creatures. Early one morning I picked up my shoes, not worn for a long time, and swore that I caught a glimpse of a giant creepy arachnid inside one of them. My aversion to spiders renewed, I dropped them instantly and raced for the Doom, wondering aloud what purpose spiders *that* big have. After cautiously carrying the shoes outside, I could see nothing out of the ordinary. I shook each shoe vigorously. I banged them on the ground. I 'Doomed' inside them. Yet nothing happened. Convinced that I must have imagined the whole episode, I picked them up and walked back inside.

While still in my hands, a monster baboon spider emerged from one shoe, climbing slowly up and over the tongue. The hairs on my arms stand up even now as I relive the experience. I began to believe that I'd been singled out for something – and it was not divine favour.

After a night of imaginary creepy things crawling over my skin I pulled back a curtain, only to exercise my lungs once again. But it turned out to be just Garry the gecko. As far as geckos go, he was the hugest one I'd ever seen and if he was supposed to eat spiders, I thought to myself with a frown, he hadn't been doing his job very well.

Out in the field, at Kanondo, there lived a princely male bushbuck who, a few months earlier, I'd named Trust. His ears were a little tattered, his horns worn, and the hair on the back of his neck was balding, but he was a handsome gentleman nonetheless.

I'd been sitting in my 4x4 one afternoon, door open, for over an hour. Trust was enjoying the fresh water running into Kanondo pan, nibbling on the new spring leaves, always within 20 metres of my vehicle. I couldn't bear to disturb him – so peaceful was he – that I had no desire to start my engine for fear of frightening him. Instead, I watched. He drank and browsed and stood quietly in the shade of a bush, having covered his horns with mud. Then came an encounter that I'll never forget.

Trust walked straight towards my vehicle (while I fumbled with my camera) and put his nose to the petrol tank. He moved slowly towards me, as I sat side-on in the driver's seat, my legs dangling out of my open door. As he came closer and closer I wondered, bewildered and moving only my eyes, if he was perhaps blind or deaf. No more than 20 centimetres away from my knee now, his head inside my vehicle, he sniffed the elephant identification folders behind my seat. Then retracting his head just a little, he gazed up into my eyes. His own eyes were huge liquid pools of trust.

I held my breath. I dared not move even my eyelids. He was definitely not blind. He looked old and wise. Slowly, I moved a finger towards him, unbelievably close to his handsome face. He twitched his moist nose, but still did not move. I sat awestruck, barely able to think.

It's a terrible habit; this overwhelming urge to photograph everything. I remembered the camera on my lap, already knowing that my lens was much too long to photograph even his eye. He stayed next to my leg as I very slowly put the camera to my face. I knew that it wouldn't focus, but the photographer in me had to try. He jumped back, startled by the noise of this strange machine. Yet still he stayed close by.

Eventually, he moved off slowly into the bush while I sat mesmerised by what had just happened. My heart pounded in my chest, my hands were shaking and I had pins and needles in my arms. Apart from the elephants, this was the first wild animal that had ever initiated such intimate contact with me. I didn't believe that it could happen quite like this.

Trust, I'd called him. And I felt humbled, and privileged beyond words.

However, Kanondo didn't always bring such cheerful encounters. In fact my most terrifying encounter with a snake happened there one afternoon.

Seeking shade, I'd parked under the sprawling branches of a tall acacia tree, laden with the scruffy nests of sparrow weavers and the large communal nests of red-billed buffalo weavers. I was whiling away the heat of the day, working on my laptop, while waiting for the elephants to arrive.

The loud thud of something hitting Nicki Mukuru's bonnet startled me and I looked up in alarm. There, covering more than the length of the bonnet, its body in a curl, was a horribly long, mottled, greenish snake. Its head held aloft, very close to my wipers now, it was about to slither up and over my windscreen.

I gasped, shouted unrepeatable expletives and banged on the glass of the windscreen, my other hand already opening my door, preparing an escape route.

The snake – a deadly boomslang perhaps, known to prey on birds' eggs and fledglings – turned and slid quickly out of sight.

I jumped out, terrified that it might now be coiled somewhere underneath my 4x4, but I could find no sign of it. Hesitantly, I climbed back into the driver's seat and looked high above my head. If the snake had fallen just one metre further back, it would have landed right on top of me, through my open roof. I wondered how long it had been hovering above me in those branches. My heart pounding, I put foot, and determined never to park under that tree, or perhaps any tree, ever again. Death by sunstroke was preferable to death by snake, I decided.

Snakes aside, I always found it fascinating to witness first-hand the obvious differences between the animal species. When an infant elephant so much as stumbles accidentally into a shallow water trough, there's much screaming and concern from the rest of the elephant family, all of whom immediately join in to rescue, and then comfort, the youngster. When a female kudu was stuck, belly-deep in mud at Kanondo, the other kudus with her showed no concern and made no attempt to assist. After a few frantic minutes she managed to free herself, her body now completely covered in thick grey mud, but there was no one, except me, that even acknowledged her potentially deadly ordeal.

I always found the birdlife entertaining. A flock of more than 40 guineafowl sometimes raced along in front of my vehicle at sundown, spindly legs kicking up puffs of sand, apparently forgetting that they could fly. Perhaps it was exhaustion that eventually reminded them, for momentarily they would take flight, only to land straight back on the road in front of me. It was a comical, though irritating, routine that was repeated time and again.

I often mused that if God created the weird-looking warthogs on a day when he was bored then he must certainly have created the marabou storks on a day when he was in an awfully dark mood. Wrapped in a cloak of black, they are sinister-looking and really rather ugly. I often stared at them for a long time, trying to find something pleasing about their appearance, but I always failed. Still, I was pleased to have the privilege of their presence. When they took to the skies, their wing-beats sounded like loud squeaky doors.

I always took great pleasure in the antics of the banded mongooses. One family visited me frequently at my rondavel – *in* my rondavel sometimes, although that really was stretching the friendship a little. They would lie on their bellies with legs outstretched, on my grass mat, until I chased them outside. They came for water from my birdbaths, and for bread or banana from my hand, if I had some to offer. As with the elephants, I tried to tell them apart – to find some distinguishing feature to identify them. Mostly, I failed. In time I decided that they all belonged to what must have been the G family, since they were all known to me simply as Greedy. They reminded me of otters as they slithered around in the largest of my birdbaths on sweltering days. Then, bedraggled, they pulled themselves along on their bellies over the grass, as if both back legs were injured. They chattered to each other incessantly, while I sat trying to decipher their conversations. I would close my eyes, listening, light-heartedly wondering if they were, perhaps, from another planet! They certainly sounded like they could be. I envisaged them transmitting valuable findings back from planet Earth. I liked to imagine that mongooses really were little men, spies no less, from Mars.

Learning about Elephants

Since the 1970s Cynthia Moss and Joyce Poole, both legendary in the world of elephants, have been studying the grey giants of Amboseli National Park in Kenya. Cynthia and Joyce, who are both American, have spent most of their adult lives among elephants in Africa.

One day I went to visit them.

Staring at the genitals of baby elephants was, once upon a time, not how I'd envisaged spending my life, yet there I was in Amboseli doing just that. I spent two weeks living among the elephants there, practising sexing new-born elephants and aging known-age older ones. At that time, the Amboseli elephants had been known intimately for 30 years, many since they were born, and so there was no disputing their real age. From the Amboseli project I learned what a 10, 15, 20 and 30-year-old elephant *really* looked like. It's strange to recall it now, but back then I was still confusing female babies with male, although this was quickly remedied.

Over the years the Amboseli research project dispelled many myths about elephants, and uncovered many fascinating facts. I admired Cynthia and Joyce's supreme dedication and craved their vast knowledge. Devoted indigenous Kenyans also shared with me their intimate understanding and love of the elephants.

The splash of icing atop Mount Kilimanjaro provided the perfect backdrop. The purple sunsets were dramatic, the last rays of sunlight illuminating the snowcap with golden light. I awoke in the mornings under canvas in a palm grove, to the call of fish eagles, and to buffalos, hyenas and elephants wandering through camp.

The tusks of the Amboseli elephants bear little resemblance to those of the Hwange elephants. I have enduring memories of splendid tusks

129

almost reaching the ground, of elephants exuding an air of elegance and polite charm. Not so, though, one of the musth bulls, his adversary serenely unaware of impending disaster.

Few sights are as awesome, and frightening, as a serious musth bull fight. A clash of ivory, no longer a pleasing playful sound, signals the start of a battle. This particular battle left one of the musth bulls dead, having suffered a fatal tusk wound to his head. His own imposing tusks were over two metres long. It was a dreadful shock to Cynthia and others who'd known him for almost 30 years, ever since he was a cheeky teenager. I walked up to his body, lying still and noble on the ground, and placed some grass in his mouth.

'For your journey,' I whispered sadly to him.

Over lunch in camp one day, Cynthia and Joyce asked after some of the people who'd been involved in Zimbabwe's past elephant projects, but I was unable to shed much light. I was aware, though, that Zimbabwe's elephant management stance, and associated elephant understanding, was not always well regarded by others, and I sat hoping that they wouldn't tar me with the same tainted brush.

At the historic 1989 Lausanne meeting of CITES (Convention on International Trade in Endangered Species – the body that regulates world trade in animal products), elephants were placed on Appendix 1, banning all international trade in ivory. Elephants were being slaughtered for their tusks, but now they had finally won a reprieve. Zimbabwe, though, had pushed for the trade to remain open. The then deputy director of research from Zimbabwe's Department of National Parks didn't win the confidence of many. He'd stated, in assemblies leading up to this celebrated meeting, that Zimbabwe's elephants first conceive at seven years of age and subsequently give birth at age nine. The response to this was incredulous laughter from some of the elephant experts in the room. They were well aware that the free-roaming female African elephant typically didn't reach sexual maturity until her teens. A distinguished European biologist was quoted in Allan Thornton and Dave Currey's book *To Save An Elephant*, as saying scathingly, 'As a biologist I congratulate Zimbabwe's elephants on reproducing so young. Maybe they are born with their tusks!'

I cannot imagine how Zimbabwe's elephant 'experts' at the time came up with such exaggerated statistics. To many, this grandstanding had more to do with career building than with conservation. Nonetheless, already back then, Zimbabwe was trying to convince the world that it had too many elephants; that the population growth rate was extremely high; that they should be allowed to kill elephants and sell the ivory.

During my first seven years with Zimbabwe's elephants the youngest one I ever witnessed give birth was Lesley, Lady's daughter. Based on known ages of her younger siblings and her estimated age when I first met her, Lesley was at least 11 when she had her first calf. But most became first-time mothers when they were considerably older than Lesley.

In response to the number of elephants said to be in Zimbabwe at the time of this 1989 CITES meeting, one conservationist was reported to have asked, 'Are Zimbabwe's elephants on fertility drugs, or don't they know how to count in Zimbabwe?'

I have to admit to regularly wondering the same thing.

I often found myself in the field listening to and pondering comments made by both tourists and residents. It was always interesting to note how many of the 'townies', who visited the bush for a week or so each year, believed themselves to be experts in all things wild.

'We've seen *so many* elephants over the past few days,' some would say. Others repeated what they'd read in the government newspapers, 'There are *too many* elephants...'

With the culling controversy constantly raising its ugly head in Zimbabwe, I would sit and wonder how many *different* elephants these visitors to the bush actually saw.

People's perceptions vary widely. For some, just 30 elephants are considered '*so many* elephants'. Others don't realise how frequently they see the *same* elephants in the morning, again in the evening, and yet again on subsequent days. I would, for example, regularly see the same elephants in the Khatshana area during the morning, in the Kanondo area that afternoon, and on the vlei the next morning. At other times, the same elephant family might linger around just one of these areas for many days in succession. What's more, when seeing a group of 40 'unknown' elephants in the morning, and a group of 20 in the afternoon, you cannot, even then, categorically declare them to be *different* groups of elephants. Although their numbers are different, they may well be the same elephants. Groups often split, sometimes for just a few hours, or minutes, other times for a few days or longer, their numbers temporarily fluctuating. Unfortunately for the elephants in Zimbabwe, it was usually only I who realised that they were indeed the *same* elephants.

As a result, the number of (different) elephants seen was often inadvertently exaggerated. While this is clearly of little consequence to tourists who understandably just wish to enjoy them, it *is* important when it comes to talking about elephant management requirements based on perceptions of elephant numbers.

Casual assessments are very often skewed. Only if the elephants are seen in great aggregations, or are known as individuals, can you be sure of what you're seeing. There are often not as many *different* elephants as there might appear to be.

I also overheard such remarks as, 'There are *hundreds* of elephants here.' A quick count regularly revealed this assessment to be 50-300 per cent inflated, the elephants' size belying their actual numbers.

When annual game-counters sit for 24 hours around the most popular pumped pans and watercourses in Hwange National Park, counting elephants in the hottest, driest month of October (when they will not wander far from palatable water and will, I know for certain, drink *multiple* times during a 24-hour period, resulting in many being counted more than once), the counts are still always *tens and tens of thousands* of elephants short of the 75 000-plus sometimes said to be in the park.

Where are these *tens and tens of thousands* of 'missing' elephants? Seeing a group of just *300* elephants together is a truly imposing sight. Imagine then, if you can, up to *60 000* 'missing' elephants! Are they out there unseen, these fussy beasts that are known to seek out the very freshest of water, not drinking from the most palatable water sources at this scorching time of year? Are they concealed in bush too thick to enable sightings of them, the very bush they have reputedly destroyed?

Away from the perceptions of the layperson, even formal processes leave me confused. Aerial counts are typically only done in the dry season, and often appear to be extrapolated blindly, on the basis that the same numbers of elephants counted close to water sources will be found away from them. This is not sensible dry season logic. These official counts are also not carried out simultaneously in adjoining areas or countries, so that the double-counting of wandering elephant groups must also surely inflate numbers – these elephants very probably appearing on the tallies of more than one area, and indeed more than one country. Furthermore, until disproved without extrapolations, predictions or assumptions, can the indisputable 30-year-strong Amboseli data be ignored? It reveals that wild free-roaming elephant populations are likely to increase at an average rate of around 3,75 per cent per annum[1] – well below that often touted.

The number of elephants said to reside in Zimbabwe, particularly the number said to inhabit Hwange National Park, leaves me disbelieving and confused. And immediately a saying springs to my mind: 'Never trust anyone whose explanations leave you confused.'

Zimbabwe's stance on other wildlife matters also regularly leaves me confused.

Authorised *ration*-hunting, and worse still, authorised ration-hunting in photographic tourist areas, seems to me to be such a paradox. The very people employed to protect the wildlife are, in many places in Zimbabwe, the reason that the elephants and other wildlife species are being killed. If 20 animals are saved from the poachers' snares every week, but 10 are slaughtered to feed the National Parks game scouts – the gunshots terrifying scores more – what has really been achieved? Ordinary law-abiding citizens must go to a butchery to buy *domestic* meat to eat. Why shouldn't the same apply to those employed to *protect* the wild animals? Why should *they* be allowed to kill and eat the wild animals living inside a 'protected' national park – a park that is supposed to be a safe haven for wildlife, and a place of peace for tourists?

It's a situation I still don't understand; a logic that I cannot fathom; a practice I cannot defend. It is also a practice not always properly monitored and, in recent times, has become excessive. In 2001, even

I (not alone) was witness to after-hours ration-hunting gunfire only metres from the tourists' favourite Nyamandlovu platform, inside of Hwange National Park. Naturally, the following morning there was not an animal in sight for the tourists to enjoy. And yet it seemed that everyone routinely blamed *the elephants* for the decline of other species. Few questioned the impact of all the ration-hunting gunfire in tourism areas.

Any type of hunting, I believed, should surely be restricted to designated *hunting* areas, but this, still today, is not the case. Animals inside of Zimbabwe's national parks continue to be slaughtered for meat to feed Parks staff.

One of the most disturbing facts for me is that *female* elephants – despite my pleas – are also regularly placed on approved hunting quotas. It's known that bonds among elephant family members are exceptionally strong, and research in Amboseli National Park has proven that no free-roaming calves under two years old are likely to survive the death of their mother. Only 30 per cent of calves aged between two and five are likely to survive such a tragedy, as are only 50 per cent of those aged between five and 10.[2] Hence, given an elephant calf's very long reliance on its mother, the repercussions of shooting an adult female elephant are catastrophic, with up to three young offspring left to die a slow, cruel death without their mother. But this obviously doesn't matter to those who set the hunting quotas. In particular, Zimbabwe wishes to rid itself of tuskless female elephants (like Inkosikazi) since these, with no ivory to harvest for profit, are considered an undesirable gene pool and are routinely placed on hunting quotas.

Government-controlled newspapers were regularly used as a mouthpiece to seek public support for a cull, with reports often reflecting the 'elephants are negatively impacting other species' speculative stance. Eventually though, this argument was dealt a crushing blow. Scientific studies in neighbouring Botswana confirmed that – despite their elephant numbers, which are said to surpass even the most extreme estimates for Zimbabwe – numbers of smaller species there continued to increase.[3] So why was Zimbabwe apparently different? Why were other species declining here? Should the elephants really be blamed?

Could the decline be due, rather, to fewer sources of permanent water in recurring drought years? Other climate changes? The out-of-control snaring? Or had excessive gunfire taken its toll?

People's attention was being diverted, and poachers – together with some National Parks personnel and higher officials, it seemed to me – were being given a cover for their shameful acts.

Eventually, in late 2006, a three-year scientific study undertaken within Zimbabwe's Hwange National Park concluded that elephants certainly modify vegetation, but it was found that other species actually *benefit* from their presence. It was established that animals adapt to elephant presence at waterholes, and many select sites modified by elephants. No real competition was found.[4]

It was another blow to the pro-cull lobby.

Also in 2006, as part of another scientific study undertaken by the same French research establishment, it was concluded that the Hwange elephant population was in fact *stabilising* with a total of around 35 000 elephants – a far cry from the 50 000 to 75 000, with added annual growth, regularly touted.[5] It was yet another blow to those who preferred to exaggerate. Many, though, conveniently chose to ignore the results of these two in-depth studies.

Elephants seem to be blamed for everything, including the frequent ringbarking of trees. In fact it was once established that porcupines, not elephants, were destroying the *Cordyla africanas* in the Lowveld, ringbarking them near ground level. And I've observed countless times – and indeed have video evidence – that it is baboons, not elephants, that destroy many of the *Acacia eriolobas* in Acacia Grove, tearing off great slabs of bark in search of insects.

Now, with a better understanding of the social structure of the Presidential Elephants, the reality of what must surely happen, even when the most professional of culls takes place, causes me unease. Extended family groups often, but not always, move as one. What might their group structure be on the day of a cull?

Given their proven communications ability over many kilometres using infrasound, the elephants no doubt have a different perception as to who is in their group at any one time. We mere humans, with no infrasound ability, can only perceive group composition *visually*, no doubt making mistakes along the way.

Will the elephants be split temporarily, resulting in the slaughter of part of their bond group? For those of us who've witnessed the sheer joy of the greeting ceremonies that regularly occur when such members reunite after time apart, it's alarming to think of them never being able to reunite again. When elephants join up after days (or perhaps only hours) apart, they greet each other with boisterous, celebratory, open-mouthed vocalisations combined with excited urination, defecation, ear flapping, head rubbing and trunk entwining – this rapture causing liquid to stream from their temporal glands.

It was decreed that the Presidential Elephants should never be culled, but more and more often my thoughts drifted to those 'unknown' elephants; those who had no voice; the ones no one knew very much about.

Zimbabwe's elephants, it seemed to me, had few friends in their own country, white or black. How could sound management policies be formulated and implemented, I often wondered, when so many seemed to want to do little other than have elephants killed for their meat and ivory; to have elephants killed for profit?

It was often distressing to work with a species that few seemed to care about, and worse still, a species that was so very often the target of misinformation; of far more fiction than fact.

1   Moss, Cynthia J (2001) The demography of an African elephant population in Amboseli, Kenya, *Journal of Zoology* 255, pp145-156 (London)
2   Poole, Joyce (1996) *Coming of Age with Elephants* Hodder & Stoughton, London, pp200-201
3   Skarpe, C et al (2004) The return of the Giants: ecological effects of an increasing elephant population *Ambio* 23, pp276-282
4   Valeix, M (2006) Insights into processes structuring large herbivore communities: the role of elephants in the functioning of an African savanna – habitat changes and interference for water access. PhD thesis, University of Paris, France
5   Chamaillé-Jammes S, Fritz H, Valeix M *et al* (2008) Resource variability, aggregation and direct density dependence in an open context: the local regulation of an African elephant population, *Journal of Animal Ecology* 77, pp135-144

PART V

Land Reform Hits Home

The Ongoing
Poaching Nightmare

It was a long-cherished dream to be able to spend my days among elephants, but more and more often now the dream was infused with nightmares.

Poaching continued to cause great concern. There'd been an adult elephant with an over-sized snare around his chest, only seen once. Two zebras, six buffalos and six sables were all found too late one day. All had been snared; all of them were dead. And there was another elephant, shot dead.

Time and again, with a heavy heart, I wondered where it would all end.

The loading of a rifle is a sound that I don't particularly like, but there were dangerous animals out there, and dangerous people. It was a necessary precaution when searching for poachers.

I walked into the bush with two armed guides.

We stopped abruptly. Branches chopped off a tree signalled that something was amiss. A few metres away were crossbeams, set high in a tree. It was a structure used for drying meat. The long horns of a sable, impressive no longer, were aloft in the branches. The sable's head, body not attached, was on the ground. We spotted a yellow-billed kite in the sky above. I knew that, even before the vultures, kites discovered fresh meat. Further on, a buffalo lay dead. Across the sandy road the poachers had boldly set up camp, leaving behind them a plastic mealie meal bag on the ground, ashes from a recent campfire and more structures for drying meat. There was a zebra skin and a buffalo skin.

Forewarned perhaps, the poachers had fled, at least for now.

Fresh spoor around broken snares was disturbing proof that elephants had recently encountered these death traps. I fought an overwhelming urge to somehow be able to take the snare off the leg of the innocent giraffe, seen one recent morning, and wrap it tight – tighter – around the legs of these poachers, leaving it there to fester and debilitate, day after day. Would this be punishment enough, I wondered?

Occasionally, conflicting emotions raced around in my mind.

Jabulani and his men had been sitting quietly in ambush for days, waiting for someone to return to the snares they'd expertly uncovered. This time someone did return, and the team was successful in capturing him. The poacher was old, short and extremely thin. He had no teeth, at least not in the front of his mouth. His grubby trousers hung to his ankles, bare hardened feet poking out below.

At first the old man professed his innocence and refused to talk. A few less-than-subtle intimations changed his mind, and now he was ready, he said, to talk to the police. It was late by the time he was escorted to the police station, so it would be morning before his full cooperation was required.

After a night in jail he'd once again changed his mind. Now he was innocent, he declared. Nevertheless, under the escort of two policemen and the manager of the anti-poaching unit, we all tramped back into the bush. The warnings to him were becoming increasingly less subtle, as patience wore thin.

Eventually he cooperated, leading us to more of his snares set for guineafowl and antelope and, under order, destroyed each snare. Fresh duiker spoor surrounded one of his traps, yet he seemed undaunted that he'd very nearly had another fresh kill, right there in front of the police. He admitted to snaring buffalos and sables, leaving the skins and horns behind in the bush. Sable meat, he admitted, was currently drying in his house.

We drove to his small mud shack not far off the tarred road. The tiniest, oddest-looking brown dog ran around, wagging its tail. A bigger one, skeletal with skin clinging tightly to clearly visible ribs, did too. Inside the dark hut was the stench of death. Fly-covered meat hung from the roof, close to the poacher's ruffled bed.

He handed over the lower legs of the recently butchered sable. Then, while still being interrogated by the police, he casually bent down and brazenly gave the smaller dog some of the dried poached meat.

He'd been a lorry driver, he told us. He was divorced. He'd been poaching regularly for the past two years. The meat was sold and bartered in his village, he said. His own dubious story changed often as he told it but even so, looking around me, I found myself feeling a sense of sorrow.

He went on to speak of some of the inside goings-on within this criminal world of poaching, but he wouldn't rat on his mates. Clearly he had accomplices and knew of other teams of poachers.

'I can set snares up to pole 138,' he stated. The poachers had given the telegraph poles numbers. Like lions, they had their own territories to work within.

While the police searched other huts I sat and waited in the 4x4, looking at and *really* seeing the poverty that surrounded me. The gaunt-looking poacher walked, scruffy and barefoot, into his mud hut. He reappeared with a handful of wild berries. He gummed on them loudly, as I watched him walk towards me. He held out his hand, this desperately poor man with no teeth, and offered me some of his berries.

Wearily, I closed my eyes. And very slowly shook my head.

There was little doubt that this poacher had illegally killed and maimed probably hundreds of animals. More than 30 snares had been destroyed that very morning. He'd been stopped, at least temporarily. After leaving him in the hands of the police, I drove out into the field with my head spinning. I was having some difficulty reconciling the events of the morning.

Then, at Kanondo, I saw my first elephant of the day – a teenage bull with a small 'w' notch in his left ear. He is just one of too many elephants who has more than the two fingers of his trunk sliced off. I recalled the horror and the human-inflicted suffering, and I could see it all clearly once again. A snare set for a duiker or an impala can rip off an elephant's trunk. A snare set for a sable or a buffalo can also horribly maim, and even kill, an elephant. It's an irrefutable fact that snares are despicably cruel, and deadly, to all that encounter them. I was convinced that handing poachers – all types of poachers – over to the police was the right thing to do.

The animals had few friends, I reminded myself. I knew that we needed to continue to make sure that snares were destroyed, and that poachers were arrested. It was also glaringly obvious to me now that there were other fundamental problems that someone, somehow, somewhere, must strive to solve. Nonetheless, it was essential for the anti-poaching team to continue its crucial patrols.

A solar eclipse brought a welcome diversion from the poaching. I chose to forgo driving 100 kilometres deep into Hwange National Park with friends to witness the total eclipse. Instead I hoped that my friends, leathered and feathered, would join me for a partial eclipse at Kanondo pan.

By 8am the light was fading. More than 50 elephants were unexpectedly around the pan. At the darkest point, they appeared completely bewildered. There was an eerie silence – prolonged moments of mystery and intrigue. The elephants bunched together and took on an almost purple glow. Their illusory colour was mysterious, and an absolute pleasure. They moved their heads from side to side, trying to make sense of this strange phenomenon, but made no audible sound. I was conscious that the loudest sound I could hear was the excited thumping of my own heart.

Through protective eye-wear I could see the almost total blackout of the sun; just a thin crescent shape remained. I wished that I had another two sets of eyes. I wanted to watch the elephants. I wanted to watch the sun. I wanted to watch the saddlebill stork pair, the zebras, waterbucks, kudus, impalas and sables that were all around me. Noiseless hooves. I'd forgotten that they were even there.

'F*ck, this is absolutely incredible!' I couldn't help repeating out loud to myself.

Overawed, I'd forgotten to switch off my video camera and from the seat beside me, I realised only later, these words I'd used to express my awe and wonder were recorded for posterity.

As incredible as I thought this occasion was, many of my African friends believed a solar eclipse to be a sign of evil things in store; a dire warning that bad would now overtake the good, for many years to come. I dismissed this notion without a second thought, rolling my eyes at the seemingly endless superstitions of those around me.

Perhaps, though, they knew something that I did not. Indeed, since then, I've learned not to be so insensitive to the beliefs of others.

Instead of spending Christmas of that year with Julia and Carol in Harare, I spent it searching for the 17th snared elephant that I'd encountered to date. Distressed and disheartened, I'd begun to think that all this snaring might never stop.

More and more often I felt a need to try and escape it all. At times like these I sat and watched the sun nudge the horizon, imagining what it would sound like if elephants could laugh...

Six months later, the snaring problem on the Hwange Estate was under better control. Fewer snares were being uncovered, and I wasn't finding as many snared animals. It appeared that, finally, we were winning the battle.

Yet while we toiled to make the animals' world a better and safer place, little did I know that others, soon to float in on a sea of greedy intentions, were scheming to take it all for themselves.

Cry of Kanondo

It was a sultry night in early October 2003 when there was an unexpected knock at the door of my rondavel. Standing there was a man who delivered a message to me, in the laid-back, accepting way of Africa. The area of Kanondo, and the adjoining area of Khatshana had been claimed, he said, by the governor of this province; the very government official responsible for land redistribution in these parts. He had allocated this prime land, abundant with wildlife, to himself and to his relatives – and they'd managed to obtain licences to sport-hunt. The Parks and Wildlife Management Authority (formerly the Department of National Parks) had issued them with a hunting quota, renewable annually, allowing them and their hunting clients to legally kill a specified number of each species, including elephant.

I stood stunned, listening to him with growing disbelief.

This was an area that had not been hunted for more than 30 years. This was an area of habituated wildlife. This was the key home range of the protected Presidential Elephants of Zimbabwe. This was an important tourism area. This was not a white-owned farm. In fact Kanondo, on all the certified maps, was classified as 'state land' – land that, at least some in the government, had clearly stated could not be claimed.

But none of it mattered. This was Zimbabwe, after all.

From tomorrow, I was told, I must no longer drive in the Kanondo area. From tomorrow, the tourists and the anti-poaching team must no longer go there either. From tomorrow, they would hunt there.

Rich foreigners pay tens of thousands of US dollars to come to Africa and bag for themselves animal heads to hang on the walls of their homes. Since there were so many prime animal species already on this land, this was easy money – nothing but a greedy 'get rich quick' scam – and it made me shudder with fear and horror.

So many joys, I knew, flourished only in the peace and quiet of the African bush, now to be shattered by gunfire. As if the snaring wasn't bad enough.

'What about the "protected" Presidential Elephants?' I challenged. There was no response. 'Who is doing what to try to fix this?' I pleaded. Still, there was no response.

Was it *really* all over, just like that? It was inconceivable.

Although I immediately set about informing all those who I thought might be able to help, there was no stopping what was going to happen the next day.

The whole situation held the promise of true pain, and I tried to shake the horror.

I'd left Kanondo pan that very afternoon, not realising it wouldn't be there again the next day in the same way that it had always been. Looking back, I realise that I left Kanondo that day, and in some essential sense, I've never really returned. Not to the Kanondo that it once was, wild and free. I'd never known any place so evocative. A light that was often indescribable. A place not of conflict but of peace. A place of life. Kanondo's wildness called out to so many, who left with unforgettable memories of the Presidential Elephants and of all the habituated wildlife. Shooting with cameras; never with guns.

I knew my body would eventually recover from the shock, the disillusionment and the tragedy – but my heart and mind wouldn't heal nearly as quickly. Another part of my Africa was gone forever. This part, however, was no accident.

In my mind, day and night, I heard the distant cry of Kanondo.

For the first time ever it was not a happy meeting. The next morning I found Lady in Acacia Grove and I put my hand on her trunk. Her family was so often in the Kanondo area. Born wild. Living wild. Like all of the Presidential Elephants, they were extraordinarily trusting of human beings.

I could manage to say to her only two words, 'I'm sorry...'

Ten days passed. Not unlike me, the gods were angry. Deafening cracks of thunder boomed continuously in the night, and then the rain finally came. And it came early. 'Let it rain. Let it rain. Let it rain,' I begged.

Let the habituated wildlife disperse, away from all the hunters. I wanted it not to stop. It did stop, but not before the pans, turned dry and cracked by the burning sun months earlier, once again held some water. It was good news for the wildlife, the animals no longer forced to congregate around just the few pumped pans which, before the downpour, were the only ones still holding life-giving water.

This first deluge of rain doesn't permeate very deeply into the baked ground, the fresh run-off water in the pans not lasting for long without supplementary rain, but these first downpours are important, preparing the pans, enhancing their water retention capacity for when next the rain comes. The smell of these first rains is a delightful aroma, etched into the minds of all of us who live in the African bush. The lingering dust of the long dry months is washed away. But this year, I barely noticed.

Out in the field, close to Acacia Grove, I was not the only one taking an interest in the mating lions, dozing now only metres from my vehicle. Both male and female radiated a wild energy as they mated over and over again, muscles bulging around their necks.

A hunting vehicle, complete with white hunters, had the audacity to pull up beside these lions too, in this one small area that had escaped being redesignated for hunting.

By now I thought my capacity for astonishment had been exhausted, but this was a photographic area – one of the very few photographic areas left now – and their blasé presence *did* astonish me. These men had been seen a few days earlier examining lion spoor. They wanted this lion – to hang on a wall. Hunting in an area full of habituated wildlife, I could practically see them salivating.

Were they hunters or simply killers, I wondered? Where was the ancient skill of the indigenous warrior? There was no need here to track an animal for days, or weeks perhaps. There was no skill involved in these hunts. So many of the animals here walked right up to you – or at least they used to, before the gunfire started.

These were, I concluded as I watched them, nothing but soulless greedy men, in cahoots with others of similar character.

They moved off, not soon enough, leaving my mind full of a thousand resentments. I tried to enjoy the setting sun as it cast a stunning light on the lion lovers. They rolled on their backs in lazy abandon, mouths wide with yawns of indifference. Thousands of white moths erupted from the damp earth, fluttering like snowflakes around them. It was beautiful, but my mind was elsewhere.

Suddenly I felt afraid, *very* afraid. By now it was painfully apparent that there were only a few people who gave more than a cursory acknowledgement to the wildlife tragedy that was unfolding here.

'This is Africa,' I was told repeatedly. And they knew the risks of getting involved.

I didn't care that this was Africa; I didn't care who owned land in this country; and I didn't care who these settlers were. But I did care about the Presidential Elephants and about all the wildlife that I'd come to know so well over the past three years.

Given that the head settler was considered 'a big man' (that is, a politically connected man) – with an unsavoury reputation – most people were afraid of getting too involved.

Thankfully, though, there *were* some who were genuinely concerned. There was *some* support on this fearful road, the wildlife not having to walk it entirely alone.

Back at my rondavel that night, there was no power. Thousands of flying ants, making their regular appearance after the first rain, swarmed around the few lodge lights powered by a generator. A toad jumped against my leg, giving me a slimy fright. Now *all* of the wildlife seemed to belong, and I was definitely on *their* side. My spirit hadn't quite failed me yet. By candlelight, a glass of Amarula (six times the price it was 12 months before) warmed what hope was left within me.

Yet sightings of the Presidential Elephant families decreased markedly. They did not like the sound of gunshots, and neither did I.

While out in the field, my mind now needing to escape the looming wildlife tragedy, I read Laurens van der Post's *Flamingo Feather* while waiting for the elephants to appear from the bush.

It was just one sentence, '… his life will achieve… something which is greater than happiness and unhappiness: and that is meaning', but it struck a chord.

I read these words once, and then a second, a third time. The call of the rainbird interrupted the profound effect they were having on me, taking me back to times long ago, to my childhood home in south-east Queensland, Australia. My rural parents always linked this distinctive call with the rain that farmers so depend on. I didn't even know then if 'the rainbird' had another name. It was always just 'the rainbird' to me, with vivid childhood memories of it calling, unseen, from the mulberry tree in our leafy, well-tended backyard. I listened to this same call now, in this different era and distant land, far removed from the years of my youth, longing for the rain to return; longing for the hunters to leave.

I was, I knew now with certainty, a million miles from my childhood world.

The silence became intolerably loud inside my head. Fearing reprisal, so very few people were willing to speak out. This was not often a country of 'free and fair', and everyone knew it. Although I was aware that my permit could be cancelled at a moment's notice, I couldn't turn a blind eye and so I continued to recount disturbing events to wildlife conservation organisations within Zimbabwe and abroad.

My thoughts and feelings were sometimes so intense they became unbearable. My disillusionment grew daily. It was a heavy burden that those of us who cared deeply for the Presidential Elephants, and for all of the habituated wildlife, had to carry. I knew that, somehow, I must continue in spite of it.

Now though, everything was soured with fear. And I was stricken with unease and deep sorrow. I took comfort in those prophetic words and applied them to myself, '... his [my] life will achieve... something which is greater than happiness and unhappiness: and that is meaning'.

My desire to be out in the field for the six to eight hours that I used to spend so devotedly, each and every day, was gone. I now dreaded what I might see, and what I might not. Which of the elephant families were still around? Which were running from the sound of gunshots?

Did I *really* want to know? My spirit was beaten and bruised; was I strong enough to cope with the reality?

Few things are more distressing to me than watching a family of magnificent giants bunched tightly together, running terrified from the sound of gunshots. Sometimes the shots were not audible to my ears, but the elephants heard them, or maybe others that were closer-by warned of the danger, passing information in a chain of communication to those further away. Whatever the case, they fled at high speed. It was horrifying to see normally placid elephants racing across the vlei, grabbing a trunkful of water as they ran, not game to stop for more.

With the hunting, and without access to Kanondo, my days with the elephants couldn't be what they used to be. Their key home range was now inaccessible, their behaviour changed. Encountering the hunting vehicles elsewhere on the estate – a wildlife estate that was previously purely for the photographic tourist – was a sad and awfully disturbing sight. In three years, I had never *not* yearned to be out all day in the field with the elephants. Occasionally now, I didn't even go out at all. Too often, the elephants were not around, and I knew it wasn't only the rain that had chased them away. Outwardly, I tried to behave as if little had happened to ruin my world – the wildlife's world – but inwardly something was broken.

It has been said that you can't live with animals without heartbreak. But heartbreak at the hands of greedy humans is so much worse to endure. My regrets were for the elephants. Despite the pain though, I could not bemoan my time with them. I recognised that I'd been happier with the elephants than I'd ever been – although now, possibly more sad. Perhaps it was inevitable, I consoled myself, that I would encounter the dark side of Africa.

Yet I came to realise, with renewed clarity, that I no longer had any real place in a sophisticated Western environment. It was a life for which I'd lost enthusiasm, the wildness of Africa having called out to the deep wildness in my heart. Three years before, I'd finally found the courage to jump, and I couldn't imagine going back. Zimbabwe, with all its troubles, had still managed to keep hold of my soul.

An adopted child of Africa, that's what I was now, and there was no running away.

The elephants had become an important part of me that I wasn't ready to lose. By now I knew nearly 200 of them as individuals and family members. They had, in some ways, taken the place of people. Helping the snared elephants and learning more about the lives of the elephant families was a long-awaited aspiration that somehow I needed to hold onto – for myself, but mostly for the elephants.

During the last months of 2003 I regularly sat and watched the sun touch the horizon, contemplating the unpredictable current of events in Zimbabwe. In the past, when chaos was someone else's and not mine, I'd had a boundless capacity for optimism. Now though, I was more worldly-wise, far less naive. Disenchanted, I still nourished hope that things would somehow come right for the wildlife on the Hwange Estate.

The hunting went on, much too close to the Hwange Safari Lodge, while I waited impatiently for sanity to intervene. But alas, as I knew only too well by now, things take time in Africa.

In an attempt to ease my troubled mind I searched for diversions, while the habituated wildlife continued to be slaughtered.

The glorious full moon nights temporarily dulled the painful reality of what was happening around me, and I crept to Mpofu pan (now also 'owned' by the settlers) to watch the sunset.

The beauty of the fading day pierced me like an arrow.

The sunken sun in the west had left the horizon orange and the warm glow of the full moon was visible in the east. The dusk symphony began. A saddlebill stork flew low from the pan, landing in a dead tree close by. Bare, contorted branches decorated the moon, the saddlebill exquisitely silhouetted in the middle of this distant yellow ball.

Everything was still. Their perfect reflections in the pan were the only evidence that the four elephants were there. I managed to disappear into my imagination. For a short time, while watching the twilight die, everything was right with the world.

I drove back to my rondavel, recalling with a sharp stab of alarm, that everything was far from right on the Hwange Estate. Yet it had been a distraction, an escape. I found it so healing (temporarily anyway) that I returned late the next afternoon.

Just a few elephants rested at the edge of the pan, now orange with the reflection of the sun just gone. Heavy grey clouds, with a touch of deep blue, hung in the sky above a band of vivid orange, and there were three elongated woolly clouds in the most wonderful hot-pink colours, completing a magnificent scene. There were soft elephant rumbles and the familiar sound of dung balls hitting the ground. Sheet lightning was visible behind the heavy cloud cover, and the rainbird was calling. Eventually, the roosting commotion of the guineafowls ended my quiet escape.

Back in my rondavel, sleep no longer came easily. I thought about all the snaring, and constantly now about the hunting. I thought about the last three years, which had passed more quickly than I could ever recall. When I looked back on certain events, they seemed so very long ago, while other long-gone events seemed to have happened just the day before.

I realised there was something missing of the person that I'd been three years before. I had, since then, been part of the wonderful – and the dreadful. In order to manage over the last 12 months or so, I'd distanced myself from negative forces, physically when I could, emotionally when I could not. Taking people at face value was sometimes, now, unusually difficult for me.

I'd learned, quite late in life perhaps, that there could be hidden agendas behind certain faces and that self-preservation, at the expense of others, did exist for some. I'd also discovered that there was a very long history of trials, tribulations and insincerity – often well disguised, and sometimes not so – between many of the egos that came and went in this small, surprisingly competitive, wildlife environment. Perhaps as a consequence of being isolated for long stretches from news and happenings of the world beyond the bush, gossip mongering was alive and well. Hearing the negative gossip had been inconsequential, even amusing, years before while visiting, but living in the midst of it could be tiresome. Things were often not as they appeared on the surface, with the sour taste of gossip frequently lingering in the air.

I'd once been told about 'the stench of ego', but only now did I really understand. I'd anticipated a more sincerely unified, genuinely close-knit, conservation/research community. I had, however, come to accept the personal drawbacks of living day-to-day in 'tiny town' surroundings where there was limited choice of friendship and, at the time, a lot of petty infighting. Despite this, I still loved my chosen lifestyle, and really learned to treasure those who were true friends.

By now Julia and I were focusing our energies in different directions, and we heard from each other only occasionally. She eventually left her hyena research work in Hwange National Park in early 2004, telling me in a Christmas message that it was 'too heartbreaking' for her to remain in Zimbabwe.

Most of the other academics working in the area at the time, focused on their degrees, cared little and knew less about what was going on just a few kilometres down the road from them. Even if they had, it would have meant risking the permits enabling them to do their research work (and therefore their careers), to speak out.

His pension worth a pittance – given the continuing decline of the Zimbabwean dollar – John had left the country, as had many white Zimbabweans. He left his dilapidated home in the Hwange bush in late 2002 and joined Del in Bulawayo. Eventually, they moved to a retirement home in South Africa. I heard from him rarely after that, but understood just how much the move must have cost him emotionally.

Soon after John's departure from the bush, the house that he'd lived in was fully renovated by its owners – and then the settlers claimed it as their own, and moved in.

My close friends e-mailed regularly, but they were hours, or oceans, away. For the most part, I knew, I would have to get through this on my own. I'd learned long before to be self-reliant.

I looked for Lady around Acacia Grove, the only part of the Hwange Estate not claimed by the settlers. She had no hand for me to hold, but I wanted to hold her trunk; to tell her that everything would be okay; to beg her to stay safe.

I realised there was no turning back. There was no running away, and no giving up. In an elephant's rumble, and in the feel of living ivory, I'd found a life of meaning from which there could be no escape. Not now anyway.

During this hunting period, Limp was still suffering through the aftermath of his snare injury. His leg was hideously swollen, a complication of his human-inflicted injury, and I feared for his life. Coordinating a sighting of him with someone on call to dart, so that we could look more closely at what was wrong, proved frustratingly difficult.

Having made Limp's condition clear to the settlers, they eventually gave me permission to drive to Kanondo one afternoon to search for him. But there was no sign of him – or much of anything else. Kanondo *looked* well, leafy and green after the earlier rain, but it was deserted. A few impalas and waterbucks, previously unconcerned, ran at my approach. There was little evidence of any other mammals. The elephant dung was all old, scattered by baboons and dung beetles. Thunder rumbled in the distance and a few drops of rain fell. My throat tightened. My hand was on my chest. There was an ache in my heart. A pair of Egyptian geese honked, and I shared their loud concern.

I could taste and feel the utter immorality that Kanondo had been exposed to. It had been hunted, that was evident, and I felt deeply sad.

It was an awful time, my emotions constantly oscillating between hope and dread. Would the hunting *ever* be stopped, I wondered? Would the land ever be returned? Mostly the days passed in a blur of disbelief, outrage and grief. There'd been several months of hunting, and the parties working with the settlers were dubious, at best. One of the hunting companies was an external one, banned from Zimbabwe, although they still managed to operate here underhandedly. 'You must know how corrupt a hunter has to be to be banned from *Zimbabwe*,' I heard someone state one day, and I cringed at the reality.

Searching my mind for some thread of hope, I recalled my mother once telling me about a highway in Australia that was being diverted 'because a frog lives there'. I'd gazed at my mother with a grin, rolling my eyes at her playful sarcasm. It was clearly not just one frog; not just any old frog. A unique family of frogs. Frogs, and their habitat, deemed worthy of preservation.

It had worked for the frogs. Would it work for the Presidential Elephants?

So very often when the hunting was underway, I needed to sit back and *make* myself see the beauty. As always, it was the little things that helped sustain me.

I regularly took time now just to enjoy my small garden. Hovering above the water of my largest birdbath there was often a paradise flycatcher, his long tail-feather curled like a silk streamer, illuminated by the early morning sun. A brightly coloured kingfisher, his head movements imitating those of a vervet monkey, darted in and out of the shallow water. The masked weavers adopted a much more leisurely approach, splashing endlessly in the cool water, momentarily taking the shine off their bright yellow bodies. They were frantically building their nests on a many-stemmed acacia bush close by. It was incredibly intricate workmanship. The bush was laden with over 100 nests, each hanging from the tip of a flimsy limb like an oversized, perfectly woven Christmas ball. So many nests, built high in the trees, was said to be a sign of good rains to come. Heartened, I walked over to investigate a fallen one. Extraordinarily chic and cosy-looking inside, the woven grass nest had been expertly lined with the beautiful black, white and fluffy grey feathers of a guineafowl.

The tiny powder blue waxbills and the deep pink fire finches loved to cool off in my birdbaths too. They kept company with the citrus swallowtail butterflies that balanced on the mass of hot-pink flowers on my coral creeper – which, incidentally, an elephant had demolished one night but which grew back in all its colourful glory – alongside the deep purple bougainvillea. The mongoose family was often nearby, chattering incessantly in that secret language that I so wished I understood. Frequently, I could see vervet monkeys playing in the flowering teak trees, mother monkeys with babies on their bellies. Infected with their zest for life, they always helped me to feel re-energised. Tiny antelope spoor and the odd porcupine quill were certain proof of those who visited my garden unseen in the night, consuming all that was edible.

Everything I did in my rondavel was to the accompaniment of

peaceful music, but when the rain came I wanted to hear nothing else. It's a gift in wild Africa that one learns to cherish. I would switch off my cassette player and listen, luxuriating in its sweet joy. The birdlife always rejoiced after a brief storm passed, dragonflies joining in the celebrations. The dual transparent wings of flying ants fluttered rapidly, like colonies of tiny fairies, against the dull sky. The dust once again washed from the leaves of the trees, everything looked exceptionally green, and I regularly delighted in the tinkling voices of the many frogs.

After the first rain, bright red fireballs always appeared in my thriving garden of succulents, bringing a welcome dash of colour. It seemed incredible to me that the bulbs hadn't rotted, despite my garden beds – unlike the natural bush – having been watered regularly during the seven-month dry spell. I found it even more incredible that, in spite of this constant watering, these balls of fire came up only after the first natural rains, in concert with those everywhere in the unattended bush.

The beauty was still there, without even leaving my rondavel. But the foreboding was still there too, now ever-present.

Out in the field the foamy white nests of tree frogs hung once again from logs and branches above the fresh water in the pans. They looked not unlike what you might scoop up in your hands from a bubble bath. The brand new baby impalas looked like they'd just stepped out of this bubble bath, their coats still wet and matted. Soon, the tree frog nests would resemble dried fairy-floss, hardened by the rays of the sun, and the newborn impala fawns would quickly dry off too.

Warthogs revelled in the muddy hollows, compliments of the recent rain. Still with four of last year's piglets, the mother warthog would soon have a new brood of little ones at her heels. I drove past zebras and impalas, heavy with fawn. Before long, I knew, infant life would abound. But would it make up for the terror, and for the lives already lost?

There were no elephants around, although there were signs of them. I stopped and picked up a piece of ivory from the ground. It felt like an omen, however I wasn't sure that it was a *good* one. Probably broken off in a clash of tusks, or perhaps when being used as a lever, I thought about the feel of ivory on a living elephant, and how extraordinary it was that I could experience this sensation by placing my hand on the tusks of some of the wild Presidential Elephants. Would this still be possible, I wondered, now that their trust in humans had been injured?

Lazy baboons lounged on the soft sandy road, in poses reminiscent of beach beauties immersed in the late afternoon sun's soothing rays. I envied their laid-back existence amid the wildlife turmoil going on around them. Alone, a big daddy baboon climbed high on a tree branch. He sat on the very end of this sturdy leafless limb, rocking himself as if on a spring. A grove of acacias was all around him, and from that vantage point he could see up and down the vlei. What better reason did he have to climb all the way up there, I mused, other than to enjoy the view? I wanted to climb up there with him.

The baboon troop was joined in the golden afternoon light by guineafowls and a family of banded mongoose. It was a perfect, if odd, potpourri of energy. With the lush green grass as a canvas, they clowned around together unexpectedly well, seemingly the most agreeable of companions. A baboon and a mongoose sat together on top of a tall termite mound in front of the acacia trees, tumbling off in unison. Three baboons chased each other around and around the trunk of a tree. Guineafowls leapt into the air at the approach of the baboons and the mongooses. It was a comedy of note, and I felt the scene beginning to revive my senses.

The anxiety and turbulence of the past few months was temporarily pushed aside by the beauty surrounding me. Finally, I remembered. It felt like such a long time since I could see it clearly. I was living a blessed existence among the wild animals of Africa. I appreciated, even more so now, this unusual privilege, and I was enriched by it.

Eventually, I was allowed to spend another day at Kanondo looking for Limp. It was only the second time in several months that I'd been granted permission to return. And my fears were paper tigers – at least for now. With no hunting having taken place just recently, it was a little like it used to be. With a big heart, no longer untouched but not yet damaged beyond hope, Kanondo had seemingly forgiven some of the events of the past few months. There'd been no steady rain, but the few welcome downpours meant that there was currently good food, water and mud for the wildlife.

A small group of elephants revelled in the luxuriant surroundings, countless dragonflies airborne among them. The familiar sweet straw-like pungency of fresh elephant dung pervaded my senses, making me feel instantly at home. It's such a distinctive smell, indelibly etched in my memory; an inoffensive aroma impossible to do justice with a simple description.

Sables and waterbucks were there, as well as zebras and giraffes. Crowned cranes, Egyptian geese and jacanas were joined by knob-billed ducks, spur-winged geese and white-faced whistling ducks. Behind them, the water in the pan sparkled when the sun's intermittent rays touched its surface.

This was the Kanondo that I knew and loved; a place where the great pachyderms chose to spend hours leisurely going about their elephantine business. I longed to be able to monitor their lives again in this open, welcoming environment. I did not want to leave.

In the knowledge that the settlers had refused my request to return again the next day, I stayed for as long as I could, despite there being no sign of Limp or any of the L family. The reflections of the kudus in the pan were stunning. They stopped to drink, slurping at their mirror images. Soon though, I had no choice but to give in to the inevitability of the sunset. The sun disappeared, abandoning the almost full moon that already sat high in the sky.

Something odd happens to the elephants around full moon – they always seem a little moonstruck. That invisible man sprinkles his moon dust and his magic, and the elephants become a little crazy. They are often, at this special time of the month, more visible, more social and more vocal. They are somewhat infected, I think, by the exquisite beauty of these round moon nights.

As I lingered just another few moments, tusks gleamed in the failing light while the white-faced ducks whistled their three-syllable farewell to the day just past. I could stay no longer.

The fact that Kanondo still existed as it had before was reassuring. My mind turned to the settlers, who had the ability to rectify everything. I pondered the legality of the land acquisitions, and could only conclude that perhaps no one is really an owner here. We are all just passing through. And we owe it to Nature not to fail her. I wanted to accept implicitly the recent report that hunting on the Hwange Estate would not be allowed to continue in 2004. After a splendid day at Kanondo pan I felt the freedom to be impractical, and I drove home in the moonlight, hopeful, enjoying the peace and quiet of my illusion.

There'd been so many trials and so many tribulations, and then one day soon after, as the year drew to a close, I found myself faced with another, considerably less worrying one. It was the first time in years that I'd had to admit defeat in the bush.

While driving along a little-used road, essentially to show my presence to poachers, I'd driven over a log, hidden by long grass. Somehow it had dislodged my rubber fuel pipe and had ripped it in two.

'What a schlep!' I muttered to myself, and to the animals no doubt wandering about in the thick bush.

I realised I wasn't going anywhere unless I could rejoin that rubber tube. Two clothes pegs (used to fasten the mosquito net that I always carried in my 4x4 in case I was forced to stay out overnight) kept the rubber pipe bent and secured so that no more precious fuel would be lost. Some handy all-purpose putty and tape from my toolbox didn't help in rejoining it, although I tried various imaginative fixes for over an hour. I felt surprisingly happy, pleased with my resourcefulness, although realising that I was going to fail.

I knew of only one vehicle that might pass my way, but I also knew that it could be days before I might see the dust of this approach. It was almost mid-afternoon. I'd given up trying to repair the pipe, lying now on the sandy road looking up at it – as if that perhaps might help. I decided to lock my field equipment in my vehicle, leave a note on the windscreen and set off. I planned to take my water bottle, my little high-pitched air-horn, which would hopefully help to frighten off anything threatening, and my one-and-a-half-metre-long hollow metal pipe that John had given me to use over my wheel spanner to help loosen tight wheel nuts. They seemed like sensible protection devices to have on hand; a false sense of security perhaps, but better than nothing.

I thought about John and fondly recalled the day that he'd made me an expert in tyre changing, and I wondered wistfully if he'd ever imagined that I'd be using his length of pipe for a purpose such as this.

I reasoned that it would be a one-hour brisk walk to the nearest lodge. I had my 'weapons'. I felt okay. Then, fortuitously, I heard that vehicle. It was, just this once, an infinitely preferable sound to the silence that surrounded me. A tow rope, never yet used but always in my 4x4, meant that I was quickly rescued. Previously, Nicki Mukuru had always managed to limp back to base, but not this time. Resident mechanics, exercising their superb bush skills, had me mobile again within minutes and I was soon heading back into the bush, smelling distinctly of petrol.

Although it sometimes felt like Nicki Mukuru was held together only by wire and optimism, she was, for the most part, an extremely reliable bush vehicle – albeit with unenviably high fuel consumption. She also had one or two little foibles.

During one of my visits to Bulawayo I asked Ernie, a kind friend of mine, to help me source some brake fluid, so often in short supply. Soon after, he returned with a small pot.

'What's *that?*' I asked sarcastically.

'It's brake fluid,' he replied.

'That will last me for *two weeks*,' I stated, perplexed.

Ernie turned to his companion and simply shook his head. 'She's got the only vehicle in the world,' he eventually sniggered, 'that runs on brake fluid.'

With the local currency continuing to devalue by the day, it was sometimes difficult to pay for what was needed to satisfy Nicki Mukuru's voracious appetite. I recalled the recent response from the computer on the Hwange Safari Lodge reception desk; a response that was indicative of a country in crisis.

'Two hundred and fifty thousand US dollars is how many Zimbabwe dollars?' I asked the receptionist one evening. I'd just heard that this was the minimum amount the settlers wanted for their newly acquired land.

Numbers were punched into the computer, but it was too much even for the computer. It displayed no numbers, but responded instead with just two telling words: 'Numerical overload.'

The Dark Side of Africa

My relentless campaign to safeguard the Presidential Elephants had continued during late 2003, and by year-end the Parks Authority was forced to withdraw the hunting quota that it had so rashly issued to the settlers. It was pleasing news, and I felt greatly relieved.

There were, fortunately, some influential officials in the government who were well aware of the Presidential Elephants, despite many in the Parks Authority pleading ignorance. A few concerned people in Zimbabwe's conservation organisations had helped me to remind those in high places that this was the land of the Presidential Elephants and that they were protected by a 'presidential decree'.

Although we succeeded in getting the hunting quota revoked, the settlers remained on the land and it looked as if they were here to stay. I'd asked my supporters to be discreet, which they were. This meant that the settlers were unaware that I had urged for their hunting quota to be withdrawn, and I was not about to enlighten them.

In January 2004 the head settler agreed to meet me in his offices in Bulawayo. A small rickety lift landed me in a nondescript reception area. Soon I was sitting at a large wooden table with a few of his extended family members. I couldn't help but notice that they were all extremely well fed, in this country where so many go without.

Who owned what land in Zimbabwe was still of no concern to me. I certainly did care about the Presidential Elephants though, and now that these settlers had no approval to hunt, I thought there was no reason that I couldn't work with them.

The meeting went well. In fact it lasted for several hours, and we talked and even laughed. They were exceedingly polite. Perhaps, I thought hopefully at the time, these men may not be as ruthless as many people claim they are.

'Just be careful,' I was warned time and again. Even so, I was ready to give them a chance. There was, however, one statement that kept racing around in my mind; one thing that set off alarm bells; one sentence that made me doubt their integrity... 'We do not *want* to hunt,' the head settler had said.

Although I sat quietly listening, I knew this to be a lie. I knew that the Parks Authority was no longer *allowing* them to sport-hunt in the Kanondo and Khatshana areas, despite their application to continue to do so. I also knew that this man had already allocated himself and his extended family at least two other farms, on which they were hunting. But in Africa, as I also knew, many things are all about not 'losing face'. So I said nothing.

For a few months after this meeting my life returned to a degree of normality. Although I'd been granted permission to return, it was very worrying that tourists were still not permitted in these Kanondo and Khatshana areas, and the anti-poaching team was still not allowed to patrol. I did not see many elephants during my daily rounds, but I didn't regard this as too unusual because sightings always did decrease during the rainy months.

I constantly wondered where the elephants disappeared to during the greater part of each wet season. Were they following centuries-old migratory instincts? Was there perhaps a favoured plant – a tree, a flower, a pod, a particular type of grass – that they went in search of? Or were they just hidden in thick bush? Regardless, when the dry season arrived, the elephants should have returned. But they did not. Kanondo was often void of elephants – of any animals in fact – day after day, week after week. And I became increasingly suspicious.

I returned to Australia for a surprise visit, arriving on my birthday on the 3rd of May. A visit, especially to see my family, was long overdue – I hadn't been back for over two years. Besides that, I needed a break. Only two of my sisters, Deborah and Catherine, knew of my impending arrival since we thought it would be fun to keep it a secret.

Deborah fetched me from Brisbane airport, and drove me the hour and a half to Grantham. She'd bought me an extra-large packet of cheese Twisties (a favourite snack from my childhood) and a McDonald's cheeseburger, with fries inside the bun. She knew I'd been craving this 'comfort food'. We arrived at our childhood home in darkness. Deborah walked up the stairs and went inside, where our parents were clearing up after dinner. I remained quietly downstairs listening to her reminding them that it was my birthday; asking if they'd made contact to wish me a happy one.

At the right time, I appeared without warning. One should probably never do that to parents in their 70s! My eldest sister Genevieve, and my nieces and nephews, were equally bowled over by me being there so unexpectedly.

I found it difficult to speak about all that had been happening in Zimbabwe, in a way that my family and friends could relate to. I spoke of things that I knew were incomprehensible to those living in a stable country where life is fair, where shops supply your every need, where everything functions as it should, and you can say whatever you like, to whoever you like, without fear of repercussions. Sitting in my parents' living room, my words suddenly seemed unfathomable, even to me. It became easier not to talk too much about it, and besides, for just these few weeks, I wanted to forget.

After a rejuvenating month of fine food, rest and relaxation I returned to Zimbabwe, fearing the worst.

Back on the Hwange Estate it didn't take long for my worst fears to be realised. The hunting vehicles that I saw on the land after my return were just 'sightseeing', I was told. When I caught one hunting party at Kanondo, on foot with their guns, I was informed that they were 'after a wounded elephant bull'. Never during my time on the estate had I known anyone to be following an animal at Kanondo that had been wounded elsewhere by a hunting client. When this happened more than once I became more than just suspicious. When I left Kanondo another day, returning without warning a few hours later, I found one of the settler vehicles driving around Kanondo pan. The gun-toting occupants were clearly looking for an animal to shoot, and I was incredulous.

I would give the devil my soul, I declared to myself, rather than close my eyes to what I was seeing. It was another risk that I'd have to take. I told only those who needed to know, and asked again that they handle my feedback with discretion. This was a country where some simply 'disposed of' those who were in their way, and even though these settlers did not have a good reputation, I tried not to worry unduly about the possible consequences.

I was constantly distraught now about how little wildlife I was seeing, day after day after day. July came, and there was no sign of 'reunion month' at Kanondo pan. For the first time in four years, the majority of the elephants stayed away. With so little wildlife activity, the once pristine Kanondo pan was rapidly becoming choked with weed and reeds.

There was, however, one day when Lady and her family appeared there. I was so happy to see them, as they seemed to be to see me, and they surrounded my vehicle to sleep. I'd just been singing 'Amazing Grace', when all of a sudden the entire family raced off in complete silence, with tails up, into the bush, alarmed by a sound or smell that was beyond my human senses. I sat bewildered and saddened, presuming that they'd heard a distant gunshot. But it was a settler vehicle that appeared in the open not 30 seconds later. It was further evidence of what was going on unseen – the elephants clearly associating the sound and smell of it with danger. Beneath the surface, I was incensed.

I frequently worried now that in letting the elephants (and indeed all the animals) become so accustomed to me, they would be more trusting of humans than they otherwise would be, with potentially fatal consequences. This began to trouble me more and more. Were they safer fearing humans?

What happened the next month was of even greater concern.

I raced from Kanondo to phone for darting assistance immediately after I saw Wholesome, three-year-old son of Whole, with a snare wrapped tightly around his little head and neck. But, hearing him gasping for breath, I realised I was probably too late. He died in front of my eyes some 30 minutes later, before assistance arrived. I'd known Wholesome since he was just days old.

His elder sister, Whosit, was particularly grief stricken, as was mother Whole. They used their trunks and tusks to try and hold him upright, and then to lift him. Eventually his little lifeless body ended up in the water.

Mother and sister, together with grandmother Wendy, remained close by the little elephant that had been such an important part of their lives. Later, Whole and Whosit returned to his carcass again and again. The way mother Whole held her head, her mouth, her eyes; everything about her spelt intense grief. Whosit resolutely refused to leave her dead brother, even when all other family members had wandered a short distance off into the bush. My body ached for them all.

Tuskless Debbie and Delight and others from the D family later passed by, spending eerily quiet time beside Wholesome's body. By then it was dark, and I drove home dejectedly. Spoor around Wholesome's body the next morning confirmed that many elephants had visited him during the night. The settlers had then, uncaringly, butchered Wholesome's little body, taking his hide, his ears, his tail and the meat – for sale. Humans had killed him, and humans had greedily taken all that they could.

Elephants have a sense of death, like few other animals. They will walk straight past the remains of another animal, but will always stop at the new remains of one of their own kind. Family, bond group and clan members stopped frequently at Wholesome's butchered carcass, touching it gently with their trunks. It was Anne and Andrea, and others from the A family who now spent time beside his remains. They silently backed into their dead companion, and slowly moved a hind foot in a circling motion over the carcass, in a chilling gesture of awareness. As I watched them, moved and saddened, I vowed that Wholesome's death would not be in vain. He would help to highlight the plight of the remaining Presidential Elephants.

I sent around graphic photographs and the story of Wholesome's death. I didn't send them to the press, but somehow they ended up there. Without my knowledge or approval, one of the tightly controlled government newspapers published the story. Obviously they didn't know who the settlers were, since articles were never published that were disparaging to those in positions of power. And the settlers were not pleased.

By early September 2004, after the story of Wholesome's death had appeared in the press, I was targeted by the settlers as the person they needed to get rid of, if they were to survive on this land. I had the police, from the nearby town of Dete, searching for me, asking endless questions and demanding to see my passport and permits. The head settler was using his political weight to try to have me expelled from the country. Clearly now, I was persona non grata.

Out in the field I battled with thornbush roadblocks erected to deter me, and regular shouts of abuse. This was one of the most fearful times that I faced in Zimbabwe. I'd heard all about threats and intimidation in Africa. I never expected though, to be on the receiving end of them.

Carol and others arrived out of the blue one morning and, sensing my anxiety, kindly whisked me away to 'The Hide' safari camp, far enough away to be peaceful, for a few nights of rest and recreation. This is the land where Andy is buried. It is Carol's great pleasure to spoil her friends, and I was exceedingly grateful for this thoughtful deed. However, the police were waiting for me on my return.

Yet the settlers had nothing on me. My permits were in order. I'd worked with these protected elephants for the past three-and-a-half years. Even so, the harassment continued. At one stage I was advised by a concerned colleague to leave the country, if only temporarily. I thought this surely wasn't necessary, but after listening to the tale of his talks with another in the know, I decided that perhaps I should. But very soon afterwards I received other frantic advice. 'You may not make it to the airport,' he said anxiously. 'Stay where you are.'

It was what my Zimbabwean friends had told me used to happen regularly in the post-war period. 'Death by puma', it was called. People often met with 'accidents', a heavy army truck – a puma truck – would run them off the road. I thought people's imaginations were getting the better of them, but I couldn't be certain. They'd lived in this country far longer than I had, and they knew better what some were capable of.

'Never be at your rondavel on a Friday afternoon,' I was warned by another with first-hand knowledge. 'If they lock you up then, you'll spend the entire weekend in jail. And you don't want to spend that long in a Zimbabwean jail.'

All this was not just bewildering to me. It was shocking.

I hadn't done anything wrong. In fact I was the one – and one of the very few, it seemed to me – trying to do the *right* thing by the wildlife.

But this was Zimbabwe. It did not matter.

I'd somehow found myself embroiled in games that I had no stomach for, struggling against powerful adversaries. It was something I'd never bargained on.

Around the pans, I gazed at the crocodiles. I imagined my body floating in a pan, chewed on by crocodiles, with it somehow having been made to look like a careless accident on my part. So it was that I warned my friends, rather than worry my family. 'If something like this ever happens, don't you believe it,' I cautioned.

The Australian Embassy in Harare was alerted to my situation, and I felt better knowing that people at least knew.

All of this, though, was draining away my spirit and my zest for being with the elephants. I longed for things to be as they were before the settler invasions. There were awful days when I could no longer see any beauty at all.

'Did you really think it would stay as it was?' a friend asked me one evening.

I remembered that line from the movie *Out of Africa*, and my reply was the same, 'I thought it might…' I whispered sadly.

The Kanondo of wishes, of sanity, of peace. It was gone.

My days of sheer enchantment were long gone too. The nights were the worst, filled with torrid dreams. I wanted to be the eyes of the owls, watching what bad things were going on out there under cover of darkness. It was at night that I, and others, heard most of the gunshots. And I felt an unspeakable despair. I would close my eyes, only to see the ruins of my fallen-down world, and I would weep in grief and frustration at what was going on around me.

I remained disheartened that so few people were speaking out.

Sometimes it was as if there was an echoless void out there – so few willing to get involved. They knew well the dangers of doing so.

The safe, carefree land of seafood and chocolate and everything else one could ever want, across the sea in Australia, seemed so far away. I could be there, I knew. But no wild elephants live in Australia; my elephants there were made only of stone. And the actions and intimidation tactics of these settlers triggered in me a dogged determination to stay, for the sake of the animals that I love.

My surroundings had once seemed so seductive, serene and untainted. Now I was constantly alert to the possible presence of illegal or unethical hunters, and other unsavoury individuals, behind every bush and around every corner. I ceased to harbour even the slightest romantic notion of what life was *really* like in darkest Zimbabwe. I mustered my resolve and battled on. But the harassment continued.

Four-legged predators, I knew, lived in the bush. Now the greedy two-legged ones lived there too, trying their best to destroy it all. The most dangerous predator in Africa, I came to realise, is not the lion. Nor can the hippo, the buffalo or the elephant hope to compete. Clearly, the most dangerous animal is *man*.

At one stage I had a visit from *six* officials. This sizeable delegation, some from the immigration department and others believed to be from the Central Intelligence Organisation (CIO) – no doubt acting on instructions from the head settler – had travelled all of the way from Harare, on the other side of the country, to speak to me. They seemed to realise that I didn't have anything to hide though, and they left quietly after a short meeting. Even so, I eventually felt that I had no choice but to go with an influential man – who had a long and ongoing interest in the Presidential Elephants – to Harare, to the offices of three government ministers. These ministers, whose names I was advised not to flaunt publicly, were colleagues of the head settler.

Two of these three government offices were large and relatively plush, all of the staff, friendly and welcoming. The ministers listened attentively to what we had to say, and I had no reason to doubt their sincerity. 'Don't be afraid,' said the most high-ranking of them, holding my hand between his. 'Your work is crucial. It must be allowed to continue.'

Without the support of this man (one of the most powerful men in the country at the time), the Presidential Elephants had no future. Until then, he hadn't heard of our problems and concerns. Continued support for the Presidential Elephants was pledged. My permit was to be renewed. The settlers would be dealt with.

Yet back on the Hwange Estate I still battled with thornbush roadblocks, and another order from the settlers that I was banned from 'their' land. Sightings of the elephants had reduced from an average of eight families in one day, to eight families in one *month* – if I was lucky. For the past 12 months the veld had been disturbingly quiet.

The situation dragged on for more long weeks, the days blurred with uncertainties, until finally, still banned from the land by the settlers, I climbed into my 4x4 and drove to Kanondo. On the way my troubled mind battled with unsettling images of possible ambushes, snipers and tyre spikes, but a sixth sense had told me that something was very wrong and I needed to find out what it was. And there, at Kanondo, I was met with a huge tract of felled trees.

This, for all those involved in the fight for the Presidential Elephants, was the final straw.

PART VI

The Aftermath

Awaiting the
Return of the Land

Despite everything, 2004 had been a fulfilling year. I'd endured hardships and faced events totally alien to most in the First World, but I'd also experienced the sheer privilege and joy of being accepted by the animals of the wild. This sustained me, and helped restore my energy.

I dared not think about what might have happened to the Presidential Elephants had someone not been there to plead their case, and I felt proud to have contributed to their future, which now seemed more assured. But although my Zimbabwean life was ribboned with beauty, it was frayed now with fear and disillusionment.

I was aware of the saying that the earth was made round to ensure that we couldn't see too far down the road. If I'd indeed been able to see further down my already bumpy path, perhaps I would have left Zimbabwe at once. For now though, I remained apprehensive – yet still hopeful – about what 2005 might bring.

It was a hot morning in late December 2004, when a young man who dreamed of studying law arrived on my doorstep, wanting to talk. He hadn't seen an elephant for eight years, and longed to see one during this, his Christmas visit to the Hwange Estate.

We both knew that the chances of this happening had, during the past year, been significantly reduced. We spoke of the ongoing restricted access to the Presidential Elephants, a situation that was being enforced by the settlers. His dark, intelligent eyes expressed confusion and sadness.

'*Okungapheliyo kuyahlola,*' he said in Sindebele. A statement of consolation and encouragement – 'nothing bad lasts forever'.

Then, pondering the concept of 'freedom of speech', he exclaimed, '*Eisshhhh!*... little freedom after speech sometimes...'

Eventually he offered me his prayers, and I wished him well.

'Remember *Okungapheliyo kuyahlola,*' he urged as he walked away – nothing bad lasts forever.

I could only hope.

I saw movement high in the sky. Something was riding the thermals of the summer storm. Perhaps it was Dasher and Dancer, Prancer and Vixen, Comet and Cupid, and Donner and Blitzen!

It was in fact a flock of hundreds of migratory white storks, feathered visitors that – like the Christmas clients visiting the photographic safari lodges – stayed for just a few days. When I asked the lodge workers if they thought that Santa and his reindeers would make it to the Hwange bush this year they looked a little downcast and simply shook their heads.

Remember *Okungapheliyo kuyahlola*. Maybe next year?

The voices of the night, usually audible from my rondavel, had all but vanished. The lions' bellows, once frequent in the still of the night, had been silenced. The 'big pride', 17 members strong when I arrived in 2001, was no longer. Many of them, it was feared, had fallen victim to hunters, both legal and illegal. The elephants too were scarce and wary. My sleep was rarely disturbed by natural sounds any more. Instead, it was now disturbed by what the grave silence meant.

A special friend of mine in New Zealand, Eileen – who regularly acknowledged my deep love of wild Africa, once observing that my eyes always sparkled when I spoke of the elephants – wrote with heartfelt concern: 'Come home.'

But where was home? Australia? New Zealand? Zimbabwe? I no longer knew. And I could not yet bring myself to abandon the elephants. I could not yet give up.

It had been 15 months since this land was claimed, sinking the tourism industry and the Presidential Elephants, further and further into decline. But there was a renewed glimmer of hope, and I tried once more to find the beauty. It was still out there – not as abundant as it once was, but it was there ready to rally, if only given the chance.

Stunning two-tone red and yellow flame lilies – that flower for just a few weeks – were in bloom along the roadsides, reminding me that it was nearly Christmas. They always seemed to radiate my hopes for the coming year.

I hadn't ventured into neighbouring Hwange National Park for months, and there was something invigorating about having decided to overnight inside the park with my French friend Marion (one of Mathieu's colleagues), who always provided cheerful company and with whom I could share childlike pleasures and wonderment. There, perhaps, away from the still troubled Hwange Estate, things would be clearer.

I needed to rest the bones of the old year.

What struck me most about our excursion was how much I loved it all. Still. We made our way to Ngweshla pan, a lengthy encounter with a white rhino bull secured along the way. His huge form eventually disappeared, the lush vegetation swallowing him whole.

I recalled, with a grin, an American visitor's response to my question, posed earlier that year, as to whether we were looking at the backside of a black or a white rhino. 'This rhino is *grey*!' she had exclaimed. Indeed, she had a good point – both the black and the white rhinos are certainly grey. A wide mouth rather than a pointy one distinguishes the white grey tank from the black one.

The many tortoises on the sandy road prepared us for the spectacle of Ngweshla at sunset: waterbucks, impalas, kudus, elephants, zebras, giraffes... even some ostriches and a huge known herd of more than 800 buffalos. No sooner had we settled ourselves – G&T in hand, with other small luxuries of olives, smoked mussels and cheese to be savoured – than we were surrounded, 360 degrees, by the buffalo herd. It was as though no other humans existed in the world, and this we respected with silence. Watchful and wise, the buffalos made a wide grand circle around us, before breaking off and moving away. What had been their message, I wondered?

Carefully avoiding the many nightjars and the occasional springhare sitting on the road, we found a place inside the national park to rest our heads. First though, we shared our wine – and our stories. We spent our days, it seemed, in such an improbable way. Our incessant talking, now quite foreign to my solitary existence, didn't drive away the tranquillity. It was wonderful that, though we'd spent thousands of days and nights in the African veld, we both still truly treasured the sublime beauty that surrounded us, even under cover of darkness.

An encounter with a pride of lions was Marion's parting gift from Hwange National Park the next morning, before she returned temporarily to France.

The birdlife on the Hwange Estate during these wet season months was always spectacular. The bare branches of a small tree festooned with flamboyant carmine bee-eaters outdid any Christmas tree full of ornaments that I could ever have assembled. A goshawk clung to the opening of a weaver nest, preying on the ill-fated victims inside. Those hundreds and hundreds of stunning white storks, once again riding the thermals of a late afternoon storm, were equally impressive when they landed on the vlei. A martial eagle demonstrated his prowess, a cover of pristine white stork feathers scattered on the ground close by. It was 'white', but it was indeed a far cry from the storybook 'white Christmas'.

Christmas Day that year was a special one in the field. I unexpectedly came across Lady and her family in an area where I'd never seen them before. I hadn't encountered them for more than eight weeks. Toddling among those so familiar to me were two wee packages of pure pleasure – a dashing little boy for Leanne, and another for Louise.

I could hardly contain my excitement, yet Limp (the snare injury on his leg no longer bothering him too badly) seemed uninterested in his new baby brother. Both youngsters were probably already about six weeks old, and played together around a rainwater pan. The great matriarch, Lady, herself heavily pregnant, came to share her mud with me. I'd seen her in oestrus twice during 2003, and assumed that she'd conceived during her second session (when she was mated by a musth bull named King). Based on this, I expected her to give birth in just over three months.

As I rubbed my hand hard over the corrugated surface of Lady's trunk, I thought about the first time that I'd placed my fingers, so very tentatively, on her long, rough nose. That was well over two years ago now.

When Lady led her family into thick bush, I drove on, elated. It had been such an unexpected encounter, leaving me with a renewed sense of wonder and possibility. After emerging from a thick canopy of leaves I was showered with raindrops, and treated to a stunning display of jade, yellow, pink and purple, which enveloped the vlei. I always find these rainbow moments of simultaneous shower and sunshine intoxicating, but this one had no equal. I marvelled at the curve of incredible colour, and my spirit soared higher. A fleeting encounter with a zebra family – lush green at their feet and a perfect arc of brilliant colours above – was dazzling.

It was hauntingly beautiful. It was Christmas in the Hwange bush.

I thought about my family celebrating Christmas in Australia, and recalled the numerous children in the Western World who receive so many gifts that they flit from one to another, barely appreciating any of them. Many times I'd watched the African children race behind old car tyres, which they pushed along sandy tracks. I'd watched them play hopscotch, the outline for their game etched with a stick in the damp ground. I'd watched them throw balls that were nothing more than a plastic shopping bag, stuffed with more plastic bags, shaped round. I'd watched them high-jump over a crossbar of twig, supported by two sticks pushed into the ground. And to me, it seemed that these children, who received no material gifts, but were endowed with a natural ability to create their own fun, were not really missing out on that much at Christmas.

On Boxing Day, I realised it had been over six months since I'd seen a lion on the estate. The lions, especially those found wandering in surrounding sport-hunting areas, were being persecuted relentlessly. So it was that I casually got out of my 4x4, unconcerned, to walk a few metres to photograph the crinkly white flower of a bauhinia. Satisfied that I'd captured my delicate dew-spangled subject, which glistened in the early morning light, I took the camera away from my eye – and caught a glimpse of tawny colour. It had been so long since I'd seen one in these parts that I barely registered what it was. Then along came another three. Now I was sure! And I was out of my vehicle.

They seemed more afraid of me than I was of them. Nevertheless, I quickly retreated to my open door. As it turned out, it was a collared mother and her three grown cubs. The three adolescents were playful, climbing high on the dead branches of every fallen tree they came across. That morning and again in the evening, I saw them attempt a kill four times. Each time they were unsuccessful, despite the bounty of the wet season when so many vulnerable babies are around. The adolescents, not quite as tall as their mother and still sporting spotted coats, seemed too eager, always pouncing too soon. The lioness hung back, trying to rectify what her offspring had done, to no avail. My sympathies usually rested with the prey, yet I found myself feeling sorry for this desperately hungry four. I wondered why there were no other adults to help them kill. Were they always alone? Had something happened to their pride?

In addition to the pleasure of wildlife encounters like these, I always delighted in the variety of plants and flowers to be seen in the veld. The charming pendulous, two-tone – mauve-pink and yellow – flowers of the dichrostachys (also known as sickle bush), hung limp and colourless. Christmas had passed and this, the 'Kalahari Christmas tree', had passed its prime. When in its peak the flowers hold an irresistible appeal, reminding me of little ballerinas – a fluffy mauve-pink tutu above a bright yellow body.

The seed pods were now forming on the *Acacia eriolobas*. Peering through binoculars at the miniature pods, I hoped that they would cling on tightly another few months to maturity, when they'd become sought-after elephant delicacies. I recalled other fascinating pods forming on trees further afield. The fruits of the sausage tree are particularly impressive, dangling from great heights on rope-like stalks. As they can grow up to one metre long and weigh up to 10 kilograms, it's preferable not to be standing under the umbrella of this tree when these sausage-shaped capsules decide to disengage from their stalks. 'Killed by a sausage' would be a rather frightful epitaph after all.

In an attempt to sustain my spirit, which had been bruised – indeed, shattered – by the events of the past 15 months, I often got up at sunrise to enjoy the area around Acacia Grove, still the only portion of the Hwange Estate not adversely affected by settlers and hunters. Impala babies formed crèches, resting together in the tall green grass, a cluster of little heads barely visible. The black-backed jackal numbers were staggering, 15 my highest tally, including two litters recently born. Painted hunting dogs made an occasional appearance, adding an extra thrill to my outing. And then, one still morning, the realisation dawned on me: I was drawn to the wilds of Africa by a wish for freedom; a wish for peace and tranquillity.

A few days later I was sitting on the rooftop of my 4x4, admiring a sizeable zebra herd, dramatic against a backdrop of green-topped acacias and bulbous grey storm clouds. The zebra herds always seemed to enjoy this area around Acacia Grove and the nearby Hwange Safari Lodge. The lush green grass was often bent by a gentle late-afternoon breeze that seemed to deliver messages from distant places, if you paused long enough to hear them.

The quiet beauty was broken abruptly by another gruesome snare injury. The sub-adult zebra, the stripes on her rump not yet jet-black, wore the death trap around her neck. The ring of wire dug in deeply, the wound so horrific that I needed to turn away. But, having watched young Wholesome die, I knew that I could now bear anything. Harder to stomach was the knowledge that the anti-poaching team was still not allowed to patrol this estate. What was there to hide, I wondered?

The Animal Rescue team darted this snared zebra the following morning. It was a horrific wound that you'd expect to see only on a *dead* animal. Her neck had been deeply sliced. The maggots were nauseating, the snare difficult to remove, a loop of wire wrapped hideously around her windpipe. I feared that she would not survive the ordeal. Antiseptic washes, ointments and antibiotics were used liberally.

After the reversal drug was administered, she (somewhat remarkably) got to her feet and rejoined her mother and the four others that had put their heads to hers, concerned, when she first fell to the ground under the effect of the immobilising drug. Once they were back together again, they all began to feed.

Lady's daughter, Lesley, enjoys a dust bath. Dust protects an elephant's skin from the blazing sun.

Lesley, thin from the 2005 drought, gave birth to a tiny boy who was christened Lancelot.

Lesley rests her trunk on the bonnet of Nicki Mukuru.

The three generations in 2005: Lesley (Lady's daughter); Lancelot (Lesley's son and Lady's grandson); with Lady - and her youngest calf Libby.

Mud, water and dust temporarily turned this rhino at Kanondo into a three-toned work of art.

The elephants enjoy the natural mineral licks at Kanondo.

Lesley comes to say hello, with baby Lancelot (who preferred to play in one of the mineral lick excavations).

I place my hand on Leanne's tusk, while her sister Lady and other family members doze. Leanne disappeared in 2007. I fear she was shot.

Zebras enjoy the vlei, and the shade of the Acacia eriolobas *(on the left) in Acacia Grove.*

After regularly being splattered with mud myself, I learned to stay further back from mud-bathing elephants.

Jabulani (centre) led the estate anti-poaching team. Here they hold a deadly wire snare found in the bush.

For immobilised Future, I say a silent prayer to the god of wild things – but it was to be in vain.

A successful snare removal. I'm beside immobilised Victory. His mother Vee is 'standing immobilised' in the background, a dart protruding from her left-hand side.

Victory, one year after his snare removal, the scar on his back right leg still visible.

Loopy, Lady's son, with a tight wire snare around his head, mud-bathing in an attempt to get some relief.

Unlike other species that often die in snares, elephants regularly escape, with dreadful injuries. Bubble's trunk injury is one of the less gruesome ones.

I had an unforgettable encounter with this bushbuck, that I'd named Trust.

My home in the Hwange bush.

Whole gives me a trunk-to-hand greeting beside the Kanondo water trough. Her family is closeby.

A dry season view from the Hwange Safari Lodge game-viewing platform; the elephants heading down the vlei.

Due to neglect, dry season water on the estate is now so scarce that the elephants are forced to fight over water from tiny seepages (caused by leaking pipes).

The once lavish Mpofu pan, on the Khatshana side of the estate, no longer even exists. It used to be the estate's second-busiest pan.

Young elephants love to climb all over each other, building elephant castles, reaching for the sky.

The antics of the elephants enthrall.

Youngsters revel in the wet season surface water.

The Presidential Elephants approach to greet you.

Holding trunks.

Pink behind the ears, for the first few weeks of life.

Dust particles, separated and snaking, sometimes landing all over me.

Elephants greet and caress each other.

An elephant fountain. I learned to stay further back from these cheeky elephants too.

Tuskless Cathy, suckling her calf from human-like breasts.

In 2008, Lee became the fourth snare victim in the L family. First he lost his mother (Leanne), and then he lost the lower portion of his trunk in a snare.

I always experienced a great sense of relief, knowing that we had done what we could to treat the human-inflicted injury. Nothing could ever make it right, but we could continue to try to make it better.

By now it was New Year's Eve; soon to be 2005.

As the New Year loomed I found myself reflecting on the year 1997 – the year that I'd branded, just prior to its arrival, 'The Year of Change'. Perhaps predestined by my naming of it, it certainly turned out to be just that. It was when I first decided to take extended time off from my busy corporate life to volunteer on wildlife projects in Africa. It was the year that Africa truly took hold of my soul. I sat wondering where these past eight years had gone. Managing 'millennium bug' fixes – indeed all of my former life in IT – seemed like a lifetime ago, and in many ways, I guess it was.

Five years into the new millennium, I understood that the coming year might well be 'The Year of Difficult Decisions'.

In an e-mail received from New Zealand, my good friend Bobby – worried about my wellbeing – asked, 'When and how do you make the decision to stay or leave?' I wasn't sure *how* but it was during 2005, I decided, that I'd need to make up my mind if it was worth staying on in Zimbabwe. I sat pensively, contemplating my life.

I used to believe that dreams were free, but not any more. Nothing in this world was entirely free – not even dreams. And it seemed to me in my grief that someone was always waiting around the corner, ready to *steal* your dreams.

Time in the *peaceful* African bush had drifted along, and I used to find myself not taking much notice of it.

As a child, I used to ask my father, 'When are we leaving?'

'Half-past,' he'd always reply playfully.

'Half-past *what?*' I would demand.

'Around *half-past...* Whatever, whenever, we'll leave at *half-past.*'

Like in those childhood days, time was largely irrelevant. I came in from the field after the elephants disappeared, not caring what time it was. I rarely knew what day it was, and definitely not what date it was. It was often amusing when I sat in the field trying to *work out* what day it was. It was an odd existence I suppose. A weekend was no different from a weekday. There were no accrued days off. There was no lunch break, no finishing time; each day flowed into the next. During the wet season I became aware that a week had already passed by the need to take my next dose of anti-malaria *muti*. In the dry season it was the realisation that I really should shave my legs again.

Now, however, the days were much more troubled and I was hindered from doing what I'd come to do. Time raced on, with things that needed to be done not getting done. Not *allowed* to be done. The settlers were *still* around. It wasn't a First World situation. There were different problems, different priorities and different protocols, and a very different pace. I had some tough decisions ahead. Alone with nature, I would have to make them.

I had such grand plans to toast the new year at *three* different times that New Year's Eve. Firstly at 1pm when friends in my old home New Zealand would be popping champagne corks; again at 4pm when family and friends in Australia would be celebrating; and again at midnight Zimbabwean time. But a snared elephant sighting – another gruesome neck wound, this time on a youngster in the M family – ensured that 1pm and 4pm passed without me even noticing.

That same afternoon, I was at least able to confirm that police were now living on the Hwange Estate, in both Kanondo and Khatshana lodges. I could not yet be certain that this was a good thing, although I hoped desperately – my New Year's wish – that they were on the *right* side. The side of the wildlife. It did appear that the settlers had finally been displaced, at least for now. Yet still I remained sceptical.

With no one available to provide darting assistance, I took three of the policemen to see the young snared elephant at Kanondo pan. I could hear my little grey friend struggling to breathe. It was a horrifying sound that I'd heard before, too often.

I came in from the field, distressed by this latest tragedy, and set about organising the necessary help to be on standby the next day. Then I checked my e-mails and received more upsetting news. The tsunami disaster in Asia, which had struck on Boxing Day and claimed several hundred thousand lives, had hit my circle of friends. Two white Zimbabweans, known to me only through stories, but who were dear friends of friends, had been caught up in the tragedy. One lay in intensive care in Thailand, his partner feared (and later confirmed) drowned.

It was another nail in the coffin of the old year, a reminder of the fragility of life.

Feeling a mixture of melancholy and hope it was time to rest my weary head – well before midnight. First, though, a moment of prayer and positive thoughts was desperately needed. I lit a candle.

By early January, there was no sign of the snared youngster among the M family. I'd not yet been able to work out who the mother of the snared calf was, and therefore the name of the calf, but I had to assume that her lifeless body lay somewhere unseen. This grim reality sapped my vitality and I couldn't help feeling indescribably sad. I was also sorely aware that the hopefulness and resilience of my youth was fading fast.

A mature teak tree, a familiar sight on my regular route through the veld, stood wounded. Some uncaring people had hacked out its sturdy trunk, which once stood proud by the roadside, nearly toppling the towering tree in the process. Bees still worked inside the remainder of the trunk, which confirmed that they had been on a quest for honey. Lured there, perhaps, by the 'greater honeyguide' (a dull-looking but clever bird, renowned for deliberately leading people to beehives), the robbers clearly had no qualms about destroying this prime specimen for a pot of illegal honey. Aghast, I could only hope that they did *not* leave a portion of their find for the honeyguide, and therefore, as legend has it, evil would befall them on their next trip into the bush.

Further on, at Kanondo, a friend and I stumbled upon a handmade contraption of wire and netting, clearly being used to catch small fish from the pan.

'This is all getting too much,' he said, giving voice to my silent thoughts.

The unexpected reappearance of some of the settlers brought profound unease. By now it was very clear that they believed themselves to be above the law. And I was so tired of their ongoing harassment. Poaching – of all kinds – was once again on the increase. Soon, I hoped, if the evictions were real, the anti-poaching team would be able to resume its patrols.

I watched the flight of the white-faced whistling ducks across the evening sky. Pensively, I closed my eyes, seeking the peace and contentment that Kanondo had once brought. But, still being a troubled place, serenity was not within reach.

It was one week later that official notification was received at last. The areas of Kanondo and Khatshana were to be returned to the original owners, and photographic safaris were to recommence on the Hwange Estate.

Although thrilled, I remained wary. My heart still heavy, I recalled that I'd heard this all before. There'd been so many assurances, worth little thus far. The assemblage of police, though, suggested that perhaps this time it *was* for real. I needed to believe that it was true. I headed to Kanondo to celebrate. Would she celebrate with me, I wondered?

It was late afternoon when the elephants arrived unexpectedly in all their glory. Significantly perhaps, tuskless Inkosikazi led in her family. Other Presidential families followed, massive grey bodies swaying to the music of the dusk symphony. They mingled in the golden afternoon light, little Inky, daughter of Inkosikazi, just as cheeky and playful as any little one-year-old. For 50-something-year-old Inkosikazi this would be one of her last offspring. Mother and daughter dug for minerals, a ball of fire their backdrop.

Then I savoured yet another surprise encounter. As the long grass – tinged gold by the setting sun – danced in the wind, two male cheetahs appeared from nowhere in perfect silence. Never before had I seen cheetahs walk so casually among elephants. Their spotted coats seemed luminous under the glow of the sinking sun. Exuding an air of elegance and grace they paused at a termite mound and lay down, one on either side of this tall chimney of sand.

Were they all *really* now safe from the hunters' and poachers' bullets?

The new moon, so full of promise, was once again lying on her back. With my arms outstretched to this slither of silver, I whispered a thank-you. But I was still wary. I had already climbed *many* ladders of hope.

The rungs of those ladders had not held for long. This time, I needed more convincing that all was really well, and that it would indeed stay that way. The painful memories of the past 15 (almost 16) months were still fresh in my mind, my previous optimism unrewarded.

It was around this time that an e-mail arrived from England, crammed with kind words of encouragement. Having read some of my writings, this thoughtful Zimbabwean, unknown to me, considered that we might well be 'kindred spirits'. He recalled the almost painful beauty of an African sunset, which clearly he longed to see again. Rather than *Ndlovu*, the Sindebele word for elephant, he used the Shona word, *Nzou*, and he shared with me a Shona word that I'd not yet heard, '*Mashambanzou*' – 'When the elephant bathes' – the Shona word for dusk, he said.

It should indeed have been the word for dusk, since that's when the elephants regularly bathe, but it is, I've been assured, the Shona word for dawn.

I sat on the rooftop of Nicki Mukuru at Kanondo pan (the police still occupying the tourist lodge hidden by trees behind me), absorbing the beauty of my surroundings. Elephants bathed under the grandeur of the setting sun.

'*Mashambanzou*,' I whispered to myself. And a shiver ran down my spine.

Yes, I thought, what a wonderful word for *dusk*.

Dawn brought more small pleasures. Still regularly enjoying that first hour or two after sunrise, when the world seems born anew, I watched playful young jackals climb on fallen branches in Acacia Grove to the accompaniment of the mournful chirping of a young tawny eagle, the cooing of numerous doves and the twittering of countless other birds. On the floor of the grove, zebras rolled on their backs in the dirt, four legs upright in the air. The young zebra with the gruesome neck wound had survived her torture. Still easily identifiable by her damaged mane, I considered her to be a symbol of courage and determination.

Finally, a few days before the end of January, for the first time in 16 months, a photographic safari operator drove tourists around the

Kanondo and Khatshana areas. It was a victory for tourism; a victory for The Presidential Elephants of Zimbabwe.

The settlers were gone.

Perhaps now, I thought, sanity would prevail.

My own sanity though, had been somewhat affected by everything that had gone on. Years before my life in Africa began, and even during the honeymoon period of my time in Zimbabwe, I would read, with discord in my heart, the writings of foreigners who'd lived in wild Africa for many years. I'd always been baffled, even a little offended, when they told of the protocols and eccentricities they'd once found amusing but which later infuriated them; of the extraordinary surroundings in which they could no longer take pleasure; of the fear and loathing; the dark side of Africa. Then, I didn't know much about the dark side of Africa. I didn't understand their sentiments. It took several years – for this does not happen quickly – but now I finally understood.

During the past 16 tumultuous months I'd discovered powers of resilience I didn't know I had. The need to be in the bush with the elephants was intrinsic to the wellbeing of my soul. I knew that to part with it would be to die a little, but the situation was becoming unendurable.

Now everything seemed to melt into a hope that, with time, the Presidential Elephants would return to their former glory on the Hwange Estate. It must be true, I thought (prematurely). *Okungapheliyo kuyahlola* – nothing bad lasts forever.

A few days later one of the policemen, who was still living in the lodge on the Khatshana side of the estate, exclaimed, 'Arrhhh Arrhhh. He is *too* big. It's my first time to see one.' While we'd been walking back from destroying a wire snare found in the bush close to the lodge, a bull elephant had arrived to drink from a nearby pan. The young policeman was in his 20s, raised in the Midlands. He'd never seen an elephant before. His eyes wide, he exclaimed again and again, 'Arrhhh. He is *too* big.'

To the Shona people he is '*Mhukahuru*' – the hugest animal of them all.

Two days later at Kanondo, another of the policemen looked deep into my eyes and said, 'One day, Mandlo, the elephants will speak to you, but only to *you*. It will be a miracle.'

I smiled. Perhaps, I thought, the elephants already *do* speak to me, in their own unique way. If only, though, they could speak my language, or me theirs.

'Where have you all *been*?' I asked longingly of matriarch Disc when I saw her at Kanondo the next day. I hadn't seen the D family for many months.

I received, of course, no comprehensible response. Their secret was safe with them.

The Ds had brought with them a whiff of the great elephant mystery, and I longed for all the elephants to return to their former stomping ground around Kanondo pan. All the wildlife, I hoped, would eventually learn that it was, once again, safe. The tranquillity had been driven away, but now I believed it would return. However, I'd learned many hard lessons, and I knew well the pain associated with being *overly* optimistic.

By now it was February. The wet season would soon be at a close, and not nearly enough rain had fallen. Drought looked likely, and that was definitely not what we needed right now. I longed for the soft patter of gentle rain on the heart-shaped pads of the water lilies, but even the lilies were scarce that year, the musical voices of the frogs also strangely silent.

The settlers had left many of the pans to dry up, and some of them, despite it being near the end of the wet season, were still bone dry. There was much to be done to get the Hwange Estate back to its former glory.

It was still, however, a sanctuary of great enchantment and I tried once more to find the beauty. While driving through the veld I stopped frequently to look at the trees, the flowers and the birds. The ever-changing detail of the smaller life forms, in all their delicacy, always brings intense delight. Somehow, they're often overlooked. Yet they are, in their own way, as dramatic as the elephants walking proudly across the plains.

On the vlei, scores of impalas raced after each other, leaping gracefully from the ground. Sometimes, with their full weight on their front legs, both back legs spring high into the air, their agile bodies seeming to bounce in the breeze. Males chase males, males chase females, and females chase each other. Rutting to establish dominance, mock fights, courtship or just fun, they race after each other, tails erect, the showy white hairs on their under-tails flared. They all like to join in, the loud harsh sounds emanating from the males often belying their elegance and grace.

I was deeply thankful to those government ministers who'd displayed wisdom and courage, helping to restore peace and calm on the Hwange Estate. It was indeed heartening to know that there *were* some in high places who recognised the need to preserve wild places, and wild things.

It was a time of wonder and wonderment; a time to rediscover the gentleness of the wild.

Tranquillity or
More Trouble?

Although the settlers were gone from the Kanondo and Khatshana areas, things did not turn around quickly. I sat at Kanondo for hours, at various times of the day, always with very little wildlife around. This left me pensive, wondering if it would ever fully revert to its former magnificence.

One day I was focused on my tree book and on one of the acacias, struggling to identify it, when I heard a strange sound. With my eyes half closed and one ear facing the direction of the sound, straining to hear better, I still couldn't make out what it was. It wasn't an elephant ripping grass. It sounded more like a *crunch, crunch, crunch,* something like lions or hyenas gnawing on bone. I was about to start my 4x4, responding to an overwhelming urge to locate this odd noise, when there it was, another 'never before'.

From behind a bush, just a few metres away, appeared the huge form of a white rhino. My pulse quickened. I'd never seen a rhino at Kanondo in four years of spending thousands of hours there. The mysterious sound was nothing other than the rhino bull munching, right to left, left to right, right to left, his wide mouth keeping constant contact with the grass that he was mowing. It was something I never expected to hear or see at Kanondo, yet there was something warm and natural about his presence. It was, indeed, *the* best rhino sighting I'd ever had.

Perhaps, I thought, someone was trying to tell me something. Perhaps everything *was* going to be okay.

The rhino bull stayed clearly visible for well over an hour, proudly displaying his unique colouring. Mud, water and dust had temporarily turned him into a fanciful three-toned work of art. His legs, belly, mouth and horn were *dark* grey with mud. A strip of *light* grey appeared above the dark grey, and on top of this, a strip of *dusty* grey. He was indeed a splendidly coloured rhino, until he decided to immerse himself completely in mud, his unique stripes vanishing instantly.

He evoked images of a prehistoric age. Looking at him, I was overcome by a primeval feeling of having lived a very long time ago. There was something treasured and familiar about him, yet he didn't seem to belong to this time. I was elated, though, that he *did* still walk this earth – and that he did, indeed, belong to my time.

Just as the rhino was about to disappear into the bush, elephant families appeared. The smell of elephant dung – the sweet scent of untamed Africa – filled my nostrils. Some were National Park families, clearly agitated. I found myself pondering once again, as I did so often, what these unknown families must have been exposed to, for them to have become so skittish.

Then, along came the Ws.

Since the death of Wholesome, son of Whole, from that strangling neck snare, I'd worried about this family. Neither Whole nor Wendy was present, and both of them had appeared so ill after Wholesome's death. The family was not entirely visible from where I sat however, so I didn't fear the worst.

It is always difficult to compile family trees that include the mother/daughter relationships of the older female elephants, especially when they already have several adult offspring of their own. Nevertheless, based on the intensity of greeting ceremonies I'd seen, age estimates, and the obvious closeness of their relationship, I believed that Wendy was Whole's mother. Not having known them as youngsters though, it was impossible to be certain. I realised there was a chance that they were merely close sisters or perhaps very close friends.

Among those there that afternoon was Wiona, with a dear little baby girl less than a month old. Full of blind hope, I immediately named her Win because, I thought, the Hwange Estate wildlife *had* won. At least for now.

Other well-known elephants that I'd seen in oestrus before the settler invasions were also giving birth around this time, and it was exciting to see the results of their matings.

It is during and just after the November to March wet season each year, when conditions are at their most favourable, that many of the elephant cows come into oestrus, stimulated by the abundant food and water. It follows therefore – given a gestation period of some 22 months – that after mating in the wet season, their calves will also be born in, or just before, the wet season, two years later.

When the A family appeared at Kanondo I searched for Anne, and found her with a tiny baby. I'd seen her alone with the bulls, clearly in oestrus and in consort with a musth bull named Arthur, on the 29th, 30th, and 31st of March 2003. Her baby, who I named Aimee, had indeed been born 22 months after her rendezvous with Arthur. I calculated there to be a comparatively short interval of three years and two months between Anne's youngest calves (who were probably only half-sisters in actual fact, given that it's unlikely one female's calves, conceived so many years apart, would be fathered by the same bull).

Among Anne's family members there that day were Africa, with a little boy less than a week old, and Askew, also with a young boy approximately six weeks old.

Oestrous females are known to prefer to mate with males in musth, so – given that I knew Arthur came into musth during February every year, and stayed in musth during March and April – it was fairly likely that he'd also fathered the babies of Africa and Askew. Instead of cousins, this would make these three new A family babies half-brothers or half-sisters on their father's side. But, not having seen their parents mating, there's no way I could be sure.

Arriving much later at Kanondo pan was the adult female Adele, easily identifiable by a thin strand of skin that hangs from her ragged right ear, and now sporting a broken right tusk. (Adele was one of the elephants who took an acacia pod from my hand on the odd occasion when one was on offer.) The higher-ranking female named Anya – probably Adele's mother – had already been wandering around the pan for some hours. Adele and Anya were rarely separated, as they had been on this day. Although they were still hundreds of metres apart, I could see them both through my binoculars. Anya quickly became aware that Adele was approaching and I knew instantly what would happen – an elephant greeting ceremony.

The intensity of these ceremonies varies, depending on how long the elephants have been apart and how closely they're related. Even so, they're among the most special things you can witness in the wild. Adele and Anya ran towards each other, their offspring in tow. Loud open-mouthed rumbles filled the air. They urinated and defecated elatedly, waved their ears enthusiastically and pushed their trunks together affectionately. In the excitement of the moment, liquid streamed from their temporal glands. Clearly, they were delighted to be back together again.

While gazing at Anya I noticed that her breasts – which are very human-like on adult female elephants, and are located between the front legs – were full, her form huge. I knew that her youngest calf was at least five years old. Although I didn't see her in oestrus, I fully expected her to give birth any day.

Another of the A family females was, years earlier, named Andrea, after a special Kiwi friend of mine. Andrea's new little calf, born in March, was subsequently named Alessandra, after that same friend's young daughter. I e-mailed a digital image of proud mother and young calf. Andrea's reply drifted back across the ocean, bringing a smile to my face. 'Alessandra is soooo gorgeous,' she wrote. 'In fact I'm not too bad-looking myself! If you have a look between my legs I've got great breasts (not that they should really be between my legs but it's a major size improvement on what I have now!) …'

The M family was at Kanondo too. The gentle giant Misty lost her baby in November 2002, when it was just a few weeks old. In November 2004 Misty gave birth again, to a charming wee boy I named Merlin, confirming that she'd come back into oestrus quickly after losing her previous little one. Misty and Merlin ambled up to my open window just to say hello, and I was relieved to see them both safe and well. Mortality is high during the first few years of life. It was always so sad to notice someone missing, and I often wondered just how many of these little ones died in wire snares.

Wandering among the family groups that day was a musth male, unknown to me. Temporal gland secretion ran down from behind his eyes to his chin, as is usual for a male in full musth. His temporal glands were swollen, as is also usual at this time, but they were swollen to a degree that I'd never seen before. He appeared to have basketballs under his skin, extending from behind to above each eye, gargantuan round 'blisters' that looked ready to explode. His appearance was rather alarming, although his condition didn't seem to be bothering him. He was simply in deep musth. He strode happily among the family groups, dribbling urine and using his trunk to test the adult females for signs of oestrus.

It was a sad fact that I no longer liked to get to know the bulls too well. Tragically, most of the musth bulls that I'd become acquainted with from 2001 to 2003 had disappeared. Significantly, known bulls with small or broken tusks still roamed the estate. I was always pleased to see broken tusks. *All* elephants are magnificent to me, and broken tusks ensured that they were less attractive to the sport-hunters and the poachers.

Occasionally, when I drove down the vlei, the 'tear-stained' faces of the two (semi-resident) male cheetahs popped up unexpectedly from the long green grass, just for a few seconds before disappearing in the lush vegetation. I always looked up and down the vlei, wondering how many other creatures lay hidden in the tall grass.

Luckily for the cheetahs, a troop of baboons was not always around to betray their presence. The predators, I thought, must surely loathe these vigilant creatures. One afternoon a mother cheetah and her two young cubs were relaxing on the vlei. She was a glorious vision of stealth and speed, her cubs picture perfect. Then barks from the baboons echoed around the vlei. This alerted the impalas, ensuring that none of them were on the cheetahs' dinner menu that day.

I dreaded the recommencement of the sport-hunting season, which would soon be underway, fearing that these cheetahs might well wander onto nearby hunting concessions, which could seal their fate –

regardless of whether their kind was on quota.

At Kanondo, a little more than one month after the settlers had left, the antelope were learning once more to enjoy the open pan and mineral lick areas. Although still skittish when vehicles approached too closely, they were slowly regaining confidence in their surroundings. Kudus were often there, as well as impalas, waterbucks, sables and roans. It was a welcome spectacle under stormy skies, a signal that tranquillity was returning.

And my spirit found comfort.

I searched for other signs of life. Two lilac-breasted rollers sunbathed on the sandy road, their colouring even more exquisite with their brilliant blue wings spread. Having had his fill of sun, one sat just above my open rooftop, preening himself and singing with his mouth wide open, a loud, harsh song. Why is it that the most beautiful of birds so often has the least beautiful of calls, I wondered?

A tiny frog sat on a contorted stem of a water lily, then jumped onto one of the stunning flowers as I approached, lingering there momentarily. Would he, I mused, turn into a handsome prince if I kissed him? The ear flapping of a lone musth bull, an 'ear wave' unique to a male in musth, added to the music of the veld.

I was quietly hopeful that all would now be okay.

The weather, though, was not so pleasing. During February and March it was still disagreeably reminiscent of October. Clouds built up mockingly, thunder rumbled in the distance, but little rain fell. The days were extremely hot, surface water sadly lacking. With the wet season rapidly coming to an end, I longed for the rain that we so desperately needed. But still it didn't come.

I recalled having read a book entitled *Sometimes When It Rains* by Keith Meadows, in which an African man is quoted as saying: 'Sometimes when it rains, when it rains really hard, then the bad things get washed away.' I longed for it to rain *really* hard, to wash away all the bad things.

At the end of March my thoughts drifted to Karen Blixen – the author of *Out of Africa*, and one-time owner of a farm at the foot of the Ngong Hills in Kenya – who wrote in 1919, 'I have a feeling that wherever I may be in the future, I will be wondering whether there is rain at Ngong'. Almost a century on, I realised that I had similar feelings. The joy of the rain had crept into my veins too, and now ran there. No matter where I was in the future, I felt sure that I'd always wonder whether there had been rain at Hwange.

The wet season had still not really materialised. Although a child of farmers, I'd acquired no true appreciation for the rain when I was small, except that it meant I could play in the mud. I often noticed my parents on the veranda of our Queensland farmhouse, leaning against the wooden railings, watching a still distant storm – hungry for rain. Yet I didn't fully understand. Years later, while working in the cities, the rain or lack thereof didn't trouble me either. Perhaps there were water restrictions occasionally, but I didn't fret over them unduly. Now, the lack of rain pulled at my heartstrings so intensely that I felt a physical ache in my chest.

Day after day I looked longingly at the heavy dark clouds, from which nothing fell. This year, I felt sure, I would watch the wildlife suffer shortages of water and vegetation. The frogs, from the beginning of this wet season, had been unnervingly quiet. The black cuckoo – 'the rainbird' – didn't sing his song of rain. Did they know something we did not? Did they know the rain wouldn't come? It was nearly April. Unless something unusual happened soon, we couldn't expect rain for another seven long months.

Frequently, in this time of drought, Matabele ants (known by the Ndebele as *impolompolo*) could be seen crossing the sandy roads in long wide columns. These staggering processions of outsized army ants always seemed never-ending, the atmosphere electric with the eerie sound of millions of little legs marching in unison.

In my bathroom area, I often stared at the countless smaller ants that had crawled up the drainpipe and into the concrete tray of my shower. From across the ocean in Queensland I could hear my rural parents saying, as they'd so often said when they spotted ants inside, 'Perhaps it will rain.' When there were many ants, for days on end, they'd say, 'Perhaps it will flood.'

Tired of putting down ant-kill, I scowled at these thousands of ants that kept invading my shower tray, telling them that they were tricksters. But just six hours later the rain began to fall; the best rain we'd had all year. I was at Kanondo, watching (as had become routine that year) the dark heavy storm clouds that encircled me. The wind picked up, the tall yellow grass dancing to a song that I didn't yet recognise. Nothing significant had resulted from equally threatening conditions all year.

The rain came with such force that I laughed out loud, the fat drops pelting my hot skin, as I crawled around inside Nicki Mukuru frantically closing roof and windows. Parked at an angle now, so that all this unfamiliar 'wet stuff' didn't pour into my partially open window, I watched the spectacle. The rain pelted down for over an hour, the trees a few hundred metres away, barely visible.

When it finally reduced to a drizzle, I stepped out of my 4x4 and ran, barefoot and elated, through the many fresh puddles on the road. All the mineral lick excavations were full of water. Two frogs croaked a duet. A family of impalas, still as statues, stood in the light rain with backs arched and tails tucked in tightly, both ears pulled back. Several waterbucks sat in the long grass, chewing their cud, looking exceptionally pleased with themselves. Eight ground hornbills were also celebrating, two of them singing their repetitive duet, which I'd come to love – a deep vibration tangible in the moist air. She (with a blue patch on her bright red throat pouch) provided the first three notes. He (without a blue patch, but with his red throat pouch inflated) provided the final two.

One afternoon of rain wasn't going to solve our water problems, but it was glorious nonetheless. 'Please come again,' I whispered, looking skyward.

Back at the Hwange Safari Lodge an acquaintance uttered his usual greeting, 'Mandlo!' he exclaimed, his head slightly bowed and his hands clasped in a gesture of respect, 'How is Kanondo?'

'*Wet!*' I responded excitedly, punching the air.

But no further rain fell.

Often on the vlei at twilight the sky was filled with a magical light. An elephant family might be there, moving with silent agility while feeding ravenously on the grass, the clouds above them tinted stunningly pink. Impalas, guineafowls and jackals were always going about their evening business. The baboons were often there too, babies straddling their mothers' backs. At this time of year the air was usually still and warm. I'd experienced it all a thousand times before, but no amount of familiarity could breed contempt. So great was the feeling of all-pervading peace which sunset often brought that I stepped out of my 4x4 to savour the moment.

Once again there was beauty and magic in the air – the beauty and magic of wild Africa.

Presidential Elephant sightings, though, continued to be few.

Ominously too, these sightings were now not consistent with their 2001–2003 patterns. While unharassed and with nothing to fear (in these years before the settler invasions), my data confirms that sightings on the Hwange Estate used to be most frequent between the hours of 11am and 3pm. This differed from sightings within Hwange National Park where elephants typically emerge in large numbers just before sunset. Some believe that the reason the National Park elephants drink primarily in the safety of the fading day is that older family members have not forgotten daylight culling operations.

Those Presidential Elephants that were still around had altered their previous routine, now also appearing in the open predominantly at dusk. 'I hope this is not permanent,' I heard myself say out loud to no one. Had these elephants, too, learned to be wary?

I also had other concerns. During the period that the settlers were on the land I'd observed female elephants come into oestrus up to four times before they conceived, instead of the usual once or twice. Was the stress of so much gunfire having a negative impact on elephant conception rates – and perhaps on the conception rates of *all* the wildlife species?

With many unanswered questions rolling around in my mind, I frequently sat on the rooftop of my 4x4 longing for the carefree splendour of times past.

Deadly Snares Galore

Days of carefree splendour were now few and far between.

It was April 2005 when I realised we once again had a serious snaring problem. Some days we seemed to be losing the battle, with wire snares everywhere. Sadly, we were playing 'catch up' after the late-2003 to early-2005 period when the settlers had prohibited patrols. Jabulani and the anti-poaching team once again searched tirelessly, destroying all the snares they came across. Without these men the situation would have been much worse. However, the bush was thick and vast, and they couldn't possibly uncover *every* death trap. They continued to destroy snares and apprehend poachers, and together we carried on liaising with the police, but penalties were simply not harsh enough to deter poachers for long.

Tragically, one morning, I saw yet another snare on a zebra. Thankfully it was a relatively loose copper wire, but it needed to be removed before it tightened around its neck. Once again, though, there was no one available to dart.

I'd suffered this same ache in the pit of my stomach too often over the past few years. I felt downcast and let down, and knew that I should try to do the drugs course myself. (In Zimbabwe one doesn't have to be a vet in order to hold a drugs licence.) However, attending the course is expensive, the dart gun and drugs necessary to always have immediately on hand, even more so. It was hardly a luxury, but it wasn't within my means. Besides, I reminded myself, the darter was not the only important person in this process. It was also the vigilant eyes and ears of others that made many of the snare removals possible, and with Presidential Elephant dartings I was always preoccupied keeping a close eye on known family members.

Incredibly, this snared zebra turned out to be the same one that had been darted in December – the one that suffered the gruesome neck wound. I was certain of this, given her already damaged mane and scar tissue under her neck, but it seemed beyond belief. So I took more digital photographs and compared her stripe pattern with the one on the photos I'd taken before. Every zebra's stripe pattern is unique. There was no doubt. This same zebra had been snared twice in just a few months.

I wished we could temporarily fit just a couple of satellite collars to individuals within those zebra and elephant families that had suffered multiple snare wounds, so their movements could be accurately tracked. This would help to improve the effectiveness of the anti-poaching team, since if we knew exactly which areas were frequented by these families, the men could concentrate on trying to find snares there and destroy them before the animals were caught. Yet again though, costs were prohibitive, so we made wild guesses and deployed the team as best we could.

Many of the snare wounds were truly horrific, and I found myself constantly shocked by the attitudes of some humans. It is only right, I believe, to give a snared animal a chance by removing the wire and treating the wound with antibiotics. The animal has surely been through enough human-inflicted suffering without receiving a gunshot to top it all. So my stance remains that an animal should be put down only if the situation is truly beyond help; an absolute last resort. Many people don't understand why we bother. The snare wound on our unlucky zebra, treated in December, was indeed the worst neck wound that I'd ever seen on a live animal and I had feared for her life, yet she recovered fully. The resilience of these wild creatures is incredible – something I urge others to remember when considering the fate of an injured animal, especially when the damage is human-inflicted.

I could only hope that this second snare didn't wound the zebra again, before the wire could be removed. As it turned out, this wire broke off without human intervention.

Other animals, though, were not so fortunate. Within a few months I was seeing gruesome snare wounds; horrific injuries that were killing the Presidential Elephants.

'We're finding hardly any snares, and we haven't seen a snared animal for a very long time,' declared a spokesman for a nearby anti-poaching unit (which operated in adjoining areas), intent on keeping their reputation intact.

'Well you'd better open your eyes,' was all that I could say.

It was difficult to believe that even some of the so-called 'white conservationists' in the area were denying the problem. It was as though they thought it would reflect badly on them if they acknowledged the truth. So for many long weeks they refused to see it. Some seemed more intent on defending themselves, while trying to discredit me and my attempts to raise awareness. They also tried to discredit the Hwange Estate anti-poaching team. These were the self-important, blind to the input of others. It was a sad fact that most of them spent relatively little time in the field, but thought they knew it all; thought, wrongly, that everything was under control. But eventually no one could deny the snaring problem around Hwange National Park. It was there. And it was getting increasingly worse.

One day at Kanondo there were three elephants with partially severed trunks, one with tendons dangling hideously from what was left of her vital appendage; new wounds that I hadn't seen before. Another day I came upon 80 elephants, from three different Presidential families. Of these, I saw *seven* with shortened or sliced trunks. There was Brandy and Bubble and Bobby's six-year-old son, Bailey. There was Grace and Tarnie's four-year-old daughter, Tabitha, and there were two adult bulls. Some were old injuries, in spite of which the elephants managed remarkably well. Other injuries were reasonably new, and it would be a waiting game to see whether these elephants managed to survive. It was a distressing fact that no Hwange Estate elephants that had lost half or more of their trunk in a snare had ever survived for long.

Calls for assistance started, tragically, to overlap. Over one three-day period, seven different snared animals were seen. How I longed for a period of respite.

The Presidential Elephants were no longer as predictable as they'd once been, making it more difficult to locate the snared ones. When preparing to dart snared Limp back in 2002, I'd told the team that he'd been arriving with his family at Kanondo at midday. We assembled the next day at noon, and the L family arrived just four minutes later. On another day in early 2003 I recall waiting with a friend at Mpofu pan, having told her confidently that the M family was likely to arrive around 2pm. She looked at me doubtfully – these were wild elephants after all. The Ms arrived at 2.03pm.

But the settler invasions had disrupted the elephants' carefree routines.

One morning, at Kanondo, there was a youngster wandering alone. I watched her for hours, not knowing what would be the best thing to do. She was no more than 12 months old and appeared healthy, but without her mother she would not survive for long. With no identifiable ear notches, I couldn't be sure that she was a Presidential Elephant, and there was no way of knowing whether her family would wander by to collect her.

By now I was far from convinced that calves such as these had been abandoned – a term that many choose to use. How can we assume, in unknown family groups, that the mother is still alive and that she has abandoned her calf? In my experience, it's far more likely that the mother of the calf has raced away from gunfire or some other terrifying thing and, in the panic and pandemonium, mother and calf have become separated. Or perhaps the mother is very ill or dead. The lone calf is unlikely to be suckled sufficiently by any of the other elephants within its family, all the breeding females preoccupied with the welfare of their own youngest calves. Although females do suckle each other's calves, there is typically not enough milk to fully sustain a second hungry baby. I suspect that a calf wanders dejectedly, searching for its mother, eventually separating itself from its own family. Finding itself lost and alone, it tries to join other families passing by, but it is unwelcome and lags behind. This appears to the casual observer that it is being abandoned, when in reality, the calf probably doesn't belong to the family it's seen trailing – a foreign family not interested in adopting it. In all likelihood the lone calf, and indeed its mother, has a horror story that we cannot know.

By early evening many families had come and gone and I could no longer see the lone calf. I'd heard many greeting ceremonies throughout the day and hoped that by some miracle the calf had found her mother. Without her, she was sure to die.

Just a few days later I came across a three-year-old named Plucka, from the P family, with the most horrific leg snare. Plucka was thin and thirsty and could put no weight on her foot. Her lower leg was hideously gashed and raw, repugnantly swollen from the tight wire. But it was too late in the day to dart.

I was sickened and disheartened.

The next day I waited at Kanondo hoping that the P family would arrive again. And arrive they did – but *without* Plucka and her mother Priscilla. I stayed on for hours. Every time I heard a rustle, I looked hopefully into the bush, but they didn't appear. There was a rainbow in the sky. The three-quarter moon had risen in the east and the sinking sun had given a purple hue to the heavy cloud in the western sky. There may have been beauty, but there was no sign of Priscilla and Plucka.

I couldn't accept that Plucka might already be dead. After seeing her snared for the first time just the day before, that would be too cruel. Yet where were they? The family had stayed around the Kanondo area for the past 24 hours. Tuskless Precious, who was always close by Priscilla, had been there. Clearly there was something very wrong for Priscilla and Plucka not to have arrived to drink with the others.

Cousin Pookie was there, with mother Paula, to lift my spirit just a little. Three years before, Pookie, then only a few months old, had been the victim of a dreadful head snare. It was a wire wrapped tightly under her chin, running up to her ear, culminating in a disgusting bow of wire on top of her head. Mercifully, that snare somehow managed to break off without intervention, no doubt with assistance from Paula. Pookie had only a badly deformed left ear in memory of this awful ordeal. She was one of the 'lucky' ones.

The next day, I decided, I would try again to find Plucka, praying that I wouldn't see any vultures in the meantime.

After driving the sandy roads I sat alone, waiting at Kanondo, hoping that she would reappear. It was too difficult to write, or read, or do anything other than wait, and the wait was long. At 4.40pm

Priscilla finally appeared – without Plucka. Overcome by emotion, I watched Priscilla drink. She should not be without her youngest calf, and I imagined the worst. But 10 minutes later Plucka, having great difficulty walking now, appeared at the tree line. The snare wound was truly horrific. Without hesitation, I drove back to the Hwange Safari Lodge with reckless speed (our radios not operational once again), to ring Jerry, a darter I'd got to know quite well. By then it was five o'clock. As Jerry had no immediate access to a vehicle, he decided it was too late for him to try to get to Kanondo, prepare the darts required for mother and calf, and carry out the operation. At this time of year it was already dark by 6 o'clock, and I cursed the onset of winter with its shortened days.

I returned to Kanondo in the sunset, disappointed and dejected, but hopeful in the knowledge that Jerry (and rifle support) had agreed to wait *with* me in the field the following day from 3.30pm. This was the only way to avoid delays in getting to any snared animal. I drove among the P family while little Plucka stood beside her mother with her foot raised. As this was not one of the very habituated Presidential Elephant families, I wanted them to become more accustomed to my voice and my vehicle.

The next afternoon we waited as a team – me in Nicki Mukuru, Jerry, rifle support and a back-up vehicle – ready to carry out the operation. Incessantly, I watched the sun lowering itself in the western sky. We could hear rustles in the bush nearby.

'What time is it?' I asked.

'Five o'clock.'

Hours seemed to pass.

'What time is it?'

'Five minutes past five.'

More hours seemed to pass.

'What time is it?'

'It's six minutes after you last asked,' Jerry answered softly, smiling sympathetically.

I got the message.

The first of the P family arrived at 5.20pm. If only Plucka had appeared then, we were determined to try darting in the failing light. There was, however, no sign of her or her mother, although I felt sure that they must still be around.

The following afternoon we all waited once again. The W family appeared in the late afternoon and, in an attempt to add a little relief to our anxious wait, I took Jerry to meet Whole. Jerry is an ex-National Parks warden, with many years of bush experience. He has shot many an elephant. It was he who I'd rung for darting assistance just before Wholesome died before my eyes the previous year.

We approached to within a few metres of Whole, who initially reacted with a little concern at the sight and smell of this strange person in my 4x4. I crooned to her, calling her by name, 'Hey Whole. Good girl Whole. Come here girl.'

She loomed large towards the passenger side window, stopping just half a metre away. Jerry took a deep breath and froze, peeping at her only out of the corner of his eyes.

'It's *toooo* close,' he whispered to me anxiously, barely game to move his lips.

I put my hand on his arm in reassurance (resisting the urge to tell him that Whole was not an 'it'), and left it there while I continued to croon. 'Hey, Whole. Hey my girl. Good girl Whole.' Jerry relaxed a little and looked into Whole's eyes. He was clearly awestruck.

When eventually we pulled away from Whole, his first words were, 'Could I bring my family one day?' This is what it's all about. These extraordinary Presidential Elephants of Zimbabwe.

'Those pupils!' he exclaimed, still clearly spellbound. 'We looked each other straight in the eye. Imagine!' Jerry would not forget his encounter with Whole, the first wild, fully alert, *live* elephant he'd observed at such close quarters.

The excitement quickly subsided when the first of the P family appeared.

'What time is it?'

How I hated the answers to these questions. It was 5.30pm. It was too late yet again. We needed at least 45 minutes of daylight, and even by nightfall Plucka and her mother had not appeared from the bush.

Were they merely moving slowly, impaired by the injury, well behind the other family members? Or had the family group split? Was Plucka still alive? It was unusual to see the same family at the same pan for five days in a row, although it wasn't unusual for elephants to restrict their wanderings when there was an injured family member. Nor was it unusual for a family to stay by a dead member for several days before moving off. I simply didn't know what to think.

Determined to keep trying, we returned the next day. But the same scenario repeated itself yet again. During the afternoon we saw a little two-year-old in the F family with no trunk to speak of, appallingly left behind in a snare, but there was nothing we could do right now for him. Jerry left for home, and I waited alone after dark with a spotlight, to see if Plucka came to drink. The Southern Cross was already high in the sky when the full fiery moon rose to the right of a big old acacia tree. I wished that I could appreciate the beauty a little more, but my heart was heavy.

The skittish buffalos, which had arrived in the late afternoon, finally drank at the pan. I couldn't see any wires, although I knew that six snared buffalos had previously been seen, but in which herds, I had no idea. Unlike the elephants, I didn't know the buffalo herds well enough to distinguish between them.

Eventually Pookie, with her torn left ear, arrived with her mother well after dark, as did other P family members. By 8pm it was freezing and my spotlight was fading. The members of the P family that had arrived earlier were now out of sight. Perhaps other Ps would still appear, but I decided dejectedly to go home. Although the moon was shedding light it had become difficult to distinguish ear patterns, and difficult therefore to make positive identifications. There was still no sign of Plucka or her mother, but the P family was definitely still in the same area. At least some of them were.

The same thing happened on the seventh day, when I waited alone at Kanondo yet again, driving intermittently to nearby watering areas and up and down nearby roads.

Now I was losing hope, but I continued to try.

Another four days passed. During the first two, the partial P family continued to arrive at Kanondo pan, and I kept searching neighbouring areas alone. And then there was no sign of the P family at all. Now, they had *all* moved off.

Was Plucka still alive? Was she still suffering that horrific injury?

I couldn't know for sure, although I seriously doubted that she was still alive. Her family was a group that, in past years, I'd typically seen only once every week or two. Since the settler invasions, encounters had become even less frequent – all of the elephants still regaining confidence and trust after the disturbing events of late-2003 and 2004. I realised that I may not know for an agonisingly long time.

I wished little Plucka no pain. I wished that I had not seen.

Plucka was never seen again.

Grim Future

The areas of Kanondo and Khatshana had been returned, but there were countless other struggles to cope with, in addition to the snaring.

'I'm taking the old Dete Road,' one of the helpers called to me one bushfire-filled evening, over the drone of our 4x4 engines. 'Watch out for me on your way home. I'm running on air.'

Keeping a watchful eye on the needle of my own fuel gauge, I drove home with the setting sun – a ball of hazy fire cloaked by a glowing aura of orange – behind me, and the almost full moon – round and hazy pink – ahead. I looked again at my fuel gauge. The cost of black market fuel was crippling me, talk of assistance rarely materialising, and I wondered how much longer I could keep this up.

When unable to source a delivery of fuel I sometimes had no choice but to queue in the town of Dete, 40 kilometres return journey from my rondavel, on the very odd occasions when this filling station actually had fuel.

'How long is the queue?' I always enquired.

Every time, the response was the same – 'Arrhhh, it is not very long.'

I'm not sure why I bothered to ask, since I'd always sit in the queue for at least five hours, wondering if I was patient by nature. Being out in the field with elephants for thousands and thousands of hours, perhaps I'd learned to be. In queues, though, I was always restless. This, I did not enjoy. I suspected that I was allergic to the absence of elephants!

The queue *ahead* kept lengthening, vehicles constantly barging in. 'It is our culture. You put a stone. You come back later.' What sort of culture is that, I wondered?

One time, a policeman – smartly dressed with a hat, belt and other finery – stopped by my vehicle to chat. (By now I'd come to know the police force quite well.) 'Arrhhh, Pincott,' he said, extending his hand. 'How are you?'

Given the circumstances, I didn't bother to tell him how I was, so I simply replied that I didn't like fuel queues.

'Arrhhh, but you are close now,' he assured me. Yes, I could *see* the pump now – but I was still two hours away. Why did this queue barely move, I cursed? I gazed at the old bakery to my left. Gone were the days when you could buy greasy cream buns and sweet rolls. Now it was impossible even to buy bread, the doors tightly closed. Across the road, shabby square shops of brick and tin were brightly painted, attempting to disguise, perhaps, all that was *not* available within.

By the time I reached the pump they were no longer selling a full tank of fuel. It was being rationed to 40 litres. Five hours for a mere 40 litres. What could I do but sigh and try to smile? This was Zimbabwe after all.

And still there were more problems threatening to devastate this wildlife paradise.

I'd never been to court before, and certainly not to an African court. There were people everywhere. I arrived under police escort, in June 2005, but I was not the accused. By now even the police force, and some members of the CIO, were concerned about the actions of the settlers, and when I was assaulted by the son of the head settler, a man of about 30, senior officials encouraged me to prosecute. It was odd, I suppose, that now they were on *my* side. Clearly, some of them had been spoken to by higher powers. To ensure that I got to court, and got there safely, the police had collected me and driven me the 90 kilometres to the courthouse.

The settlers were, frustratingly, still in the area of the Presidential Elephants. The head settler had allocated yet another prime piece of land to his family; a small area sandwiched between two nearby photographic safari lodges on the vlei. And once again they'd managed to secure a quota to sport-hunt. So although they'd moved out of Kanondo and Khatshana, they were still around and they were still causing problems. Together with other concerned people, I'd been urging for this third hunting quota to be withdrawn, but in the meantime they continued to hunt.

They drove in their private vehicles, and in hunting vehicles with clients, up and down the vlei, among tourists who'd come to see *live* animals, not dead ones. The very last thing, I knew, that any photographic tourist wanted to see was hunters, guns and slaughtered animals. When I saw this young settler once again driving towards the gate to the tourist vlei, I approached him on foot. After greeting him, I reminded him as politely as I could, that these were private roads, which he had no approval to use. I asked that he park his vehicle, and go and speak to the General Manager of the Safari Lodge about the situation.

Already angry about his family losing Kanondo and Khatshana (land that was, clearly, never theirs to lose), and holding me primarily responsible for this happening, he responded by thrusting his arm through his open window and punching me under my chin.

The incident left me shaken, but not seriously hurt. By now I expected no less of these men.

Inside the courthouse there was a hushed atmosphere. Both the waiting area and the courtrooms were spartan and chilly. Perhaps for my benefit, the proceedings were held in English. Without the accused present, I was asked to give my version of events. To my surprise the magistrate was writing everything down in longhand on a sheet of paper. I slowed my words, and finished my account. I was not cross-examined. Then it was the turn of the accused. He did himself no favours, initially denying that he'd assaulted me, and then constantly contradicting himself, his story making little sense.

Unusually perhaps – in a country where many are intimidated by those who wield political clout – the magistrate took no account of the accused's family connections. And justice prevailed.

The court system in Zimbabwe works strangely though. The accused, as always, got to *choose* his punishment. He was asked to choose between community service, a fine, or jail. Naturally, with plenty of money at his disposal, he chose to pay a fine. But, once again, he had the wrong magistrate.

'You are too rich. A fine will not hurt you,' said the magistrate. 'You'll learn nothing from a fine.'

So, for assault, he was sentenced to 40 hours of community service, cleaning in a clinic. I imagined that he'd never cleaned anything in his life. The African spectators in the courtroom were perhaps thinking the same thing, since murmurs and chuckles filled the air. I sat quietly, displaying no emotion.

Words from *Out of Africa* subsequently played over and over in my mind: 'If I know a song of Africa... does Africa know a song of me? ... would the eagles of Ngong look out for me?'

While the magistrate's decisions were right and commendable, they came as a surprise, and I wondered pensively whether Kanondo's eagles would now look out for me.

Back in the field, the presence of these settlers was haunting me still. They hadn't paid their Kanondo water bill for any of the 16 months that they'd been on the land, and the water had been disconnected without warning. The innocent wildlife were being punished yet again.

The settlers and their cronies kept popping up from nowhere. A little later in 2005, when the existing sport-hunting quota for the piece of land sandwiched between the two photographic lodges looked certain to be withdrawn by the Minister of Tourism, another unwelcome visitor arrived, practising his art of intimidation. A so-called 'professional hunter', this was one of the men who brought in hunting clients for the settlers. Clearly he had inside information and knew that this hunting quota was about to be withdrawn.

'You are causing us too much trouble. Do you understand?' he spat at me, his face just centimetres from my own. Too angry to care, he hadn't chosen his venue well. He had cornered me in the Hwange Safari Lodge, and there were staff all around. There were many witnesses.

Mustering all my self-control, I told him calmly that he was speaking to the wrong person; that I would find the General Manager for him. But he wasn't interested in speaking to anybody else. Ultimately he blurted out, 'You're just a f*cking white. F*cking white trash.' I looked him in the eye, slowly raised an eyebrow, and managed an incredulous snigger. Was that the best he could come up with?

By now I'd had enough, yet when I moved to walk away – uninterested in his ranting and racist name-calling – he herded me, just like I'd recently been herding a snared buffalo, and used his shoulder to impede my free movement. I could only shake my head and frown, and report the incident, which I immediately did to numerous people.

This is how unethical hunters acted at their most desperate. And this, on top of the dreadful snaring, I really didn't need.

Concerned people asked, 'Is this worth risking your life for?' I never allowed myself time to ponder an answer, although I agreed that I was of no use to the elephants as a martyr.

Not long afterwards, this sandwiched piece of land was the cause of additional concern.

It was a few months earlier (while searching for Plucka) that I'd first seen this F family youngster, his trunk ripped off by a wire snare. He was born to the Presidential Elephants in early February 2003, making him not yet three years old. Due to all that had happened in the years following his birth, he'd remained nameless. While still suckling from his mother during these past few months, he had stayed fat and seemingly healthy. But, having only a short section of trunk, unless he could adapt and become a browser, he had no chance of long-term survival. He was yet another innocent snare victim.

The next wave of tragedy struck earlier than expected. I was driving along the vlei, thinking about an approaching bushfire, smoke choking the distant air, when there he was. Alone. Abandoned – or had something happened to his mother? I could not believe that he'd been abandoned since his mother, Freida, had always been particularly protective of him, both before and after he was cruelly stripped of his trunk. The last time I'd seen them, less than two weeks before, Freida had been unconditionally tolerant of his suckling. Something seemed wrong. I would look for Freida later. Right now all I could think of was trying to save this little Presidential Elephant. He was much too young to be wandering alone, and he had no trunk to speak of. Without his mother he had absolutely no chance of survival in the wild. He was already agonisingly thin and lethargic. Clearly, he'd been wandering alone – traumatised and unseen – for some time.

I stepped out of my 4x4 and walked towards him, calling to him, remembering a newborn elephant found alone by a roadside in 2003 that had walked straight up to me, frantically trying to suckle from my arm. This little fellow, though, was older and much less trusting. He attempted a mock charge, forcing me to sidestep behind a bush. Even almost-three-year-old elephants in a weakened state could inflict harm. It would have been comical I suppose, if it hadn't been so tragic. I tried to tempt him with some *Acacia erioloba* pods, imagining that he could get down on his knees and feed with his mouth, but he just didn't know what to do with them.

By now it was late in the day. I had no choice but to leave him, praying to invisible forces that he would, in his vulnerable and fragile state, survive the night. I needed to make the necessary arrangements. He deserved a chance. We surely had to try to save him.

Plans were in place quickly. The Parks Authority gave permission for us to capture him and transfer him to a captive facility in Victoria Falls, which had kindly agreed to take him. There, at least, he would be given a chance to live – an ambassador for the Presidential Elephants, and for snare victims everywhere.

To be able to capture him though, we would have to find him again. When I'd left him in the late afternoon, he'd been heading slowly down the vlei, towards the land between the two photographic lodges. This was far from comforting knowledge. How could this little elephant know that this small piece of the vlei was currently off-limits to us all? This was the piece of land that none of us was permitted to drive across, a stance the settlers had angrily reaffirmed just a few days before. It encompassed a section of the dusty road that linked these photographic lodges with the rest of the Hwange Estate; a section of the road that had, for scores of years, been used by photographic game-drive vehicles. I imagined our little snare victim wandering, unknowingly, to this small section of sandwiched land. I imagined us needing to cross this land, leading to yet another confrontation. I was tired at just the thought of it. There always seemed to be *something*.

'If you have a problem, speak to the President…' I found myself preparing these words silently under my breath, in anticipation of yet another hostile encounter.

In the early morning I drove along the vlei searching for him, but I couldn't find him. I then asked Jabulani and the anti-poaching unit to track his spoor. It was after midday when the radio call I'd impatiently been waiting for finally came in.

Thankfully my fears had not materialised overnight. The little Presidential Elephant hadn't quite reached the claimed section of land, a hiccup in his key home range. It was a potential problem that we didn't have to face. This time.

Many had become aware of this little F family calf. I'd decided to name him Future – for the future of the Presidential Elephants, and the future of anti-poaching/snare-destruction efforts everywhere.

Some members of the Victoria Falls anti-poaching unit, and others from a facility named Elephant Camp, were immediately on their way to assist with the darting and transportation to Victoria Falls. It became necessary for me to make last minute phone calls and give further explanations, but no one tried to impede the process. Permits such as these take time, usually a very long time, but cooperation was at its best. Future was weak and any delays would certainly cost him his life.

The team arrived from Victoria Falls after a two-hour drive. The Parks Authority scouts arrived with the transportation crate. 'Will he fit in there?' I murmured, concerned.

We needed to get down the vlei. Time was running out. With a convoy of helpers in tow, we finally arrived at the place where Future was being watched. No one could tell for sure, but it was decided that the crate was in fact not tall enough. There was a frantic dash back to the Hwange Safari Lodge to find a way of cutting the top off this sturdy crate. I stayed on the vlei, concerned that the day was fading fast. Those four terrible words, 'What time is it?' were haunting me once more. I looked at my watch again and again.

Finally the radio call came in. They were on their way back down the vlei with the modified crate. It was 5.35pm. Soon the sun would set. There was no time to lose. I gave the go-ahead and the darter immediately took aim, with a reduced amount of immobilisation drug. In his weakened state, there was always a chance that Future would not survive the drug. Soon he was down. He was even thinner than I'd realised. His skin lacked lustre and his trunk was so tragically short. His breathing and heartbeat were being closely monitored. I knelt down beside him and, while touching him with my hand, whispered a quiet prayer to the god of wild things.

The helpers now moved in. A path had to be cleared to where Future was lying in the bush; the truck carrying the crate had to be reversed in; Future had to be lifted by scores of able-bodied hands onto the back of the truck; and then he had to be pushed into the crate.

Later, under moonlight, the loading work successfully complete, I looked up at little Future, his head well above the top of the crate, thankful for the foresight of others. I stepped up onto the back of the truck, placed my hand against his shortened nose, and once again wished him well.

We headed back up the vlei in darkness. Future was to be immediately transported to Victoria Falls. I watched him standing in the crate on the back of the truck, heading out of the Safari Lodge boom-gate towards his new life.

My chest was tight with quiet hope.

I telephoned the next morning to confirm that Future had indeed survived the night-time journey. Everyone was asking about his welfare. There was quiet jubilation and excited hope that he would now survive.

But Future was just too weak. Despite gallant efforts, and a drip to help him regain his strength, Future died the next evening at 6.30pm.

And a little piece of me died with him.

His mother, Freida, was never seen again.

Revival

During the trying times, I took comfort in friends, both human and non-human. While taking nothing away from the human friendships that I hold dear, the words written to me by Miriam – my American girlfriend living in Harare – rang true, 'You are happiest when among your wild friends.'

She understands me well. When among my wild friends, there's a quiet in my soul.

There were times, during and after the settler invasions, that I saw Lady and her family only once every few months. Expecting Lady to give birth during the first half of 2005, I looked for her every day, but month after month there was no sign of her and her family.

Then one day, after three months had passed, I came upon them at Kanondo. I was so relieved to see them and looked expectantly for the tiny baby that I thought might be among them. But the baby was still in Lady's belly, I could see that for certain. She was huge, her breasts full.

I pulled up just one metre from Lady while she continued, on her knees, to use her tusks to break away large chunks of minerals. In her heavily pregnant state she couldn't get enough of them. Clearly, pregnancy cravings are not limited to humankind. Lady had not seen me for three whole months, and she was completely ignoring me. Too busy eating minerals. I was indignant – but secretly honoured that a wild elephant could ignore my close presence so totally. I talked to her while she ate, telling her that I couldn't believe she didn't want to extend her usual warm hello to me; telling her too, with only a touch of sarcasm, that I was most hurt. But clearly, right now, she was a woman with priorities.

After about five minutes, having had her fill of minerals, she put her trunk inside the window of Nicki Mukuru, and gave me a friendly throaty rumble.

'Finally!' I exclaimed, my hand rubbing her trunk.

I told her that she was wicked. I told her, too, that she had a baby in her belly. She shook her huge head in response, her ears flapping like sails in the wind, as if to say, 'I've been carrying this 120 kilogram burden for 22 long months, don't you think I *know* that?'

She must surely, I assessed, give birth any day.

Less than two weeks later I was cursing the fact that a flat tyre had delayed me while I was observing a mating pair in Acacia Grove, but after crawling around in deep sand, keeping a close eye on those elephants only a few metres away that were keeping a close eye on me, I managed to get myself mobile again. Filthy now, covered in sand and grease, I drove on, frustrated that I'd lost sight of the oestrous female.

Then, after only a few hundred metres, I came upon something so much better and immediately felt extremely grateful for the flat tyre that had delayed me. It was Lady – and she had a tiny baby girl in tow. I was as thrilled as a surrogate mother would be. Lady brought her newborn to my 4x4, the little one oblivious to what this metal monster was before her, and suddenly there was a tiny trunk pressed up against my door.

'Look at your baby! You've got a *baby*,' I crooned to Lady, over and over again.

This was the most adorable elephant calf I'd ever seen, still very pink behind the ears, with bright blue eyes. Led astray by her two five-month-old cousins (Litchis, son of Leanne; and Laurie, son of Louise), at no more than 10 days old, she left her mother's side to fool around with them. She was unusually adventurous for such a young elephant and Lady made no attempt to curtail her wanderings. Beside her mother's huge form, she looked like a tiny doll, no bigger than Lady's ears. The whites of her eyes were, unusually, very prominent, giving her a permanently 'surprised' look. The soles of her feet were a very pale pink.

She was wonderful.

Carol was given the privilege of naming Lady's baby, a task that she agonised over for many days. At night she tossed and turned and deliberated, and tossed and turned again. She imagined me, out in the field, crooning to this young elephant, and needed her name to be special. And special it is.

Carol eventually named her Liberté; Libby for short.

Libby constantly surprised me. She was unquestionably the most adventurous little tot that I'd ever seen. Just like the entire L family, she will always be precious to me.

It was Andrea, my precious friend from New Zealand, who once e-mailed me to say, 'It's a movie title that I think of, when I think of you – *A Life Less Ordinary.*'

They were four words that struck a chord deep in my heart.

It was true that my life was less ordinary than it had once been, yet there were no hidden secrets, no mysterious skeletons lurking in a closet, no embellishments of the truth. I was no longer interested in making a living. Instead, I wanted to make a *life*.

It was simply the call of the wild that had first attracted me; the irresistible lure of the African wilderness – and the African elephants – that held me here. Previously, I'd enjoyed an ordinary existence, but now I lived an extraordinary safari.

Nonetheless, some liked to imply that, after all this time, I must surely be losing my grip on reality. A (rather contrary) acquaintance from Bulawayo once asked me, 'Have you been in the bush too long?' I had, I realised, come to enjoy life in a certain way – in a way that might not be considered 'normal' by some.

There were certainly times when I craved the lively and stimulating company of close friends far away, yet when given the opportunity to socialise I often now chose to avoid places with too many people, too much noise, too much talk – comfortable in my own presence. My senses sharpened by years of solitude, I found that I was quickly able to discern people's personalities: warm, generous, kind, gentle, humble, interesting. But there was also that other irritating breed: egotistical, self-important, overbearing, know-all, green-eyed. I realised I'd lost the capacity to endure unpleasant and negative behaviours. I recognised, too, that I'd lost the capacity, and the desire, to pretend; to act as if such forces are bearable. I had also lost the need to engage in endless small talk. I would sit back and listen, or sit back and let my mind wander. I was always keen to retreat into the field, into my solitude, in love with the natural world around me. It was where I was happiest.

Been in the bush too long? Perhaps, I thought, some have been in the *cities* for far too long!

When I felt alone in the world, it was my mates Down Under who I tended to miss most. They always helped, perhaps unknowingly, to bring balance to my bush life. So very far away, it was e-mail that allowed me to spend time with them.

Life in the bush without the luxury of e-mail would, I think now, be especially tough. I can't imagine the isolation that Dian Fossey, of *Gorillas in the Mist* fame, must have felt without it, while living primarily alone, in the remote Virunga Mountains in Rwanda for 13 years (before being murdered in 1985 – possibly by a paid killer). In those days, her only contact with the outside world was via a slow and unreliable postal system. After her first year or two living in the rainforest – as her new world became more routine – this must have made things particularly difficult. While in some respects the passing years do make bush life easier, in other ways they tend to make the isolation more apparent. It's easy to forget that there's a world beyond the bush – and easy, too, to become so very out of touch, especially when there's no e-mail to connect you to the outside world.

While some of my friends were having baby showers to welcome new arrivals, I was in the bush, celebrating the birth of my elephant friend's daughter Libby. The contrast between my life and those of my friends was, to say the least, startling. E-mails helped to bridge the gap, and brought me news of a life I used to know – of distant places, of parties, of corporate life, family life, love lives, shopping, fashions and food, and of world news and opinion. Every e-mail danced with dreams and ambitions, bringing a different perspective, highlighting different personalities and priorities, and asking different questions. I appreciated them all.

Three e-mails from dear (but very different) Kiwi girlfriends –

Andrea, Bobby and Eileen – underlined the diversity and reminded me of my former life – a world away, a lifetime ago.

'Don't we lead such *different* lives!' I exclaimed in my response to Andrea. When I thought more about this a little later, surrounded by the vastness of wild Africa, it seemed strange that less than 10 years before we'd led such *similar* lives. We jetted around the world together on business – Hong Kong, the UK, Scotland, Holland, Japan, Australia and within New Zealand – making recommendations for major system installations. We flew first-class, in the air and on the ground, never doing without. We giggled together during lunches overlooking the Auckland harbour, feasting on fresh seafood and award-winning wine, sharing secrets and just occasionally leaving our professionalism behind. Now she is the doting mother of two, living in a sprawling home, self-designed with tender love and care, with green rolling hills all around. She successfully juggles family life and a thriving career, and speaks still of remarkable parties and First World fun and adventure.

It was a note from Bobby that ignited a momentary ache in my chest. She and her husband had flown from the North Island to the South Island for dinner at an exceptional Greek restaurant, discovered the previous year. Occasionally, there were days when I dreamed of enjoying that sort of extravagance again.

My mind wandered back to the early 1990s. Once, when my live-in partner had been in New York on business for some weeks, he'd phoned me from his plush hotel room overlooking Central Park. 'Meet me in New York on Saturday. We'll have dinner, and go on to the theatre,' he urged. I thought about it for just one minute – and flew part-way around the world, from New Zealand to New York, for dinner. We never did make it to the theatre!

In her e-mail, Eileen mentioned (rather casually) an offsite staff meeting, sailing the vast Auckland harbour onboard an America's Cup yacht. From land-locked Zimbabwe, in the midst of a drought, I felt a pang in my heart at the thought of all that water, and all that luxury. I used to sail that same harbour – and the Sydney harbour too – champagne in hand, a million years ago.

Having read my nightly e-mails, I would crawl into my sofa bed on the floor of my rondavel, in a space not much bigger than my walk-in wardrobe used to be, having eaten a meal of three-minute noodles – with 'All Gold' sweet chilli sauce! – my thoughts with the wildlife. (Were all these things *really* going on in distant lands?) And I always felt a deep contentment – despite the many struggles – like I'd experienced in no other place.

I was even content on my birthdays, despite rarely having any celebratory food to enjoy. E-mails always arrived from Down Under to bring a smile to my face.

'Did you manage a cake? ... candle? ... *cupcake?*,' wrote Bobby one year, making me grin at her own lowered expectations.

I have another kind friend named Mandy (who lives in Melbourne), who sometimes sent me tapes filled with music for my birthday. I played them countless times. 'Born to Try' by Delta Goodrem would regularly pierce the silence, warming my little rondavel – and my heart. Mandy had chosen this song specially, with the accompanying explanation: 'You made choices about changing your life that weren't easy, sacrificing a life of luxury and security... Keep loving what you do.'

Born to try? I pondered. Perhaps this was so, but in truth it could all sometimes be intensely *trying*.

Friends closer to home, in Bulawayo and Harare, also helped me sustain a balance. In the early days I used to truly loathe leaving the bush to spend a necessary few days in town, but as the years passed and the problems grew frightening, I tended to look forward to these few days away. I would get a little 'bush crazy', distressing events making me feel that I'd had my fill of bush life, at least for a couple of days. I'd catch up with mates in Bulawayo, often staying with Shaynie, and there I would make an effort to relax – enjoying videos, pizza, ice cream and other necessities of life!

Sometimes I felt that I simply could not see one more snared animal when there was no darting assistance immediately available. I saw the injuries of the suffering snare victims and the expressions on their innocent faces, playing over and over in my mind, day and night. Occasionally, I just had to take a break from it all; take time to regain focus and strength; take time to have field radios, laptop and 4x4 repaired. However, I was sorely aware that I spent more dedicated time in the field on a daily basis, on this land bordering Hwange National Park, than did any other person. I agonised that new snares would go unseen; that more animals would suffer; that they would not be saved.

With thoughtful concern, a friend reminded me of the words that author Erma Bombeck once wrote, looking back over her life when it was too late to change anything: 'I would have [done what I needed to do for myself],' Erma wrote, 'instead of pretending the earth would go into a holding pattern if I weren't there for the day.'

It could not matter, I came to realise, if I would not be in the field for a day, a week, or two. I couldn't *always* be there.

I recalled, too, other wise words from Erma Bombeck: 'I would have burned the pink candle sculpted like a rose before it melted in storage.' With these sentiments in mind, I decided that I needed to allow myself to take pleasure in some extra little things while there was still an opportunity to enjoy them, before it was too late.

One weekend not long after, I found myself at a friend's fashionable home in Bulawayo where there were soft carpets, scented candles, exquisite ornaments, soothing music and a warming fire. I held a glass of wine in my hand. Memories of my former life flooded back; a life packed away in boxes in a room in Australia; a life that I knew I'd never return to, at least not with the same extravagance. Although feeling a little alien, a little melancholy, I allowed myself to enjoy it all once again. One day, I realised, mesmerised by the welcoming flames of the log fire, I would need to rummage through all those boxes, filled with memories of distant places and people. Now, though, there were intense new memories, lessening the need for even the most special mementos of the past. I no longer needed so many material reminders, having learned that material things quickly lose their importance.

I went on to Harare and wandered around Carol's garden; listened to bird song; stopped, literally, to smell the roses. With the overwhelming sweet smell of gardenia lingering in the air, I savoured fine food and small luxuries.

Carol and I sat quietly, reminiscing about a special encounter we'd enjoyed together at Kanondo, before the settler invasions. A glossy black-coated sable bull, with massive sweeping horns, had walked so very close to my 4x4, while we watched, silent and awed. Then he sat down on the ground, just a few metres away, totally at ease in our presence. I recalled, too, the warthog families that once grazed right beside my vehicle. It was these sorts of memorable encounters, now lost, that I longed to experience once again. But, the wildlife was no longer this trusting.

Despite the heartache of the poaching and the ongoing settler problems, I longed to be back in the bush with the elephants. Everywhere else was not my Africa. Everywhere else I didn't *really* belong.

Before I left Harare I paid a visit to a colleague who's a little older than I am, and leads a life filled with the conviction of his beliefs. We sat and chatted for an hour or two and then, as we hugged goodbye, he uttered just three words. 'You're my hero,' he said to me. At the time I felt awkward, shaking my head to dispel the embarrassment. Driving away, alone with my thoughts, the embarrassment subsided. Then, I felt humbled. I'd never been anyone's hero.

Before returning to the bush I was briefly back in Bulawayo, buying last minute supplies. So many things were 'short', as was frequently the case. Saying 'in short supply' is too much trouble in Zimbabwe. To the Zimbabweans, things are just 'short'.

Bread was short; cooking oil was short; sugar was short; flour was short; butter and margarine were short; soft drinks were short; crisps were short; long-life milk was short; tinned goods were short; soap was short; toothpaste was short; brake fluid was short; engine oil was short... and fuel was shortest of all.

A little billboard, advertising the small piles of newspapers for sale on the pavements, caught my eye. I frowned and tilted my head to one side.

'Shortage of shovels delays burials,' it read.

This time when I shook my head, it wasn't to chase away embarrassment, but to chase away disbelief. I found myself mumbling to nobody: 'You surely can't be serious.' Yet it was true. Even shovels were short.

I arrived back in the bush to find there was no water. *Four days* with no water. Perhaps, I thought fleetingly, being in the cities was not so bad after all. At least there had been only water restrictions there. And power rationing.

That night, four bull elephants once again defied the electric fence (perhaps, as happens, a forgetful someone neglected to switch it on), and immediately began to create havoc just two metres from the wall of my rondavel. Even I, who'd spent years just centimetres from hundreds of elephants, was surprised by how intimidated I felt with unknown elephants so close in the darkness. My high-pitched air-horn (used to scare away unwelcome beasties) by now kaput, I stepped outside, awed by their enormous size and vigorously banged two pots together. A horribly loud clanging resounded around me. I only managed half a smile when these grey giants merely stared down at me from across my thatched fence – a barrier that I was agonisingly aware they could stride through without effort.

'What's *your* problem?' I imagined them saying to me.

I retreated inside and closed the door, resigned to their too-close presence, yet feeling decidedly uncomfortable. Branches cracked and broke. They were clearly enjoying a veritable feast out there.

'Please don't demolish my coral creeper – again,' I begged silently.

I was cold and longed to have a bucket-wash, with water carried from afar. I was aware though, that my waste-water drained into the ground right where the 'kings of the jungle' were standing. I feared that this scarce resource would entice them to stay longer. I feared, too, for my small hot water geyser, sitting precariously above the ground on old wobbly wooden beams. One giant elephant step in the wrong direction and it would surely come toppling down. So I went to bed without a wash, hoping that I'd still have a geyser in the morning. A hot water system is, after all, indispensable on cold winter nights – when there's water.

Well after midnight, I was rudely awoken by an extraordinarily loud munching sound. The thumping of my heart ensured that I stayed awake. The elephants had moved to the other side of my rondavel. They'd walked over wire fences, and were, I assessed, in my neighbour's backyard, even closer now to the circular wall of my little home. Wrapped in a blanket on my sofa bed on the floor, I calculated that the one munching so loudly must be less than two metres from my head. His great weight against the wall of my rondavel would be enough to bring it crashing down – with me inside.

I climbed out of bed and (rather futilely) put my laptop under layers of soft pillows in case the worst happened. Then I went to walk outside. Perhaps I had a death wish! As I opened my door I heard a loud, determined voice and forceful banging on a windowpane. It seemed my neighbour, Morgan, didn't particularly want the elephants in his backyard either. He had more luck than I'd had earlier. The jumbos turned and ran, thankfully not towards me.

It was an odd feeling standing there in silky pyjamas in the moonlight, my arms folded against the cold, listening to our nocturnal visitors hurrying away, vegetation scraping their leather hides.

Morgan must have noticed my silhouette, despite me not being able to see him.

'Hello Sharon,' he said calmly in the darkness, as if this was the most natural thing in the world.

'They were *too* close,' I replied without pleasantries.

'Arrhhh yes, very very close,' he agreed.

We moaned and joked about those responsible for the electric fence, and eventually went back to bed. Curled up against the cold, I thought about the photographs that I'd had developed while I was in Bulawayo.

I always joined Austin and Patrick in the back room of Camera Centre whenever they expertly developed and printed my photos. Patrick's words, while gazing at my photograph of a particularly laid-back baboon, came floating back to me.

'Funny things happen in the jungle,' he'd said.

'Funny' things indeed.

It was Austin who viewed my photographs on screen, before pressing the button to print. He often sat there muttering and giggling to himself. 'Sh*t roller,' he chuckled one day, a trademark front tooth missing from his mouth.

'Austin!' I exclaimed, peering over his shoulder at the screen and now giggling too. 'That's a *dung beetle*.'

Later, Austin wanted to know about the animals in my country. 'Is it true that a kangaroo has a pouch here?' he asked, patting his belly. I nodded.

'Imagine if a baboon had a pouch there!' he exclaimed. 'He would stuff so many stolen mealies into it...'

It was always a relief to laugh with town friends.

Friends, Fun
and Fantasies

Despite the ongoing problems, I still managed to experience days of deep contentment. As I sat on the rooftop of Nicki Mukuru in the clear cool air one evening, with the moon shimmering on the surface of Kanondo pan, a lioness walked towards me, passing within a couple of metres of where I sat. For those few seconds I held my breath. She was picture perfect in the moonlight, but she was *close*. And there was no 'bite me' barrier separating us! She walked to just two metres in front of my vehicle, and sat herself down. She meant me no harm.

Soon after, a male sable appeared at the pan, unconcerned. I put my index finger in my mouth to wet it, and held it above my head. I felt the wind on my finger and knew that the sable wasn't yet aware of the lioness – and her three feline companions – since the breeze wasn't blowing their predatory scent towards him. The pride of lionesses, though, was not oblivious to *his* presence.

With the moon high in the sky, some of them began to stalk – but the sable was on the other side of the pan and they soon decided it was no use. Only then did the sable notice them, barking his alarm. A group of elephants approached, a young calf momentarily stealing the lionesses' attention. They made no attempt to stalk the calf though, the adult elephants having spotted the pride now crouched in the grass at the edge of the pan. The elephants let out shrill trumpets and flicked their trunks towards these apparently bothersome predatory creatures, chasing them off.

I was in my element, sitting on my rooftop in the moonlight among elephants and lions. I wished this scene would repeat itself in a week's time when Shaynie and another friend were due to arrive. But then I had second thoughts. Perhaps I shouldn't wish *quite* that, I decided. Shaynie would probably have peed her pants by now.

And she very nearly did, a number of times! The Presidential Elephants dazzled us with one of their uniquely sociable performances. Misty was the first to acquaint herself with Shaynie, perhaps a little too intimately for this, her first-time visit to them. But terror gradually evaporated into awe. Later Whole, Willa and Whosit practically sat on her lap.

A gentle disposition. A powerful placidity. Humbling, to say the very least. Unfortunately Lady, Libby and company – the most sought-after family – remained out of sight.

The star-studded sky that night was glorious and the giggles that emanated from the hyenas around Main Camp, where we were staying for the night, were contagious.

Inside Hwange National Park the following day, on our way to Ngweshla pan where we were to overnight... no clutch. Nicki Mukuru's clutch really was a problem for a year or so, when parts were impossible to source. On level ground and fully loaded, a push was necessary to help restart her. 'But I'll leave you behind,' I exclaimed. With no clutch, I couldn't stop to allow my friends back into my vehicle.

'You don't need to be stationary for us to get in...' My mate's voice sailed off into the wild blue yonder as I chugged along to a second gear start, yelling for them to jump on. Amid hysterical laughter Shaynie appeared, monkey-like, clinging to my window-frame, her heavy boots much too close to my head. I caught a glimpse of my other supremely confident friend in my rear-view mirror running for all she was worth, in a fit of giggles. She was never going to make it. I let Nicki Mukuru stall. Surrounded by less noisy, four-legged animals, we laughed and laughed, and laughed some more.

'Hey you guys, stop it,' begged Shaynie, tears of merriment in her eyes. 'I'm going to pee my pants and there are not even any lions around.' There *were* lions around. We just couldn't see them. A lioness with young cubs was known to be in the Ngweshla area.

On arrival at the campsite, everyone somehow successfully on board, I caught sight of Shaynie looking dismayed at the state of the fence that surrounded us. I must admit I looked at it too, secretly acknowledging that it was just the right height for a lion to bound over, and there were many large holes in it. She would not have slept a wink in one of the little thatched open-air shelters that I planned to use. She very definitely needed a 'bite me' barrier. I made her bed on the back seat of Nicki Mukuru, secured the roof, the windows and the doors. There she would feel – well, at least somewhat – safe.

As I walked towards Nicki Mukuru the next morning, having revelled in a night of close-by elephant trumpets and copious other wild sounds (while Shaynie slept with ear plugs), I was more than a little surprised to see one door slightly ajar. Foolishly I muttered after waking her, 'The door was open.'

'The door was *open*?' she repeated, eyes wide, a hint of panic in her voice.

'No, no, the door wasn't open,' I lied.

Back at my rondavel a few weeks later I e-mailed Marion. We were due in Bulawayo, to speak to the local wildlife society. I told her about yet another recently sighted snared animal – another sable with a wire around its neck.

'Rather than going to Bulawayo, do you think we could go to Tahiti instead?' I suggested. I was reflecting on a TV commercial from many years before, which often sprung to my mind. As I recollect, it unfolded something like this: An affluent family are in their private jumbo jet – father, mother and children, all in their own exquisite bathtubs, lathering themselves with Imperial Leather soap. Gorgeous wife is lapping up the extravagance, reading a magazine while relaxing in her gleaming white tub. She looks up and quietly says to handsome husband, 'Tahiti looks nice.'

Forever obliging handsome husband picks up the communications handset at once, and speaks to the pilot, 'Simon! Tahiti.'

Without delay – as easy as that – the glitzy private jet veers across the vast expanse of sky, a change in direction, presumably now heading for Tahiti.

Yes, I often thought during the harrowing times, Tahiti looks nice.

However, I'd have to be content just to daydream with a bar of Imperial Leather soap in hand. Any type of soap though – forget Imperial Leather – was often hard to come by. I knew in my heart that I must simply be content to *dream*.

The few days in Bulawayo brought some relief to my troubled mind. I devoured pizza and chocolate eclairs. I stared with squinting eyes at the prices of goods, baffled by the growing number of zeros.

As we returned to the bush, with armfuls of citrus fruit, cheese and chocolate, a chilly breeze blew beneath heavy clouds. An unseasonal shower of rain fell from the dark sky ahead of us. We wound down the windows of the 4x4 and breathed in the smell of rain on baked ground. A smell of life. A smell of hope.

'If you could bottle this smell,' asked Marion from the driver's seat, 'what colour would it be?'

I didn't need time to think. 'It would be pink,' I replied with a smile.

A far-away friend had recently enchanted me with the phrase 'on a pink cloud'. In love and on a pink cloud. A time of dreams, of wonderment, of starting anew, of growth and discovery. The smell of rain on baked ground? Yes, I thought again to myself, it would be *pink*.

A wave of sudden nostalgia pulsed through my being. There was an ache in my heart. It was mid-2005 and although I was still living full-time in Zimbabwe, somewhere in the back of my mind I was beginning to wonder if perhaps I would leave some day. I was already homesick at the thought of what I would leave behind if this came to pass. What of the elephants that I knew so well?

It is easy these days, in this world of high technology, to get news of friends not heard of for years. But what of Lady and Libby and Whole and Misty, and all my many other elephant friends? Were they dead or alive? Snared, hunted, culled? Or happy? I would never know. And I would always wonder. It seemed impossible to just leave; to somehow erase all this from my mind.

Some years ago I used to joke that I'd have to go into therapy if I abandoned the Presidential Elephants. Perhaps this was no longer a joke. Yet given all the disheartening things going on in Zimbabwe, could I stay on for the many more years that I'd once hoped? I realised, with a pang in my chest, that now I did not know.

People regularly expressed surprise that I was still in Zimbabwe. In response, I always told them stories about my elephant friends, and of my time on the Hwange Estate, which had strengthened in me a vast capacity to overcome, to get on with the job – even in the face of adversity, opposition, and the self-important actions and scorn of a few who could not matter. I always told them, too, of the rewards of fighting for what I believe in, and of my love for the Zimbabwean bush, which was still as strong as ever.

I was fortunate to have kind and thoughtful friends. It was late one afternoon many months later, as I returned from a day in the field, that I saw a pizza box on the doorstep of my rondavel and wondered if someone was playing a cruel joke on me. As I strode towards it, I tried to suppress my salivation: surely if there really had been a pizza inside the vervet monkeys, which were everywhere, would have eaten it. But there was indeed a pizza inside and I had, mercifully, arrived home before the monkeys, or the ants, got to it. 'A surprise for you,' Marion had written on the box. This was such a treat. Pizzas were six hours return drive away. I greedily devoured three slices, box still in hand, before I unloaded my 4x4.

I always found comfort and peace in the kindness of others. Peace also came when I sat with a group of grown-ups listening to a story being read out loud. Lol's mom, Dinks and Shaynie reintroduced me to this dying art of quiet companionship, of peaceful listening with hushed attentiveness. It's a gift so often lost in adulthood, when most choose to read aloud only to children.

It was during a more light-hearted reading from a book of animal tales that hushed attentiveness turned into loud disturbance. I was not going to let Shaynie get away with this one. Forever teasing me about my Aussie (mis)pronunciation of certain words (*gogga* and *shongololo* immediately spring to mind, my lack of throat clearing ability a definite drawback to the correct pronunciation of *gogga*), I could not let this one pass.

'Croc-eee-dile,' Shaynie read out loud, followed closely by 'porc-eee-pine'.

And this from a Zimbabwean!

We laughed and laughed, and called a truce. A gifted artist, Shaynie later signed her next elephant work, so very kindly created especially for me, with a sketch of a sweet little porcupine.

A truce maybe, but another day soon after, Shaynie screwed up her face at me and blurted, 'You can't eat *rusks* with soup!'

'Why not?' I challenged. (When I arrived in Zimbabwe I knew rusks to be something that babies sucked on when teething. Yet here, I discovered, they are thick, rectangular, hard dry biscuits – usually dipped in coffee or tea.) 'They're like oversized croutons,' I declared. 'Big, sweet croutons. They're not so bad with soup.'

Shaynie screwed up her face a bit tighter and uttered, 'You can't. You just can't...'

When I had no bread in my rondavel, which was all too regularly, I resorted to eating rusks with all sorts of things. Boxes of rusks though, imported from South Africa, were an item not often available. Like bread.

Some months later, as we walked the aisles of a grocery store, Shaynie tossed a box of plain rusks into my trolley. 'Well you at least can't eat *raisin* rusks with soup,' she insisted.

A few weeks later, after some time together in the field, a friend returned with me to my rondavel for something to eat. I had no fresh food though, and I doubted that he'd be too thrilled with my standard fare of noodles and sweet chilli sauce, but he knew the score.

I dug out some pasta and washed it, ridding it of the countless little brown bugs that find their way into everything. I picked up a can of tomato and onion mix, a little distorted-looking but seemingly useable. This would, however, be as uninteresting as noodles and sweet chilli sauce. 'What else can I add?' I mumbled to myself. 'Perhaps,' I whispered hopefully, 'there might be a tin of mushrooms somewhere.'

I pulled out cardboard boxes and searched, pretending not to notice when a friendly little shrew (now a permanent house guest) scurried across the floor. The price tag on the can that I eventually unearthed read Z\$3 000. Considering that a tin of mushrooms currently cost over Z\$180 000, I was cautious (although I knew it hadn't in fact been bought very long before). When opened, the mushrooms looked edible enough, at least to me. For dessert I had a jelly mixture, and thankfully there was water to make it up, so I removed those little brown bugs, and found a tin of peaches to mix in with it. This tin looked awfully contorted. I opened it outside, for fear that it might explode, and gasped as I looked inside. The peaches had turned white.

The tin surely wasn't *that* old. I looked more closely at the label. 'Ohhh!' I giggled. The label read 'White Peaches'. They were *supposed* to be white. My belly ached from much needed laughter and, remarkably, we were not even ill the next day. Together we contemplated that old Chinese curse: 'May you live in interesting times.'

There were countless other 'interesting' times. One day I was anticipating the arrival of a group of Australians and decided that I really should tidy myself up a little. I filed my fingernails, washed my hair, shaved my legs, lavished my skin with scented body lotion and pulled on freshly laundered clothes. I sat on the wooden bench in my garden, letting the sun dry my long, honey-blonde hair. There weren't many times in the bush when I allowed myself the luxury of feeling feminine. Then I dusted inside my rondavel, filling in time. Still waiting for my visitors to arrive, I ventured back into my garden and pottered around just a little, not wanting to work up a sweat. A fresh breeze lifted my hair and the sun shone down on my bronzed arms.

I bent down, pulling a few weeds from among the plants growing beneath the teak tree overhanging my rondavel, when something landed on my head. It took me a few moments to react. I stood up and wiped a strange liquid from my brow. I looked up into the teak tree and shrieked. A vervet monkey had peed on my head!

It wasn't the only time that a vervet monkey caused me to shriek. One afternoon I was inside my rondavel, working on my laptop. I looked up and out of my open door, into my garden, and there before my eyes was a bushbuck drinking from one of my birdbaths.

'Oh cool, look at that,' I whispered to myself. Within seconds a vervet monkey appeared, and sat right on my doorstep gazing in at me, with the bushbuck behind him. 'Oh cool, look at *that*,' I whispered again with a smile. Then, in just one leap, the little vervet was up on top of my fridge and then on top of the concrete partition that separates my living area from the bathroom. 'Not cool!' I shrieked. 'Definitely not cool... you cheeky little monster... Out! Now!' No matter how cute they appear, a wild vervet monkey's room-mate is definitely not what one aspires to be.

I never ceased to marvel at the number and variety of birds that visited my garden, the bird song always so companionable to me. Sitting together on my doorstep one afternoon, a friend and I were enchanted by more than 20 different types of feathered friends as we talked of animals and birds, turmoil and crisis, and a thousand other things. We also talked of all the problems on the Hwange Estate.

A few hours later, I found myself thinking aloud of seashells and children's sandcastles and flying kites by a rolling sea – a spark of yearning for other, carefree, things. Perhaps, I tried to convince myself, it was just the wine...

It was only a few weeks later that I gazed towards Kanondo and was struck by a feeling that I was driving towards a beach. In this year of drought there was barely any grass, and not an animal in sight. The sandy soil had been washed anew by a light overnight shower of rain, no spoor visible anywhere. The ground was an expanse of white; a cooling early morning breeze blowing gently; a few clouds dulling the sky. There were babblers, but I pretended that they were seagulls. I fought an overwhelming urge to get out of my vehicle and run, pretending to fly that kite.

What the hell, I thought. I'll do it! And it felt *good* to chase those dreams.

It was such a relief to *really* laugh again, wind in my hair. I felt young and carefree. I felt *free*. I ran and ran and ran, looking back and up at my colourful bright kite, floating high in the sky. But I was much too unfit for this, the possibility of lions a good excuse, I told myself, for not running too far. My breathing laboured, I laughed some more as I ran back to my 4x4, still flying that imaginary kite, hoping that nobody was watching me.

It may have been a crazy flight of fancy, but it relieved some of the pent-up frustrations that had been growing inside me since the settler invasions had begun. And if the beach was fantasy, I thought to myself afterwards, my need to escape the seemingly endless poaching was not.

The fantasies didn't stop there.

'I think I've found your Robert Redford,' said Shaynie one day, with a grin and a glint in her eye – as if that explained everything.

I looked at her sideways, resigned to my fate. Why were people *always* trying to do this to me? It had, I knew, been a standing joke for some years; friends determined that I should find my Robert Redford. This was not Robert Redford the movie star. It was the romantic role of Denis Finch Hatton (long-time lover of Karen Blixen) played by Robert Redford in *Out of Africa*. This movie opens with evocative music, heart-rending vistas of the vast African wilderness, and the words, 'I had a farm in Africa at the foot of the Ngong Hills...' – and already I'm in tears.

Matchmaker Shaynie hadn't seen the movie since its release 20 years earlier and, after she'd watched it again to refresh her memory, I received a message from her saying, 'I've stopped praying for a Robert Redford for you. Why would you want some ~*~*~ like that in your life?'

Even so, her mission continued. Too often though, her optical lens appeared to be scratched, not to mention somewhat warped. Mine, on the other hand, was clear, if perhaps a little tinted.

For a long time he existed only in my mind. He was a calming force, a guiding force, an apparition of fun and laughter. He was a rather strange, if vivid, creation of my imagination. I often light-heartedly turned to him, saying, 'And what do *you* think of *that*?' or wondered out loud to my friends, 'what would *he* think of *this*?'

He was whimsical and wise, with the capacity to make me think, and his imaginary presence made me giggle. Over time he began to exist for others who knew me, and now he was deemed deserving of a name.

Together with Shaynie (without even a glass of wine in hand), we conjured up what he looked like, what he wore, how he spoke and why he had that limp! He was, naturally enough, really rather dashing.

Soon, Professor Ralph VonBerg – 'the man of the mountain' – came to life. So from then on when we talked and laughed and reminisced, or on the odd occasion when something profound was uttered, I asked with a twinkle in my eyes and a grin on my lips, 'What would Professor VonBerg think of *that?*'

It was a pact made long before by Dinks, Shaynie and me, that we, the 'Rrah Rrah Sisters' – christened one memorable night under a Zimbabwean moon – would meet up again in 2007, regardless of where the winds of the intervening years may have blown us. Together, it is true, we are probably more imaginative than sensible, but I didn't doubt that what we set out to do, we would achieve. And now, I thought, Professor Ralph VonBerg would probably come too.

Not having been party to all this nonsense, a friend I hadn't seen for several months later listened bewildered to me speaking about all of this, her giggles unsuppressed. She was still trying to visualise me flying that imaginary kite!

'Yea, yea, I *know*,' I admitted amid more laughter, 'I *really* need to get out of the bush more often.' But still I left the bush only infrequently.

One time was when I was once again staying with Shaynie in Bulawayo for a few days, restocking supplies. While there, I always liked to buy a few treats – for myself and others.

'I've bought you a present,' I exclaimed one afternoon as Shaynie waltzed in from work.

'I've brought you a present too. Come!'

I suddenly found myself racing down a flight of stairs with Shaynie in the lead, towards a cardboard box. I peered inside. 'Oh my god,' was all I could say.

I'd once told her that I had never seen one. He was huge, weighing I guessed, close to a kilogram. He was oddly attractive, although I felt no desire to see if he'd turn into my handsome prince.

I had bought Shaynie a book. *She'd* brought *me* a bullfrog.

I was always grateful for the quiet company of my close girlfriends during the trying times. For many of them, I knew, life in the bush with the elephants would be a lonely existence, but for me it was truly fulfilling, despite the difficulties. There were some days of exceptional happenings when I did wish there were a male presence beside me; a caring man to share it all with. And there were days when I remembered such shared experiences, long past.

Every so often I recalled, with amusement, an invitation to a garden party. My partner at the time said he would wear his pith helmet.

'A pith helmet. You own a pith helmet?' I enquired awkwardly.

And I, he said, feeling no need to answer my apparently silly question, should wear a long flowery dress. A long flowery dress? Me? In a long flowery dress?

I'd enjoyed his company over the course of a few months, but soon realised that someone who liked to live a little like one of the colonial pioneers was definitely not for me.

I also remember, with bittersweet affection, being with a fellow wildlife enthusiast under the stars, watching the animals. I remember the unknown elephant bull that came so close we held our breath, laughing as he moved off. I remember the shared sunsets, the blending of our bodies around a pan. I remember the long talks, night after night, secret thoughts said aloud. I remember the much-desired pizza, carried for hundreds of kilometres by thoughtful hands. I remember the toasted sandwiches shared from a frying pan. I remember, at a troubled time when Zimbabwe's roads were considered unsafe to travel alone, the bonding anxiety shared while contacting every hospital and police station searching for an answer to our fear that something terrible had happened to his father (after he didn't arrive at his destination as expected). I remember the joint relief of the next day, the next night, our fears unfounded, but not forgotten. I remember the gifts of curios, candles and scented cream. I remember the campfires, and I remember the songs and the dreams.

But he was not mine. He was not free. And he was not honest with himself, or with me. Shared lives soon vanished overnight.

Months later I wished that one day I might do all that again, with the same fervour and with someone of like mind and spirit – until I no longer wished it to be. I was content with my solitude, and considered that I no longer *needed* it to be.

Then one day, a disbelieving girlfriend spoke frankly. 'Your fears are making you foolish,' she said to me with concern.

I was somewhat taken aback by this comment, although I eventually conceded that she probably did have a valid point. The dishonesty and the disdain (which seemed to swell endlessly following this earlier parting) had brought hurt – which was still there buried somewhere in the depths of my soul. I feared, it was perhaps true, a repeat performance – and so best not to risk it again just yet. Foolish maybe, but there were always far more important things to worry about.

My romantic relationships had never been particularly successful. Even as a teenager, I hadn't wanted to have children and therefore felt no pressing need for a permanent relationship. I always seemed to be in love with something else. In the early days I was in love with my career, then with Africa, and now with the elephants. For me, fulfilment came when I was among those of my friends who were not judgemental; it came among those who offered unconditional trust and support. Not surprisingly, therefore, fulfilment also came among the wildlife. It was there that I'd found such solace. Being my husband would indeed have been no bargain at all.

It was a real comfort, one day during 2005, to receive an e-mail out of the blue signed 'Spiderman'. It threw me back to days gone by, and filled me with nostalgia. It was from John, and I was thrilled to hear from him again.

'U our hero,' he wrote, speaking on behalf of Del too – words that brought a lump to my throat.

Always, such generosity of spirit overwhelms me.

I'd often wondered about them and wished they were still around so that John could teach me more about the bush. I recalled braais in dry riverbeds, campfires in new places and long talks of philosophy. I wondered if he was still sharing his bed with snakes, befriending spiders, and climbing naked onto the rooftop of his home. I was happy to hear that he still had his gift of an akubra. Of Professor Ralph VonBerg, I thought with a grin, John would approve.

John had also been a good friend of Andy and Lol. The days when we'd enjoyed such fun together in this area now seemed so very long ago.

I saw Lol only infrequently after Andy's death, but occasionally, when she was visiting her mom and dad in Bulawayo, we managed to spend some time together. Lol has a special gift for drawing. She did some exquisite pencil drawings for me, to illustrate my writings, superbly depicting the seasons of Hwange. After handing them to me one evening, she said quietly, 'Andrew would be proud of you.' It had been more than six years since Andy's death, yet in response to Lol's words, I could only blink back tears.

Karen Paolillo, who continued to stay in touch, had also known tears. The Turgwe hippos had remained safe, but she too struggled with settler problems. Like John, Karen was considered by some to be rather eccentric, yet I think she understood better than most why I stayed on. I found relief in her empathetic e-mails, and appreciated her regular concern over many years.

We had much in common. The social closeness that I shared with the elephants, Karen shared with the hippos. Neither of us was interested in them as subjects to merely advance a professional career. We both clung grimly to the hope that things would come right, but everything going on around us just became more and more hopeless.

L Family Cheer

Confucius once said, 'One joy dispels a hundred cares.' And this I now knew to be true.

Sightings of Lady and her family, with new baby Libby, always brought relief and excitement – and renewed hope.

Like all the elephants during April and May, the L family enjoyed the 2005 season of ripe *Acacia erioloba* pods. Lady used her huge bulk to shake an acacia tree, tusks positioned on either side of its slim trunk. The baboons high in the quivering branches looked down in alarm as Lady's family reaped the rewards. All except tiny Libby quickly devoured their fair share. With no pods remaining on the ground, I laughed at offspring Loopy and Lesley still searching frantically. Loopy wandered around with a tasty pod on his head, and Lesley with one on her back. None of the others seemed to notice. They were all too busy probing the ground.

I looked again at Lesley, her breasts developing. This was an indicator that she was pregnant, for the very first time. I didn't see her in oestrus, but I fully expected that she would give birth early in 2006 in what I estimated to be her 12th year. Such a cheeky one, I just couldn't imagine her being a mother. Meanwhile, Lee wore a combination headdress/necklace of bright green vine, which he was lucky enough to stumble upon at the base of an acacia tree. He looked quite dapper, his new outfit clearly to his taste – because he then proceeded to eat it. Both at almost six months of age, little Laurie and cousin Litchis were having an argument. Laurie was suckling from Leanne (Litchis' mother), and Litchis was unimpressed. He butted Laurie's backside again and again – and yet again. 'That's *my* mother,' I'm sure I heard him say! Laurie eventually got the message and moved off to his own mother, leaving Litchis finally to be able to suckle. 'This is *my* mother,' I'm sure I heard him stress once more!

It always surprised me that Lady, with her great inspiring qualities, was such a low-ranking member of the Presidential clan. Larger in size than many of the females in other families, she hangs back, always waiting her turn to drink or bathe. Perhaps it's because her family is one of the smallest that she doesn't risk a challenge. Or perhaps she's just too gentle for her own good. The L family youngsters, though, are tolerated. Little Libby and others go wandering off among the W family, despite some of the dominant W females having advanced threateningly towards Lady, forcing her and sister Leanne to wait their turn patiently. Several years earlier Leanne had been a little aggressive towards humans, but by now I could place my hand on her tusk.

Sadly, many weeks still often passed between sightings of the L family. They had not yet reverted to spending extended time at Kanondo as they'd used to, following what I'm sure must have been a harrowing encounter there. Given that I'd been spending many hours in this open area in the hope of re-encountering some of the snared animals, I had missed seeing Lady and her family. Occasionally, though, they passed by.

Little Libby was growing up fast. Whenever she walked in front of her mother, Lady lifted her trunk just above her daughter's body in a protective gesture. Ever the playful clown, Libby loved to scratch her backside on her mother's thick legs. I was always so relieved that there were no new snare wounds on them. The L family had already had its fair share of suffering.

One day in August, while parked in the shade of an *Acacia erioloba* close to the Hwange Safari Lodge, the L family came lumbering towards me when I called to them.

Lady was always the first to react to my presence, trunk swinging rhythmically as she hurried my way. Loopy was usually not far behind her, the sight of him always bringing a sense of pride, in the knowledge that he'd been saved from certain death. Limp was there, his snared leg now much better. With awesome dignity the Ls stood around my 4x4, sleeping. Gentle grey giants, at one with me.

Lesley, quite mellow now that her pregnancy was progressing, leant her small tusks and trunk against my side window, as she stood only centimetres away from my arm with her eyes closed. She appeared heavily pregnant. Perhaps, I thought, she might give birth later *this* year. Louise placed her trunk on the back of Lazareth, who leaned against Libby, who was suckling from Lady. Lee swirled his trunk around and around. Litchis and Laurie lay down on their sides in the sand. 'We're not going to *stand up* to sleep,' I'm sure they said.

Levi, who already spent extended time away from his family, slowly embarking on his new life as an independent bull, stood placidly with his trunk on my bonnet. All the other Ls were around me too. I felt like the most privileged person in the world. It was a gift straight from heaven, a delight to my heart.

Then suddenly, to destroy it all, over the top of Leanne's mammoth head, I caught sight of yet another unscrupulous hunting vehicle on this land decreed 'photographic only'.

And the peaceful world was shattered yet again.

It was another month before the official announcement finally came, banning hunting between the photographic lodges on the vlei. I felt hope; hope that at last we might *finally* be able to revert to life in the good old days, before the settler invasions.

The Minister of Tourism was quoted in a newspaper as saying, 'We have banned hunting activities in those areas where we find the Presidential Herd of elephants for sanity and order to prevail.'

The Presidential Elephants rejoiced. As did I.

I drove to Kanondo, where I always went to celebrate my joys. On the way I stumbled upon Waughty and mother Why, who was still managing fine with her dislocated hip. I shared with them the good news, and drove on elated. I couldn't wipe the smile from my lips. But that wasn't enough. I punched my arm up through my open roof and sang loudly to the animals' world, 'Ha-lle-lujah! Hallelujah! Hallelujah!'

A bateleur eagle was also in full voice, putting on a fine performance. Spirit messengers, some believe. Right then, I also believed.

These were the times when I thought that I, too, could fly.

I couldn't help it. It just came out again, 'Ha-lle-lujah! Hallelujah! Hallelujah!'

I stepped out of my 4x4 and did a little dance. Happy *mukiwa*!

But would the decision hold, I wondered? And what would the settlers have in store for me now?

The next day there was reason for me to do another little jig – 20 litres of petrol, a gift from afar, from kind folks barely known, carried by kind hands unknown until now.

'It feels like Christmas,' I said, thunderstruck, thanking him profusely. By now, fuel was almost impossible to source locally.

Doing another little dance and boasting about my good fortune, I giggled at Busi's response, 'Only in Zimbabwe,' she declared, 'can you get *that* excited about 20 litres of petrol.'

No matter what my mood, little Libby always managed to make me laugh out loud. At nearly five months old she was still the little clown. She raced flat out, her ears flapping, her front feet high off the ground, emitting a vibrating hum, looking like she just might take to the skies. She ran towards a mud bath and threw herself down the low bank with a long slippery skid, landing with a splash in the muddy water. She made no complaint of pain that I could hear, yet concerned, mother Lady ran to see if her mischievous child was okay. Reassured, Lady splashed herself with mud while Libby rolled around, completely submerged.

Lady always chose times like these to come to say hello. She arrived at my 4x4 window covered with mud, but even in this filthy state I couldn't resist her. I ran my hand up and down her mucky trunk.

One day, a voice came over my field radio. Inquisitive, Lady stretched her trunk towards the radio. 'No, no, no,' I muttered, pushing her heavy trunk back out of my open window. I wondered how I would explain the absence of my radio. 'Stolen from my hands by a wild elephant...' Who would believe *that?*

By late September drought had a firm grip on the land, the animals struggling (yet again) for survival. There was a bushfire, but I drove instead to Kanondo to check on the water levels. The main pan was depressingly dried and cracked. Crocodiles lay in thick mud. I was astounded at just how quickly this disaster had unfolded. The water pressure to the concrete trough was agonisingly low and elephants were standing around willing more water to appear.

I noticed a brand new baby elephant, a piece of umbilical cord still attached. But this was not a happy sighting. Lesley was there, with three other young teenagers from a different Presidential family, all hovering around this baby. Lady and the rest of the Ls were nowhere in sight.

I realised with horror that the baby was Lesley's – seemingly 'abducted' by the other three. Although they were slightly older and taller than Lesley, none of the three had any breast development as they hadn't yet had calves. They couldn't suckle the newborn, and they were keeping Lesley from suckling him.

I went over and over it in my mind, hoping I was wrong. Was this *really* Lesley's baby? What other explanations were there? Where were Lady and the rest of the Ls? They should be celebrating this birth.

Then Lesley urinated, ending with a gush of blood, and I knew for certain that this baby was hers. Clearly she had very recently given birth. She was the only one of the four with milk, and she was thin.

I was numb with concern. I wanted to shout at these intruders, 'What on earth are you doing? That baby is going to die. Let him suckle from his mother.'

And I wanted to shout at Lady, 'Where on earth are you? Why aren't you looking after your daughter, and your grandson?' And then I was even more concerned. Were the rest of the L family alright?

The three 'abductors' bullied Lesley. In a submissive gesture typical of lower ranked elephants, Lesley backed into them continuously, trying desperately to get closer to her baby. Just as heartbreakingly, she raced towards my 4x4 from 20 metres away and, within touching distance of me, turned abruptly and raced back towards her baby. She did this twice. She wanted me to help, but I couldn't. What could I do to help her? I was even more distressed knowing that she'd asked me to try. Why else had she raced like this towards me, and back again – twice?

I looked again at how thin she was. I doubted that she'd eaten since giving birth, perhaps some 12 hours before. I raced to collect some *Acacia erioloba* pods, and returned to her. She came to my vehicle, bringing the three other less-welcome teenagers with her, all of them wanting some pods. Then something positive happened. Having eaten the pods, Lesley stood less than one metre from my door and suckled her baby, the other three teenagers not game to come quite so close. But the baby, eyes still very red from the birth, got milk for less than a minute.

He didn't seem to know that Lesley was his mother, and Lesley also seemed confused. He walked towards the other three teenagers, and was herded away by them. He tried to suckle from each of them, but found no breasts. Occasionally lactating females passed by, curious of this newborn, and he also tried to suckle from them. They were intolerant though. He was kicked by huge feet.

Lesley continued to trail them all, looking forlorn. She was streaming from the temporal glands, a sure sign that she was stressed. She continually backed in towards the three, trying to get closer. She is such a young gentle soul, I could barely make myself sit and watch.

By now it was dark. I feared that the 'abductors' would soon wander off with their family group – the close-by Bs or possibly the Ms (I couldn't be sure which, given the indistinct ear markings of these lesser-known teenagers), taking Lesley's baby with them. I feared that I might never see this baby elephant again, and if Lesley didn't eat and drink soon, I feared for her wellbeing too. Where were Lady and the rest of the Ls? Had they gone off in search of water?

On my way home in darkness, to top off my day, another neck-snared elephant crossed my path.

Four days later I saw them from a distance and breathed a deep sigh of relief. Both Lesley and her little baby boy were alive. But they were still wandering alone, something that made me terribly uneasy. The rest of the L family was nowhere to be seen. Thankfully, Lesley's baby appeared stronger now, apparently having bonded with his mother. At almost one week old his eyes were still very red and a small piece of dried umbilical cord remained attached. He was more aware of his surroundings and used his tiny trunk to explore the bushes.

I hoped that Lesley just needed some time alone to bond properly with her first-born given that, just after his birth, he'd tried to suckle from every female in sight. I hoped, too, that Lady and the rest of the family would soon reappear to offer protection, support and playmates for this youngster. However, never having seen a young mother wandering alone with a newborn, I remained concerned for all of the Ls.

I put my hand on Lesley's soft trunk and told her to stay safe.

The privilege of naming Lesley's baby went to a kind supporter from South Africa, who remembered the legend of the magical city of Camelot, ruled by King Arthur and the Knights of the Round Table. She recalled the mystical isle of Avalon presided over by 'the Lady of the Lake', and then wrote to me, saying, '[He shall be named] Lancelot. Because he was raised by the Lady of the Lake (although Lady is not his mom, she is the matriarch)... Lancelot also because I live in the hope – no the conviction – that the country we are waiting for is just beyond the horizon, a vision and place of ideals that will not be found anywhere else in the world – just like Camelot.'

A few days later, still wandering alone with just his young mother, Lesley's baby pushed up against the door of my 4x4. I gently touched his tiny trunk and christened him Lancelot. He appeared darker now, having had a wallow in both water and sand, which would protect his sensitive pale skin from the blazing sun. Lesley had become more protective of him, using her trunk to guide him. She'd learned to place her front leg forward so that he could suckle well. I watched them both under a setting sun, and felt a little more at ease.

Two days later the veld was once again alight. Smoke choked the air, hiding the sun – a bushfire was raging dangerously close to Sable Lodge on the vlei. Birds soared, feasting on insects flushed out by the flames. The vegetation crackled and burned. There'd been more fires than usual this year, I reflected, and they were undoubtedly being deliberately lit. I suspected that people, wanting new growth for domestic stock, or perhaps wanting clear landscapes so they could more easily spot game to poach, would strike a match, not caring about the consequences.

Having turned towards home, I passed through Acacia Grove. *Finally*, there they were, some 10 days after Lancelot had been born, the three generations – son Lancelot, mother Lesley and grandmother Lady.

I looked towards the heavens and breathed another deep sigh of relief. Lady came lumbering up to my vehicle. She was a grandmother now, and I rubbed her trunk and congratulated her excitedly. But she wouldn't tell me where they'd all been, no matter how many times I asked.

It was a privilege, over the years, to watch well-known elephants grow up – from newborn to playful toddler to cheeky adolescent, or sub-adult to mature new mother.

I often watched Lady and Libby, Leanne and Litchis, Louise and Laurie, Lesley and Lancelot and all the other members of the L family, and felt the overwhelming importance of conservation activities. My 'research' data collection continued to take a back seat, never the priority. These days there were always so many more important things to focus on.

Earlier during the day on which I'd found the L family back together, I had deployed Jabulani and his anti-poaching unit into an area I'd been feeling suspicious about – right beside the Hwange Safari Lodge. Within hours, handfuls of snare wires were found and destroyed.

Too much was going on, too close to home, and I was becoming fed up with it all. I realised yet again that there were too many people who simply didn't care.

I often sat forlornly, wondering who would be the third snare victim in the L family. And I wished desperately that fear was not so familiar.

Drought and Despair

Two weeks later, in October 2005, I came upon the L family again, and was saddened that I could barely recognise the once rotund Lady from behind. She was awfully thin, as was Lesley. Clearly the effort of suckling their youngsters during this time of terrible drought was taxing.

I watched the distress of the wildlife at Kanondo, my heart tired of feeling heavy. Sables came to drink, but clearly they found the muddy water unpalatable. They returned again and again, hoping for better luck, only to find that the situation hadn't changed. Kudus appeared a little less fussy, but they, too, seemed dejected by what they found. The rotting carcass of a young crocodile lay on mounds of dry, cracked mud. Marabou storks were feasting on small fish, stranded in thick, gooey mud. Jackals wandered across dried, cracked sections where there'd been a little water just one week before. Water pressure was simply too low to keep pace.

Enthralled as always, I watched the behaviour of the elephants. The adults used their trunks to skim only the surface of the muddy water, having learned that it is more palatable. Youngsters who had not yet mastered this technique put their trunks to the mouths of the older, more experienced elephants, hoping to share some of their cleaner water.

As always, the elephants showed their intelligence. Many of those that found mud at Kanondo at lunchtime were at the next pan – the only one with decent water – five kilometres away by late afternoon. So many animals though, congregating around just one water source, could do the surrounds no good at all.

Practically every day during October new fires erupted in the veld.

243

In five years I'd never seen anything like it and I was convinced that these destructive infernos were indeed being lit deliberately. Parts of the estate were now jet black, only the termite mounds having escaped the flames. Fresh new leaves were scorched. I sat and wondered about jackal pups in dens at this time of year; the eggs in the ground-nests of the plovers; all of the smaller animals; and I suspected that there'd been many fatalities. As if there hadn't been enough death already.

Waterbucks were rarely seen in the vicinity of the Hwange Safari Lodge, but desperate for water now, the herd had left Kanondo in search of a new home. One day I noticed with alarm that one of them had fallen into the lodge sewerage pit, which has steep sloping concrete sides. The poor fellow was exhausted, sitting down now in the green slime. As I radioed for help, I wondered how long he'd been struggling in there. A concrete ramp leads down into this pond, but it is steep and slippery at its base, and the young waterbuck couldn't get a grip. When help arrived, tree branches were cut and laid in an attempt to introduce some traction, to no avail.

Then suddenly the buck was in an ideal position and the helpers were able to slip a rope over his weary head. The sound of his loud bleating was awful, especially when the rope tightened around his neck as he was pulled upwards. Soon though, it was possible to grip his horns, relieving the pressure from around his neck, and the struggling buck was heaved up and out of the slime. The noose was frantically loosened and removed before the now pugnacious buck raced off to freedom. I clapped and cheered, and slapped the helpers on their backs, greatly relieved for the young waterbuck. Positive outcomes were, it seemed to me, all too few.

That glow did not last for long however. From there I drove to an elephant carcass that vultures had led me to earlier. Judging by the shoulder height, foot measurements and molar eruption, she was about six years old, her tusks small. I couldn't positively identify her as a Presidential Elephant, given that her ear markings were nondescript, and the family group that had been standing close by had, unfortunately, been chased off before I could try to identify them. Her trunk was marked with the telltale scratches of lion claws, as were her neck and hindquarters. She was a large elephant to have been killed by lions, no doubt having been weakened by the drought.

I stayed with the carcass until evening, hoping for a glimpse of the culprits, but more importantly a glimpse of the elephant family, which I thought might return to mourn. A tuskless adult female was the first to arrive, but by then it was already quite dark and, even when using a spotlight, I couldn't make out her ear markings. Yet I felt oddly sure that I didn't know her. Probably in oestrus, accompanied only by two bulls and a youngster, she investigated the carcass with her trunk. Recalling Whole's reaction to her dead son Wholesome, I got the distinct impression that this wasn't the dead elephant's mother, but that she was merely passing by.

Under a half-moon, now shedding more light, a nearby buffalo herd panicked and I guessed that the predators were on their way. Three lions arrived within seconds. It was a collared mother and her two grown cubs. They were the same family (less one sibling, known to be dead) that had seemed so inept at hunting just nine months before. Now they were bringing down not-so-young elephants. Heads deep inside the carcass, noses bloody, this was no silver service banquet. But a feast it was, and with huffs and puffs, snarls and growls, they dined. Under a blanket of sparkling stars I could hear the sound of rasping tongues.

Soon a National Park family of elephants arrived, trumpeting loudly with their ears spread, causing the three lions to flee. The elephant family formed a solid unit and thundered after the lions – their trumpeting deafening. It was extraordinary to witness such prolonged hostility towards another species. Were *they* the family of the dead youngster? Or were they just irate with lions in general? Elephants, I knew, had no liking for carnivores.

This elephant family didn't return to the carcass, but eventually the hungry lions did. Mosquitos were driving me to distraction, so finally I retreated home, leaving the lions to their feast.

I returned at dawn to find jackals feeding, and to marabou storks, yellow-billed kites, pied crows and vultures, all after their share. I thought about the waterbuck that we'd saved the previous day and this unknown elephant, dead in front of me. Always, there is life and death, side by side, in the African veld.

The next day, I was relieved to find that the Water Authority had pumped water for the first time in days. But then, as I drove along the road to Kanondo, I noticed that a thick electricity cable had fallen, and was hanging only two metres from ground level. One touch of this cable and an adult elephant would be dead in seconds. Other elephants would try to help their fallen comrade, and soon whole families would be electrocuted. It had happened before, elsewhere. The cable was hanging low enough to also kill antelope with long horns, and of course giraffe. There were water seepages only metres away.

After days of complaining of no water, I now cursed this flowing resource. These puddles of water would, right now, draw animals to their death. I raced back to the Safari Lodge to make a phone call. The Electricity Authority reacted quickly, recognising the urgency of the situation, and immediately dispatched a team from their base 90 kilometres away. I was dismayed to find out that an employee had seen the fallen cable the day before, but had not reported it. It was the sort of thing that was now occurring much too regularly.

I drove back into the field, hopeful of being able to herd the wildlife away from the danger zone. With no animals immediately in sight, I drove on a little further to check on Kanondo. And yet again, I was dismayed. The previous day, over-zealous workers had dug out the round concrete trough that feeds Kanondo pan, which had been choked with sand. But they had, unthinkingly, dug a well much too deep for young elephants to get out of should they fall – or walk – in. I could barely raise my own leg high enough to get out of that concrete-sided trough, and the water was flowing now, filling the well.

'Turn that valve off,' I shouted to the person I'd fetched to help me.

Now I wanted the water *off* everywhere!

There we were, madly shovelling sand back *into* the trough in a frantic race to reduce its depth, before the elephants arrived. It would take forever. I radioed for extra help.

Then the team from the Electricity Authority arrived and needed to turn off the electricity to be able to fix the fallen cable. This meant that the Water Authority could no longer run its electric pumps, and so once again the animals were without water.

Everything was going round and round in circles. My head felt as if it was too.

Having guarded the electricity workers, uncomfortable with elephants so close to where they were working, I finally arrived home in the middle of the scorching day. I was hot, dirty and weary. Baboons were jumping on my thatched roof with such gusto that it was 'raining' thatch as I walked inside. I turned on a tap, desperate to wash away some of the grime and sweat. There was no water. I walked back to my 4x4 to retrieve the small amount I had in there, only to be confronted with a flat tyre.

Dejected, I sat down on the ground, head on my knees and moaned to myself. 'No wonder they call this suicide month,' I groaned. It's a term used in these parts to describe the depths of despair you might sink to while in the grip of the unrelenting October heat. Temperatures often soar above 40°C, day after day, the heavy, thick air making it difficult to take a deep breath. Those who visit only at this time of year must surely leave with the mistaken belief that the African veld is perpetually stifling, not to mention grim, drab and hostile, looking unlikely ever to recover. But, when the rains come, it *always* cools down and flourishes.

Back in the field, my flat tyre repaired, I looked again at Kanondo pan and felt a sense of desperation – tumultuous feelings over the neglect, and the hopelessness of some others to get a job done, overwhelming me. The pan was not only dry; it was also full of weed-covered silt. It must surely rain soon, I thought, and then it would be too late to scoop this important pan. Tired of waiting for those responsible to attend to it, I managed to get some diesel donated, eliminating at least this barrier. I called the painted dog project to ask if we could loan equipment that might do the job, and negotiated a deal to secure someone skilled to operate it. Cooperation was fantastic and, within hours, we were set to go.

The scorching heat of the day was relieved somewhat by puffy white clouds intermittently hiding the sun. Sables, waterbucks and kudus looked on hopefully as the scooping of Kanondo pan began. It was a long and noisy process. Much of the pan was, deceptively, still too damp beneath the layers of crumbly soil, threatening to bog down the 4x4 tractor (which unfortunately, by design, had the scoop attached behind it, forcing the tractor to go in head first). Yet the men, working through the blazing heat, did what they could, carting load after load of silt out of the pan. Soon though, the tractor was hopelessly bogged down.

'Can't you get your friends to assist?' one of the helpers asked me. It took me a moment to understand his meaning. I followed his gaze, focused a few hundred metres away on my big grey friends. 'They could pull us out easily,' he said. 'Can't you get them to help?'

Unfortunately, it was not quite that easy.

As I stood overseeing the scooping of Kanondo pan, I realised with disappointment that the job was much too big for the equipment being used, and I realised, too, that we would never finish before the rains arrived. I was also aware that the 4x4 tractor and scoop would soon need to be returned to the dog project – so that they could do work of their own – and therefore, I selected just the outer rim to concentrate on so that at least this small section would be done.

Meanwhile, a few hundred metres away, two big old sable bulls engaged in a territorial clash. Kanondo didn't seem to me to be a particularly prime piece of property right now. It was, I thought watching their chase, barely worth fighting over.

When, three days later, thunder rumbled and more powerful equipment had still not been secured to improve the Kanondo scooping process, I finally admitted defeat. A very small part of the pan had been scooped, the process long and tiresome with equipment that was simply too small for such a big job. Now, the rain could fall. The two men operating the tractor and scoop had done their best. The pan was in better shape than it had been, but plenty more could have been done with more powerful front-end equipment.

Kanondo pan, I realised with a heavy sigh, would no longer hold the quantity of water that it had in past years (indeed, from then on the pan held decent water only in the scooped outer rim). Being completely dry for the first time ever, this had been an ideal chance to return it to its original depth – to ensure that it would fill to capacity during future rains – and to rid it of the unattractive and thirsty weed that was covering its surface. I deeply regretted the loss of this opportunity. But there was little more that I could do. I had nagged enough.

A few days later, as I watched a flock of European bee-eaters, summer visitors to this land, skimming the surface of a water seepage, movement behind a distant fallen tree caught my eye. Through binoculars I could see the legs of an antelope rocking towards the sky. 'Caught in a snare' – these words spoken or thought, I no longer recall.

Conditioned by now to expect the worst, I drove with haste, my heart pounding, towards the buck. But there was no wire, and for that I was greatly relieved. The old male waterbuck was in his final death throws. Saddened, I watched him die. There was no predator spoor, but it was soon evident that he'd escaped a feline attack. There were claw marks on his hide. I knew that cheetah tended to favour the waterbuck here, even full-grown ones like this male. His injuries didn't appear to be life threatening, but they were fresh and there was little doubt that his death was associated with them. He was a grand old gentleman in good condition, his horns 65 centimetres long. At least, I reflected, it was nature's way to die.

Elsewhere on the estate, a wire was being removed from around a zebra's neck. On adjoining land, a second zebra was not so fortunate. It had been snared and butchered and, knowing well that the carcass would be found, a flippant note from the poachers had brazenly been scrawled in the sand. I'd also recently seen yet another zebra suffering the ghastly effects of a tight, deadly wire.

The battle against poaching was far from over – and still the rains did not come.

I always await the full moon with anticipation, for with it, it is said, will come a change in the weather. The night of the October full moon was practically cloudless and I searched the night skies for a hint of rain, but there was none.

At long last, one night in early November, while an unknown

elephant bull once again attempted to demolish the coral creeper in my garden, cracks of thunder split the silence. For a short while, rain pelted my thatched roof. I lay on my sofa bed on the floor of my rondavel thinking of the Ls, who I'd encountered earlier that day. The story of *Bambi* sprung to mind, and I found myself substituting words into the passages that I'd memorised in childhood.

I imagined young Libby out there in the darkness asking her mother in a wee voice, 'What's all this wet stuff?'

'Why, it's rain,' Lady replies in wonder.

'*Rain?*' little Libby questions innocently, never before having felt anything like it on her young body.

'Yes,' says Lady, 'the rains have finally come...'

So, mercifully, the drought was broken at last.

The next month, as the trees laughed in the wind, with billowy white clouds in the sky above, I caught sight of Lady and her family mud bathing on the vlei. It was always such a pleasure to see them. Lady lumbered up to me, jet black from the sludge she'd been wallowing in. She was so caked with mud that she was barely recognisable. Even her tusks were protrusions of black goo. Soon my hands were coated in it too.

To my relief, they were all fine – incredibly muddy, but fat and happy – having quickly regained condition and spirit after the rain. Libby and Lancelot raced around together, joining little Litchis and Laurie in play and then, much to my delight, I saw that they had another new playmate. Stumbling beside Lucky was a little girl, clumsy and cute, immediately named Lindsay.

By now I had determined that elephants on the Hwange Estate give birth once every four years on average. I knew, therefore, that it would be a long wait before I could record any new additions to this family.

As I drove further down the vlei, I could see on my bonnet the thick muddy print of two corrugated trunks. I was carrying, as always, on my bonnet and in my heart, fond memories of Lady and Lesley. As had become my habit, I urged them to stay safe.

It had been a special year to spend with the Ls, with all five adult females nurturing babies less than 12 months old. Their numbers had increased from 13 to 18, but Lady's eldest son, Levi, left the family permanently (as all teenage males eventually do), reducing their number to 17.

I was always surprised during this year at how often young Lancelot suckled from Lady, and how regularly he was in close proximity to her, rather than to Lesley, his mother. I imagined this had something to do with Lesley's still-developing mothering skills, and Lady's subsequent desire to help out her daughter and her grandchild. I imagined, too, that it had something to do with the close bond that had developed between Lancelot and Libby, Lady's own daughter. They always raced around together, close to Lady, looking like twins. Lancelot was growing faster than Libby (as male elephants do), and within a few months was already almost the same size as her. The casual observer could easily have believed Lady to be Lancelot's mother, rather than his grandmother, and might even have considered Libby and Lancelot to be twins. It is, regrettably, this sort of casual observation that distorts the true picture of what is *really* going on in the life of an elephant family. Only those of us who spend extended time among elephants are privileged to know the reality.

As Christmas approached, I often gazed out from my rondavel at all the mistletoe in the 'rain' trees – large clumps of greenery drooping from high boughs. It appears to favour these trees (nicknamed rain trees because of a spittle bug that sometimes infests them, secreting a clear liquid that falls from the tree like rain). Mistletoe, as Miriam once informed me, is a symbol of love and peace. Long ago it was decreed that those who pass beneath mistletoe should kiss – to proclaim the strength of love; to seal a friendship. A symbol of peace, I pondered again. Perhaps that is why I find myself so drawn to mistletoe, not just at Christmas time, with its links to holly and fir trees, but throughout the year. Only now do I understand that it signifies my relentless longing for peace and tranquillity in this, the animals' world.

I reflected on another link to Christmas that made me pensive. It was a gift from so long ago that I could no longer remember which year he'd placed it in my hand. We'd worked together at Ernst & Young, once upon a time. 'This will keep you safe,' he said to me one Christmas. Wrapped in tissue paper, now faded and deeply wrinkled with time, I still have his tiny St Christopher pendant, which travels everywhere with me, tucked away in a small grey pouch. These days it accompanies me to 'bush Christmases' in Africa, but in another life, it had accompanied me to 'white Christmases' in various destinations around the world.

Deep in the Zimbabwean bush, far removed from the traditional 'white Christmas' of the northern hemisphere, it is the sickle bush – its boughs naturally decorated with tiny Christmas lanterns of mauve-pink and yellow – together with the enchanting sight of flame lilies flowering along the roadsides, which always reminds me that Christmas is close. The sight of newborn impala and wildebeest babies, fragile and long limbed, reminds me too.

Thunder rumbled outside, and I snuggled into bed. You forget how chilly rainy nights can sometimes be, after so much unrelenting heat. I was warmed by my mug of instant cappuccino and my piece of moist fruitcake.

'It will be my Christmas cake,' I'd whispered to my friend Carmen (who always treated me like a long-lost daughter), when I accepted this thoughtful gift, wrapped in foil, when I was last in Bulawayo. So, this year, I had something delicious to remind me that Christmas was nigh.

Later that night I listened once again to the distant rumble of thunder, and was reminded of the interactive rumbles of the elephants. In her book *Silent Thunder*, American acoustic biologist Katy Payne refers to the infrasound communications between elephants (which was her discovery) – those of their extraordinary airborne communications that are below the level of human hearing, powerful vibrations that human beings cannot perceive as sound. *'Silent thunder'*... such an apt description, I thought to myself, as the storm outside intensified around me.

Peering into the night, lit only by distant sheet lightning, I wondered what elephants think of the thunder. My thoughts moved on to the private pain and bewilderment endured by Katy in 1991. Zimbabwe had, unbeknown to her at the time, culled her study elephants – five families – in the Sengwa reserve, in the centre of the country.

It was this destruction that convinced Katy that all life is sacred and, like others who intimately understand elephants' lives, she would later challenge the philosophies that support culling. Culling, she'd learned and heard first-hand, often happened for aesthetic and economic reasons – not for ecological reasons.

And I felt decidedly uneasy, as I always do when rereading her book.

My selection of books consists predominantly of true stories of Africa; of people working here among wildlife. They provide me with company when I need to feel that I'm not alone. I've read most of them multiple times. There were lots of occasions, years ago now, when I'd read these same books Down Under, envious of the lives that these mysterious people led; remarkable lives among African wildlife. It still seems odd to me – strangely surreal – that now I am one of them.

As well as the one by Katy, I have much-loved books by Kuki Gallmann, Mark and Delia Owens, Joyce Poole, Cynthia Moss, Dian Fossey, Jane Goodall, Iain and Oria Douglas-Hamilton, Richard Leakey, Gareth Patterson, Joy and George Adamson, Karen Blixen, Beryl Markham and others. Driven by their passion, I often think to myself with a grin, some of these people could perhaps be considered a little crazy for enduring all that they did.

As I reread passages of their writings, by now well known to me, I recognise that, at least in part, they remind me of me.

PART VII

Lost Hope

Spy Allegation
and Degradation

In Kenya, the Swahili-speaking people say, '*Wapiganapo tembo nyasi huumia*' – 'When elephants tussle, the grass gets hurt.'

To the indigenous Kenyans the meaning is clear, and for me the meaning had already become real: 'When officials wield their power, innocent people get hurt.'

It was early in January 2006 and the settlers were not finished with me yet.

When they discovered that the Parks Authority had, courageously, not issued them a sport-hunting quota for that year, for the land sandwiched between the two photographic lodges on the vlei, an article appeared on the back page of the Bulawayo government-controlled newspaper, and on its website.

It read, in part, 'That Sharon Pincott is bad news and until we deal with that woman once and for all, we will always have problems. She is destroying the whole conservation.'

It was a quote from the head settler's brother-in-law, and the words 'once and for all' had only one meaning in Zimbabwe. This was their attempt to gain public support, before the demise they clearly had planned for me.

All these never-ending threats and attempts at intimidation were becoming tiresome, although at least now it was in print for the world to see. After I phoned and complained to some higher authorities about this threat on my life, the article quickly disappeared from the website. Finally, though, it was very clear to those with any degree of intelligence that these 'new farmers', who had previously been empowered with hunting quotas issued by the Parks Authority, had no idea what the word 'conservation' even meant.

Just a few weeks later, in late January (one year after their forced departure from the Kanondo and Khatshana areas), the settlers played their final card.

By now the head settler was no longer a governor; he was a government minister. Taking advantage of his position, he wrote me a three-page letter – on paper with a letterhead saying 'Khanondo [sic] Safaris & Tours' – formally accusing me of being a spy; an 'agent of the Australian Government assigned with the task of frustrating [Zimbabwe's] land reform programme'.

It was a desperate, laughable allegation. It was yet another attempt to scare me out of the country – or have me expelled – in order that he, his family and their cronies could more easily continue their unethical practices.

His letter referred to me as 'an Australian reject' and called me 'illiterate'. It went on to talk of my 'local corrupt accomplices' and the 'racist white Rhodesians', whose interests I was apparently representing. It was disturbing that, 26 years after the country was renamed Zimbabwe, he referred to Rhodesians. The 'racist white' accusation was *so* old – so very, very old – and so completely unrelated to my reasons for being in Africa. How easy it was to try to turn everything into a racist issue, and to attempt to hide behind that. It was also common practice to try to make the good guy out to be the bad.

He went on to state that my 'provocation deserves to be stopped one way or the other'.

They were the words of a very desperate man. But, as I knew well by now, this was a family of men who specialised in threats and intimidation.

He claimed that my activities in Zimbabwe were 'nefarious'. It was a word that I had to look up in the thesaurus on my laptop; a word I'd never heard before.

'Evil, despicable,' my thesaurus clarified. Well, at least that explained how *he* knew the word.

He further claimed that he 'voluntarily moved out from [the

Hwange] estate after realizing that the area was infested with anti-land reform agents like you... Never was there a request or order from anybody for me to leave the area serve (sic) for your lunatic and imaginary eviction, which only exists in your mind and that of your informers... Your mission totally failed as I frustrated it during my term as governor hence your anger'.

Were any of us really *that* stupid? It was, yet again, all about trying not to lose face.

Immediately I faxed copies of this letter to my contacts, including two supportive and powerful government ministers. Both of these ministers had, supposedly, been copied on the original letter, but by now I knew how this man operated. It was just another scam. I was *supposed* to think that they'd all turned against me. That was his plan.

My problems were not with government officials in general. They were with one man, who happened to be in office, his extended family and their unethical hunting associates.

Shortly after receiving 'the spy letter', as it came to be known, I spent a pre-arranged month in Australia and New Zealand visiting family and friends. I was one of the lucky ones, able to leave Zimbabwe whenever I wished to. Many of my friends, restricted by available funds and tough visa requirements, were not so fortunate.

On my departure, a customs officer asked me if I was carrying any Zimbabwean dollars, as it had become illegal to take more than the equivalent of a few US dollars out of the country.

'Why would I *want* to take Zimbabwean dollars out of the country?' I asked, bewildered. 'I couldn't even *give* them away if I wanted to.' Pressing my point, I continued, 'They're worth almost nothing in *this* country, and they're worth absolutely nothing in every other country.'

I could tell from his self-conscious look that he'd heard it all before, no doubt millions of times. Embarrassed laughter followed and I knew that he was only doing what he'd been instructed to do.

Onboard a Qantas aircraft the song 'I Still Call Australia Home' beamed into my earphones, and I felt tears sting my eyes. By now I was more confused than ever about where home was. It was the wild spaces of Zimbabwe that held my heart, but I had to admit that I was relieved to be about to spend time in a sophisticated environment, at least for a while. With my parents and my sister Deborah, I feasted on a much longed-for seafood smorgasbord, and I ate chocolate and more chocolate, and shared excellent red wine with my father.

I also visited friends in Auckland, New Zealand – my old home town – and delighted in the sight of the sea; endless vistas of crystal clear water. Further north, I walked some incredibly beautiful beaches, digging my toes into white sand. Waves lapped at my ankles as I revelled in the quiet beauty of the rocky cliffs, the seagulls and the delicate seashells. Now, at last, I could *really* fly that kite by the rolling sea! With Eileen, I sat on a bench in an open-air restaurant built over the sparkling ocean, devouring delicious, melt-in-your-mouth calamari, and chips, the best that they could be.

Back in Zimbabwe, the ramifications of 'the spy letter' were still being dealt with. One afternoon, while relaxing in my childhood home with kookaburras laughing outside, I received a phone call from the Australian Embassy in Harare. 'We recommend that you consider not returning to Zimbabwe,' said the voice on the end of the line. It was what they *had* to say, I knew. Should something dire happen, they needed to have said what protocol required of them.

I appreciated their concern. But I'd also received other advice, 'No one is taking the … man seriously, as they see through his ulterior motives,' I was assured in writing by the man who'd previously accompanied me to Harare. 'The abuses of the past will cease.'

Perhaps, I thought, but perhaps not.

These were just words, I knew. And doubt shook me. I'd heard many such words over the past 28 months since the settlers had first laid claim to Kanondo and Khatshana. By now, I was suspicious of their truth. Yet the more the settlers pushed, the more I was determined to stay on in Zimbabwe – for the elephants, and for all of the wildlife. There'd been so many attempts to scare me out of the country, but it was the wrong sort of tactic to use on me. The more they wanted me gone, the more I was determined to stay. At least for now.

My parents, approaching their mid-seventies yet still full of life, said to me, 'If you feel good where you are, then so do we.' So I returned to Zimbabwe in March, after my month's holiday.

'How is Zimbabwe?' I asked on my return.

'Arrhhh it is not very fine,' I was told repeatedly, 'but God must have a plan.'

I could only breathe a sigh of resignation and add gently with a smile, 'I think that God went on holiday from Zimbabwe too. It sounds like He has not yet returned...'

'The spy letter' was the last communication that I had directly from the settlers. Not as powerful as they liked everyone to believe, they'd been silenced, at least in relation to me. I never saw them again, but it was not the last that I ever heard *about* them.

That August they reapplied to hunt on the small piece of land sandwiched between the two photographic lodges on the vlei. There were new personnel in the local Parks Authority office, and they clearly thought they'd try their luck. The fact that the Parks Authority was actually reinvestigating the feasibility of reissuing a quota, with total disregard to the previous directive of the Tourism Minister banning them from ever hunting there again was, for me, further evidence of ignorance and possible collusion. I circulated a plea for this issue to be dealt with 'once and for all'. But I had little faith that this would happen. Next year, and the year after that and the one after that, I thought, the issue was sure to raise its ugly head time and again.

My agitation with the whole situation grew, rather than diminished, with the passage of time. And that echoless void was back. 'Is anybody out there?' I wondered, baffled yet again by the silence surrounding me. It was becoming increasingly impossible to get any answers at all.

Not long after their reapplication to hunt, the head settler's own colleagues pushed to have him charged with contempt of Parliament, for allegedly lying under oath. While reading the related articles in the government-controlled newspaper, I could only shake my head in distaste, for there in these very press reports was that word again: *nefarious*. It was a word I'd come to know well.

The further degradation that I witnessed during 2006 was devastating. The number of pans on the Hwange Estate that held ample dry season water had by now declined from 12 to one. There were no longer caring and interested people on the ground – at least none prepared to really make an effort to resolve the problems. Even after I managed to secure donor support to assist with water and pan maintenance, nothing was done to meet the reasonable requirements of these donors, and so, unwilling to work in a one-way street, the donors walked away. Just as exasperatingly, snare removal efforts were now being frustrated by the lackadaisical attitudes of some of the people on the Hwange Estate. Without the promise of pumped water, and still recovering from all the gunfire, the Presidential Elephants had no reason to return to the estate in their previous numbers. Lengthy, unambiguous sightings of most of the family groups were by now at an all-time low.

I still felt a special unity with the elephants – with all the animals – and I tried hard to let my body and soul succumb to the magic of nature – a magic I knew was still out there, somewhere. I took what comfort I could in the birds, in the bushbuck that visited my garden, and in the playful vervet monkeys. I'd always felt free in the African veld, like I belonged to the wind. But too often now the wind, once gentle, blew wildly cyclonic.

I would make a wish on a shooting star, or on the new moon shining in a darkened sky, slim and bright. Yet my wishes, my hopes and my dreams seemed to drift away into the dark depths of nowhere. I'd been seduced by Africa; seduced by its elephants. But now my dream of living harmoniously, continuing to lend a hand to my tranquil mighty friends, seemed increasingly out of reach.

It seemed to me that there were few people around at this time who responded well to logical input. There were few people who were motivated to try to restore what once was. I was surrounded, I finally realised, by many who cared little for hope and dreams – or for animals. I was surrounded by indifference.

Once upon a time, as for so many tourists, there was no greater pleasure for me than to spend time at Kanondo. I'd once found refuge there from all that was going on around me. But not any more. It was no longer a place of solace. There was a sadness now in driving there. Even so, I still went there most days, already knowing that few elephants – indeed, few animals – were likely to be there to greet me. The main pan was still depressingly silted up, bone dry and covered with grass and weed. Kanondo had a bleak, abandoned feel to it now, and it was splattered with bad memories. There was always a dull ache in my chest; a deep-seated fear of what could happen again; of the neglect that was happening now.

Sometimes I took the opportunity to explore on foot, trying to restore my spirit. There were often small treasures to be found on the ground. The days were generally hot, the sun's rays beating down on my bare arms as I walked about, alert to any hidden dangers, trying to rediscover the essence of the African bush. The dry breeze always carried an aroma of sunbaked earth. On the ground there might be a short hair from the tail of an elephant; the rounded shiny black shell of a toktokkie beetle; a striped quill of a porcupine or a brilliant blue feather from a lilac-breasted roller. Or there might be moulted guineafowl feathers, with delicate patterns of black, white and grey, as exquisite as only nature can produce.

Memories always flooded back. There was the place, now deeply cracked and broken apart by the unrelenting sun, where the rhino had taken great pleasure in a mud bath. There was the place where the cheetahs had devoured their kill. There was the place where the lion pride had rested and the one where Loopy was saved. There were so many memories – and so many more, I still thought optimistically, just waiting to materialise.

But however indescribable, there was the unmistakeable scent of neglect lingering at Kanondo. And there was the distasteful smell of tragedy. Was this the new scent of wild Zimbabwe, I wondered sadly?

Contact with the elephants proved to be the best medicine for me, but with so little water being pumped, they were around much too infrequently. On the odd occasions when the air smelt sweet with dung, full of the promise of elephants ahead, I was elated. Once again, if only for a short while, I would fall under the spell of The Presidential Elephants of Zimbabwe.

When they were not around, I felt strangely alone, and I thought that

262

they must surely feel it too. I wondered, more and more often, who in Zimbabwe *really* cared about their welfare. Reluctantly I conceded that there were so very few who truly did; at least not enough to find their voice and help to do something constructive. So often this feeling of emptiness overwhelmed me.

I recognised that during my years with the elephants the highs had always been so very high; the lows, when they came, so very gloomy.

'You need to get your smile back,' observed a colleague one day, as we stood together in my garden. It was indeed true that the smile of my childhood, my adolescence, my early adulthood, was all but gone.

It was Easter of that year, just after we'd enjoyed a short break in the rocky hills of Matopo, that Shaynie gave me a special gift. It was a poem she'd written for me, and when placing it in my hands she asked that I keep in mind something important. 'Always remember,' she said, 'an eagle flies further when in a turbulent wind...'

Back at my rondavel, I regularly gazed at the sausage trees now growing in my garden, wondering if I would be here to see them full-grown. The hope that had once blazed like a bright star flickered endlessly. But it was still there, along with the heartache. It was difficult to consider the possibility of leaving with some goals not yet achieved, but it was also difficult to make any concrete plans. I just had to take it one day at a time.

Sometimes, in desperate need of light relief, I would try to recall amusing incidents. This one always made me laugh: We communicated mostly in sign language. He had little English, and I no Sindebele or Shona. He tried at least, which was more than I usually did with his native tongue, given that I'd never been good at languages. I'd taken him to look at the Kanondo water supply, in the days when it was running. He plunged his dark arm deep into the murky pond of water (which shouldn't have been there), and turned the tap around and around – and around. I too had done this the previous day.

'It's a problem,' I stated. Problem was a word I knew he understood.

He motioned his hand in the air, as if he was still turning the tap, and managed to blurt out three words: 'It is f*cked.' Gobsmacked, I couldn't help but laugh out loud. When coping with day-to-day life in

Zimbabwe, this was, I supposed, an English phrase worth knowing.

Perhaps to some, none of this is beautiful. One does, however, soon come to realise that it's not an *ordinary* beauty. The beauty of wild Africa goes much deeper than that. It's a feeling. A yearning. An ache in your bones. It infects you, and it steals your soul. This is the *extraordinary* beauty of the African veld.

'What happens after the elephants?' people often asked me.

'I don't know,' was usually the best that I could answer.

It's something that I've always felt; the reason I have no retirement policies or plans for my retirement. It's difficult for me to see myself making it to an old age.

I recall an e-mail from a colleague that brought a smile to my lips: 'Sh*t Sharon,' he wrote playfully, 'it often sounds like you're auditioning for a *Die Hard* movie!'

Perhaps being content with a shortened life is what gives me fortitude in difficult times.

I've had a privileged life. I haven't worked full-time in a paid job since I was 31. I retired altogether from the salaried world at age 38. How could anyone wish to change that? I would much rather, I still proclaim, be happy in my 40s doing what I truly want to do with my life, than be rich in my 60s.

'I hope someone asks you if you still think that when you're 60,' my father once declared, scolding my lack of planning for my old age. 'God will punish you,' he mused with a half-smile. 'He will make you live until you're 105!'

It was during this year of the spy allegation that I appreciated fun times with my friends more than ever before. In October I joined Carol and Miriam for some re-energising days at Makalolo, a nearby private wildlife estate run by Wilderness Safaris. It was such a pleasure to see roads maintained, and so much dry season water in pans. The poisonous ordeal trees, which are abundant in this Kalahari sand region, were producing young foliage in stunning shades of purple, making the drives through the veld especially beautiful.

One morning I walked towards the base of an umtshibi tree to collect some of its attractive cherry-colour-coated seeds from the ground. There was a large hole in its trunk, and I noticed Miriam and our guide ambling inquisitively towards it.

'Watch out,' I whispered playfully, 'there might be a black mamba in there.' The very next instant both made muted, surprised noises, and jumped back from the tree, their eyes wide. Oh no, I thought, don't tell me there really *is* a black mamba in there.

'Ssshhhh. Sssshhh. Come and look,' both gestured to me. 'There's a *genet* asleep in there.' As I turned to get a better view, I could see the beautiful black-spotted coat of a sleeping genet. This slender cat-like creature, with long thick tail, is nocturnal, known to rest during the day in shelters such as this. Having never seen a wild genet in daylight, I was enchanted.

It had been an interesting morning for holes in tree trunks. Earlier, we'd watched in fascination the activity surrounding the nest of a grey hornbill pair. Once the female hornbill was inside her hole, the male had sealed it up with mud, leaving only a small slot visible. Although we could see only her beak, we knew she was probably naked, having moulted her feathers to line the nest in preparation for the birth of her young. The male worked tirelessly outside, feeding her seeds and insects through the tiny slot, as he would continue to do until all her feathers had grown back and their chicks had hatched.

Later, after one of the first thunderstorms of the season brought a deluge of rain and an outpouring of sound, scent and colour, we watched flying ants of the pint-sized variety emerging in the sunset from slits in the now damp ground, like columns of smoke; tiny fairies floating up to the stars. Revelling in the smell of the earth reborn, I stood over them with my arms outstretched, allowing them to flutter up and around me, feeling their magic. At my feet were tiny frogs having a feast.

It was Miriam who disturbed my quiet fairyland. 'What on earth is *that?*' she shrieked loudly. I turned and walked towards her, watching her crouched in the grass.

'Oh my goodness,' I blurted out when I got there. 'Look at *that!*' By now we were both in a fit of giggles at the sight of this oversized, truly bizarre-looking creature.

'It's a Parktown Prawn,' our guide told us.

'It's a *what?*' we screeched in unison.

'It's a Parktown Prawn,' our guide repeated.

'Sounds like something you'd eat in Cape Town,' chuckled Miriam.

The tarantula-like creature, which we discovered was actually a King cricket, got its nickname because it's commonly found in the Johannesburg suburb of Parktown.

'If that's a cricket I'll eat my hat,' I muttered.

The sight of it left me aghast. Everything grows *so big* in Africa.

We took great pleasure in the extraordinary mystery of awakened life, which always follows the first rains. Tortoises had returned from the hidden nowhere of their hibernation, visible now on the sandy roads. There were toktokkie beetles and *shongololos* everywhere. The ballet of butterflies was enchanting as masses of them gathered around wet patches on the ground, proudly displaying their exquisite markings. The booming thunder and rain urged the throngs of frogs into a deafening, full-throated chorus.

It was beautiful.

Eventually, we fell into bed, drugged by fresh air and moonshine.

'I'm as tired as a stomped-on toad frog!' Miriam declared, before drifting off into a deep sleep.

On our way home to my rondavel the next morning we stopped at Makwa pan, inside Hwange National Park. Water was plentiful, and birds and other animals were there in abundance. I breathed deeply.

It was so lovely, I thought. It was Makwa pan as I remembered it; the almost forgotten Makwa of happier, more tranquil times. I quietly reminisced, recalling the day that I scattered Chloe's ashes. My thoughts moved on to Andy, Lol and Drew, who'd lived just up the road. So much had happened during the past six-and-a-half years, since Andy's death. So much had been endured, and I thought (not for the first time) that there's surely only so much one person can endure.

It had been a refreshing break full of friendship, food and laughter. But back on the Hwange Estate – Kanondo pan and most of the other pans were still bone dry – Presidential Elephant sightings remained few.

Previously I could taste hope, but now I could taste only neglect. And the aftertaste was bitter.

The 12th of Never

Like the flooded creeks of my childhood, I felt swirled and twirled around, the waters raging, their murky depths making it impossible to see anything clearly. In the darkest days I tried to recall the noble giraffe that I once saw standing grandly at the foot of a rainbow, surpassing a pot of gold. But it did little to help.

My concerns intensified, despite me reiterating them often to numerous parties. By late 2006 it seemed to me that there were few people in Zimbabwe who truly cared about the plight of their wildlife; about the plight of their flagship herd of elephants. So many were preoccupied with their own survival – which was understandable I suppose, in this crumbling economy. Others were still uneasy about speaking out publicly. Many had plenty to say in the safety of their own gatherings, but so very few did more than talk among themselves. Eventually I found myself relaying facts with a hint of bitterness.

Some now thought me to be too forthright, too fiery, too honest. Many did not like to hear or to believe the reality, much less to admit it publicly. They did not *want* to be ripped from their apathy. Yet I knew that people like myself were still not saying nearly enough. Zimbabwe's wildlife deserved better. I could count the people on one hand – sometimes with one or two fingers – who were vocal about what was happening to Zimbabwe's natural heritage. More often than not, plenty was left unsaid.

Having witnessed so much first-hand, my deep concern and irritation about the situation eventually deprived me of much caution, and I continued to set down the reality in writing, allowing my inner despair to morph into words – regardless of the consequences. Yet it still didn't really help. With the majority not willing to rock the boat, there was little public outcry (about anything) within the country itself.

There were many times, it seemed to me, that there was only a facade of caring for the wildlife. And still, sadly, there were few tourist dollars to plough back into conservation. Zimbabwe was singing a new song, and I no longer knew the words. So much was changing, and little of it, as far as I could see, was for the good of the wildlife – or for that matter, the good of anybody.

Every day now, to relieve the strain, I played a little game with myself. As I drove along the road to Kanondo I stretched my open hand out of my window, trying to repossess my dreams. But what was left of them just whizzed past, uncaught.

I stared at the passenger seat beside me, a sharp stab of realisation piercing my chest. I could see nothing but an empty space. Hope was sitting somewhere else.

I was desperately tired of dancing with despair all the time. And I was tired of being tired. There'd been many times, throughout my life, when I relished the hardships, but more and more often now all this needless suffering and neglect simply irritated me.

It was only the sight of Lady, Misty, Whole and my other elephant friends that reaffirmed for me that it had not all been for nothing.

What had happened to Zimbabwe – what was still happening – was heartbreaking and devastating. 'You've done more than your share,' I was assured by friends time and again. This did not help to lessen my grief.

'I must leave here,' I finally whispered sadly one evening, saying the words out loud at last; finally surrendering.

'Leave here? I think you'll leave here on the 12th of Never!' came the upbeat, undaunted reply. I was silent, but I knew in my heart that he was wrong.

Perhaps only I knew the true extent of the private agonies, the failed hope and the stolen dreams, and the despair that was constantly beating down on me. So, I thought, I've done what I can. Now I must do what I thought I could not. I must leave Zimbabwe.

I thought again about Karen Blixen, who died in the year that I was born. She'd been through so much in Africa and loved it dearly, yet after her enforced departure, she never returned – not once during the remaining 31 years of her life.

I could never understand it. She had loved it there so well.

Only now do I think that I understand how someone might never go back to a place so well-loved; a place where much heartache was endured; a place where, once left, you can never bring yourself to return to – the changes too vast, the pain much too deep.

Yet I know, too, the extraordinary impact that a visit to the Hwange Estate can have on a visitor who might stay for only a few days. It's still possible for tourists to leave with unforgettable memories of peaceful and magical moments, often leaving behind (by their own admission) a small slice of their hearts, and be anxious to return one day. This I understand so well, since being among the Presidential Elephants – when they're around – is an experience like no other.

When people heard of my plan to leave, the kind penned responses, received through one of Zimbabwe's conservation groups, had an identical tone, 'a sad end'; 'sad for us all'; 'I shake my head sadly'; 'so terribly sad'; 'brings sadness'; 'we are all so sad'…

Sad, sad, sad.

At least I wasn't alone in my sadness. Many of the e-mails, from thoughtful strangers, brought an increased ache to my troubled heart. One in particular, I will remember always. It read in part, 'You passed this way and touched the history of the Presidential Elephants. They would thank you if they could.'

A tight knot lived in my stomach, day and night. I didn't quite know how I would leave. I recalled a book titled *West with the Night* that Julia had given me for my birthday five years earlier. The words of Beryl Markham weighed heavily on my heart, 'I have learned that if you must leave a place that you have lived in and loved and where all your yesterdays are buried deep, leave it any way except a slow way, leave it the fastest way you can.'

These I considered to be wise words, but I knew it wouldn't be easy to heed them. At the time it seemed easier to me to leave in a *slow* way. I spent time at Kanondo – the Kanondo that I'd once loved so much; the Kanondo that I now barely recognised. I sat alone, thinking, and thinking some more, trying to be sure that my decision was the right one. I let the tides of uncertainty and disillusionment wash over me.

The new year – 2007 – materialised, and although I tried to sharpen my hopes, I found little reason to celebrate.

Eventually, hesitantly, I said my heartbreaking goodbyes to Lady and Libby and Lesley and Lancelot, to Misty, to Whole, and to so many of my other elephant friends. I wished that I could somehow make them understand. I wondered if they would eventually realise that I'd left them. I wondered if they would forgive me. I wondered if I would ever see them again. I begged them to stay safe; to stay away from the hunters and the snares.

As Lady and her family lumbered away from me, down the sandy road where I'd watched them walk so often, I saw through tears 17 shining stars falling from my world.

For more days, for more weeks, I stared at the truth that it was over. Zimbabwe and I were parting ways, and I felt deep sorrow. I felt aching grief.

I did not believe that I'd taken the wrong path all those years before, but I understood now that I needed to find another one – another one among the African wildlife that I loved. There are no real endings, I consoled myself; only new beginnings. And my future hopes and dreams, I knew, would forever embrace my giant grey Hwange friends.

I felt unable to skip or run or dance, but I would walk, wiser now, into the next phase of my life.

Afterword

As the months passed and I prepared to move to South Africa's Eastern Cape, to work with elephants there, I witnessed an increased commitment to restore what once was. Changes in personnel brought renewed enthusiasm, and renewed hope.

I found myself still on the Hwange Estate in July 2007, when a carcass from a recent illegal elephant hunt was stumbled upon. Not long before, we'd successfully removed a deadly snare from the neck of a tiny six-week-old elephant in the T family. Shortly after, a pre-planned snare bust resulted in the satisfying arrest of two men in trusted positions, both of whom I'd been increasingly suspicious of for some time.

There was still a lot going on.

Various authorities reacted positively to my subsequent pleas for assistance, and I felt more encouraged. The Parks Authority at last seemed to be taking a greater interest in the welfare of the Presidential Elephants, and I was assured that no further hunting quotas would ever be issued on the Hwange Estate. Finally, too, the landowner Zimsun (now renamed African Sun) agreed that Kanondo, and other pans, must indeed be resurrected in order to provide adequate dry season water – although nothing had yet been done to achieve this.

Zimbabwe was on its knees: no fuel, no meat, no bread, no eggs, few dairy products and empty shelves everywhere. Friends in the cities were enduring daily power cuts, often of more than eight hours in length, together with constant water outages. The exchange rate had hit Z$150 000 to US$1. Earlier, three zeros had been knocked off the currency overnight, so this was, in reality, 150 000 000 (150 million) to one.

Things seemed worse than ever, yet I found myself hesitantly agreeing to try to hold on.

It was actually a few months earlier, one day in late April, that my decision to leave first seriously began to haunt me. That was the day I discovered Lancelot had been snared. He'd been trapped around his right front leg – the third snare victim in the L family.

To my great relief Lancelot, like Limp and Loopy before him, survived.

If I could help just one more of my elephant friends to escape further terrible troubles, I thought, it would be worth it to try to stay on – wouldn't it?

Once again, I could taste something; something vaguely familiar; something sharp and sweet on my palate. It had the flavour of wonder; the flavour of longing; the flavour of renewed hope.

I soon found myself back in the Matopo Hills with Shaynie and friends, this time to watch the night-time Perseid meteor showers of August. I was pensive; still unsure of what I should be doing.

Those stolen dreams?

'Hey Sharon!' boomed Shaynie (pretending to throw something my way), '*Catch!*'

* * *

But by now many Presidential Elephants were missing. Leanne (Lady's eldest sister) was one of them. With perfectly symmetrical tusks, longer and thicker than those of most of the Presidential females, she was a prime target for the hunters and poachers – a gentle soul on whose tusks I could place my hand. Would little Litchis, not yet three years old, survive without his mother? How would Lady cope with the disintegration of her family?

My giant grey friend Leanne was never seen again.

* * *

Seven months later, in early 2008, Litchis was managing to survive. There was, however, more distressing news. Leanne's elder son, six-year-old Lee, had one quarter of his trunk ripped off by a wire snare. He was gallantly trying to learn to live with this awful human-inflicted disability. He'd lost his mother, and now he'd lost the full use of his trunk.

Four snare wounds, and one death, in what was a family of just 17. Could the odds get even worse than this?

The day I discovered Lee had lost a portion of his trunk, I was despondent. The despair I felt was deep inside me – even though several dedicated, non-commercial, anti-poaching units now patrolled the greater Hwange area, affording some hope.

In addition to the ongoing snaring and slaughter of the wildlife, it was by now becoming clear to me that the increased interest shown in mid-2007 by African Sun, to better promote and assist the Presidential Elephants, was extremely short-lived after new faces appeared in management positions. My endless offers over the years of complimentary photographs and articles to augment marketing efforts, and to chat with guests and accompany interested ones on game drives – in order to heighten their Presidential Elephant experience, while at the same time imparting valuable knowledge to the safari guides – continued to fall on deaf ears.

Carol, who has travelled Africa and indeed the world first-class, is among a growing list of people who rate a day with me among the Presidential Elephants as one of the 'top three' things they've ever done, anywhere in the world. These visitors revel in the close presence of the elephants, while getting to know them as individuals – learning to appreciate their intimate family lives, as well as how to interpret their interactions with one another and with us, their human company. Yet the indifference among others continues.

What Zimbabwe desperately needs – what the Hwange Estate desperately needs – is a photographic safari operator who understands, and fully appreciates, the value of the Presidential Elephants as a key tourism drawcard; who would promote them as such (having learned more about them than mere 'general elephant' facts) and who would properly maintain the land on which they roam.

At the time of writing, there were still people around who tried to intimidate and silence, one way or another, those who spoke out about what was happening to Zimbabwe's wildlife. It seemed to me that this was, more often than not, their unsavoury way of attempting to conceal their own dubious activities, or those of someone they knew. During my time here (and indeed before), there'd always been lies, denials, cover-ups and scare tactics – all of which I'd been exposed to. And this continued.

Emotionally, I felt that I was almost exactly where I'd been two years earlier.

That night, after seeing Lee snared, I sat out under a full moon at Kanondo, on the rooftop of Nicki Mukuru, in an attempt to restore my spirit. It was Good Friday, 2008. Parliamentary and Presidential elections were to be held in just one week's time. The exchange rate was now more than Z$40 million (which was, in reality, 40 billion) to US$1, the inflation rate more than 200 000 per cent. The country was in more trouble than ever before, with its dollar continuing to lose value on an hourly basis. Little did I know that within another five months the inflation rate would hit 50 million per cent; the exchange rate over Z$5 trillion to US$1 (which was in reality 5 quadrillion to one). Still nothing had been done to resurrect the pans on the Hwange Estate, although there was (now in late March) enough wet season surface water to attract some wildlife.

The perfect sphere of the moon shed brilliant silvery light, dimming the myriad of drifting stars. Hundreds of fireflies danced around me, to the music of elephant rumbles, the haunting howls of jackals and the frantic klink, klink, klink alarm call from the handsome blacksmith plover pair as they tried desperately to protect their three eggs from the footfalls of the elephants, who were innocently wandering within centimetres of their ground-nest. I could see the outline of the elephants clearly. When they lumbered within a few metres of my 4x4 there was enough natural light for me to tell exactly who they were. My own form (seated high on my rooftop) was perfectly silhouetted on the ground. When elephants passed so very close, it was shadowed on their bodies. Some of the adolescents pushed their trunks together, high in the bright night sky, in playful sparring. Others mock-charged an adult rhino that was grazing nearby. The air was clean and crisp, tusks gleamed in the magical night light, huge ears flapped, and the night birds sang.

It is what holds me here. At least for now.

Members of the W family were less than one metre away, feasting on minerals. Whole was giving me a trunk-to-hand greeting, the full moon glowing powerfully just above her massive back; her youngest calf, Winnie, suckling contentedly. Her 13-year-old daughter, Whosit, rested one of her small tusks, much too heavily, against my windscreen. Whole, as always, looked about innocently, pretending that cheeky Whosit was not *her* daughter. Whosit pushed down harder on my windscreen.

'Hey! Whosit!' I cried. 'I'll give you a smack.'

Which was, I suppose, a pretty silly thing to say to a wild, several-tonne elephant.

* * *

Sharon still lives and works amongst the elephants in Zimbabwe. Her goal now is to help encourage the tourists of the world to return and experience all that Zimbabwe has to offer. It is, she believes, crucial to the preservation of the wildlife.

Glossary

4x4	Four wheel drive, off-road vehicle
akubra	Legendary hat of the Australian outback
Amarula	A South African cream liqueur, made from the fruit of the marula tree (which elephants love to eat)
black mamba	A deadly snake
boma	An enclosure made of branches and thorn bush
braai	Barbeque
browser	An animal that primarily eats leaves
cull	The killing/shooting of selected animals, theoretically as a way of managing populations
curio	A rare, unusual or intriguing object (often local art)
dry season	In Zimbabwe there is no rain of significance between April and October
duiker	One of the smaller antelope
footing	A localism for walking
G&T	Gin & Tonic mixed drink
galah	A pink and grey cockatoo, native to Australia
gogga	South African slang for bugs/insects (pronounced gho-gha)
impala	A medium-sized antelope
infrasound	The way that elephants frequently communicate with one another: sound below the level of human hearing; low-frequency vocalisations/rumbles that can travel great distances. Elephants are known to have a large repertoire of infrasonic calls
inyanga	Sindebele word for 'witchdoctor'
koppie	Afrikaans word for 'rocky outcrop'
kudu	One of the larger antelope
Mandlo	Informal version of *Mandlovu*
Mandlovu	Sindebele word meaning 'Mother Elephant'
matriarch	The adult female elephant (usually the oldest female) that leads a family
mealie meal	Ground maize (corn) used to make sadza, the staple food of Zimbabwe
mukiwa	Sindebele word for 'white man'
mushi	Shona word meaning 'super', 'excellent', '*really* nice'
muti	Sindebele word for 'medicine'

Ndebele	The people of the Matabeleland province in Zimbabwe
ndlovu	Sindebele word for 'elephant'
nyoka	Sindebele word for 'snake'
pan	Waterhole
panga	Machete
poacher	Someone who illegally kills wildlife
put foot	A localism for 'hurry'
ration hunting	In Zimbabwe, quotas for hunting in protected areas (eg, inside the National Parks) are approved, to provide 'food rations' for Parks Authority staff
roan	One of the larger antelope
rondavel	Small round hut, typically with a thatched roof
rusk	A rectangular, hard, dry biscuit, usually dipped in coffee or tea
sable	One of the larger antelope
sadza	Maize (corn) meal staple of Zimbabwe
safari	Swahili word meaning 'to go on a journey'
schlep	South African slang for 'nuisance'/'effort'
shame!	Zimbabwe's regularly used version of 'oh what a shame' or 'oh I'm sorry'
Shona	Chief language of the Mashonaland province in Zimbabwe
shongololo	A large black millipede
shrew	A small mouse-like animal with a pointed nose, that feeds on insects
shumba	Shona word for 'lion'
Sindebele	Chief language of the Ndebele people, who live in the Matabeleland province of Zimbabwe
snare	Wire trapping device consisting of a noose (set by commercial and subsistence poachers), in which animals die a lingering death, and from which animals sometimes escape seriously injured, often with the strangling wire embedded in a part of their body.
spoor	Footprints
sundowners	Drinks at sunset
Thandeka	Ndebele name meaning 'much loved'
thatch	Dried grass
toktokkie	A wingless black beetle that attracts a mate by tapping its abdomen on the ground, making a 'tok-tok' sound
Umtshibi	Base of the Parks Authority 'Wildlife Capture and Relocation' unit, Hwange National Park – named after the tree *Guibourtia coleosperma* which has the same local name
veld	Afrikaans word for grassland or bush
vlei	Afrikaans word for open, seasonally marshy area
wet season	In Zimbabwe good rain typically falls only between November and March
wildebeest	One of the larger antelope

Acknowledgements

Zimbabwe-based friends have seen me through happy and sad times, offering treasured support and sharing many memorable days. I thank especially Shaynie Beswick, Dinks Adlam, Lol Searle, Drew Searle, Carol McCammon, Miriam Litchfield, John and Del Foster, Karen Paolillo, Julia Salnicki, Carmen and Ernie Deysel, Marion Valeix and Mathieu Bourgarel for being an important part of my story. A special thank-you goes to Shaynie Beswick for countless favours over many years, and for my home away from home.

Without the late Andy Searle I might never have found the courage to leave behind my comfortable life to live among the animals in the Hwange bush, and to him I remain eternally grateful.

Friends from around the world provided encouragement and kind words. I am especially thankful to my dear friends in New Zealand – Andrea McKain, Eileen Duffy and Bobby Dempsey. From Australia, Mandy Keating still shares with me her special gift of singing and songwriting. For enduring friendship, I thank Anne Waldie, Sue McMurchy and Susan Grady, as well as Karol and Paul Smith and John Diegan, who helped me in the early days.

I must also make mention of Val DeMontille, Helen Putterill, Adele Edwards, Sue Coughlan, Lindsay Ehrich, Ian Hyslop, Ed Bredenkamp, Ian Macdonald, Mark Warren, the Nel family, Bev Poor, Alan Thomson, Wayne Monks and Mary Hutton for kindness not forgotten, and Lionel Slowe, Nick Booth (who Nicki Mukuru is named after) and Mike Karasselos for sharing some memorable moments.

My parents, Stan and June Schulz, and my elder sisters Genevieve Clark and Deborah Steinhardt are always there when I need them, my life perhaps just a little odd for them to fully comprehend! My younger sister, Catherine Finch, identified with my choices and initially looked after all that I left behind in Australia. My nieces, Rebecca and Sari Steinhardt, regularly sent e-mails that made me smile.

Andrea McKain took time to review the first draft of my manuscript, and I thank her sincerely for making time for me in her hectic schedule. I also thank Nevin Weakley for valuable critical comment and for kind words of support over the years. I am also grateful to Susan Keogh for her assistance and advice.

I sincerely thank Janet Bartlet – my publisher at Jacana Media – and her colleagues, for their enthusiasm, and Gillian Warren-Brown, my editor, for her sensitive and careful guidance. Thank you for making this book a reality.

I am indebted to the late Lionel Reynolds (one-time Safari Operations Manager for Touch the Wild) who initially granted me access to The Presidential Elephants of Zimbabwe, and subsequently to Rudy Boribon (Touch the Wild's General Manager in the early 2000s) who always encouraged my efforts. I thank, too, Leonard Chihwai and Masunda Chimhamhiwa (past managers of the Hwange Safari Lodge, a Zimsun hotel) for their staunch support in these early days. Without Alan Elliott, one-time owner of Touch the Wild, these extraordinary elephants would never have been afforded their initial protection, and I thank him for his foresight.

I make special mention of Jerry Matsika (from African Encounter) for always at least trying, without complaint of wasting his time, to help save the lives of some of my elephant friends, and Jabulani Ngwenya for leading the estate anti-poaching team during the years of my story. I also thank Greg Rasmussen, Roger Perry and Peter Blinston for life-saving Presidential Elephant darting, as well as the expanded anti-poaching teams that now patrol. Additional thanks to Charles Brightman, Ian Du Preez and the late Gavin Best, who all assisted with Future, and also the Dete Animal Rescue team for carrying out some snare removals.

I especially thank Nicholas Duncan and all those associated with the SAVE Foundation of Australia which, in the later years, helped tremendously by contributing towards my vehicle and computer expenses, and who bought me chocolate and Twisties! I acknowledge, too, their support of ongoing anti-poaching and snare-removal efforts. I also sincerely thank Colin Gillies, from Wildlife Environment Zimbabwe, and Johnny Rodrigues, from the Zimbabwe Conservation Task Force, for having the courage to speak out, and for always doing what they can to help.

Gary Deysel's staff at Camera Centre in Bulawayo, which included Austin Nkomo and Patrick Mutyanda, expertly processed and printed my many wildlife photographs and I thank them for always making me feel so welcome. I thank MWeb Zimbabwe for thoughtful e-mail sponsorship and Blue Arrow for assistance with coach travel. My grateful thanks also go to Heather Gaston (Mantswane Investments), who graciously assists me with transportation to and from Bulawayo.

Touch the Wild, and then Zimsun (who, after the land was returned in 2005, took over control of my rondavel, and the Kanondo and Khatshana areas, from Touch the Wild) kindly provided me with a roof over my head. I thank Misheck Manyumwa from Zimsun (these days known as African Sun), who listened to the subsequent concerns that arose, and helped with some of them. I also thank ex-Touch the Wild mechanics Wezi Ndlovu and Sidumiso Ngwenya, and the late Nicko Banda, for skilfully attending to Nicki Mukuru when she was sick.

I am grateful to the Zimbabwean government for allowing me to call Zimbabwe 'home', and also to those government and Parks Authority personnel who understand the value of keeping The Presidential Elephants of Zimbabwe safe from harm.

To the elephants themselves I am particularly beholden, for with them I have experienced golden days and true meaning to life. I will always cherish my special grey friends, having been accepted, and affectionately named Mandlovu – *Mother Elephant* – as one of them.